Context

CONTEXT AND CONTENT

Series editor: François Recanati, Institut Nicod

Other titles in the series:

The Inessential Indexical
On the Philosophical Insignificance of Perspective and the First Person
Herman Cappelen and Josh Dever

The Mirror of the World
Subjects, Consciousness, and Self-Consciousness
Christopher Peacocke

Assessment Sensitivity
Relative Truth and its Applications
John MacFarlane

Context

Robert Stalnaker

OXFORD
UNIVERSITY PRESS

OXFORD
UNIVERSITY PRESS

Great Clarendon Street, Oxford, OX2 6DP,
United Kingdom

Oxford University Press is a department of the University of Oxford.
It furthers the University's objective of excellence in research, scholarship,
and education by publishing worldwide. Oxford is a registered trade mark of
Oxford University Press in the UK and in certain other countries

© Robert C. Stalnaker 2014

The moral rights of the author have been asserted

First Edition published in 2014
Impression: 1

All rights reserved. No part of this publication may be reproduced, stored in
a retrieval system, or transmitted, in any form or by any means, without the
prior permission in writing of Oxford University Press, or as expressly permitted
by law, by licence or under terms agreed with the appropriate reprographics
rights organization. Enquiries concerning reproduction outside the scope of the
above should be sent to the Rights Department, Oxford University Press, at the
address above

You must not circulate this work in any other form
and you must impose this same condition on any acquirer

Published in the United States of America by Oxford University Press
198 Madison Avenue, New York, NY 10016, United States of America

British Library Cataloguing in Publication Data
Data available

Library of Congress Control Number: 2013957454

ISBN 978-0-19-964516-9

As printed and bound by
CPI Group (UK) Ltd, Croydon, CR0 4YY

Links to third party websites are provided by Oxford in good faith and
for information only. Oxford disclaims any responsibility for the materials
contained in any third party website referenced in this work.

Contents

Preface   vii

Introduction   1
1. Three Notions of Context   13
2. Common Ground and Keeping Score   35
3. Presupposition Requirements   54
4. Context and Compositionality   78
5. The Essential Contextual   108
6. May, Might, If   126
7. Disagreement and Projection   161
8. Contextualism and the New Relativism   189
Appendix   208

References   237
Index   245

Preface

This book had its roots in work begun more than forty years ago on presupposition and assertion, and I have been tinkering with the ideas I sketched then, off and on, ever since. I am grateful for the opportunity provided by François Recanati to further develop these ideas in a set of lectures in his Content and Context series. I benefited from stimulating discussion at those lectures from, among others, Herb Clark, Kathrin Glüer-Pagin, Peter Pagin, François Recanati, and Isadora Stojanovic. These four lectures, given in Paris in 2010, grew to six when I gave the Gaos lectures the next year in Mexico City at the Instituto de Investigaciones Filóficas at the Universidad Nacional Autónoma de Mexico. I am grateful to the philosophers of language at the UNAM for the invitation to give these lectures, and for the stimulating discussions that I had with them during my month there. Thanks also to the philosophers at Brown University where earlier versions of three of the chapters constituted the Josiah Royce lectures, given there in 2007.

The 1970s, when I first started thinking about pragmatics, were exciting times in the philosophy of language, with a lot of fruitful interaction between philosophers and linguists, who were just inventing theoretical semantics and pragmatics as it is practiced today. Among the linguists who helped to draw me into the subject at that time and to appreciate the relevance of their work to philosophical issues were Lauri Karttunen, George Lakoff, Barbara Partee, Stan Peters, and Sally McConnell-Ginet.

Philosophers and linguists tended to go their separate ways in the decade after the 1970s, but from the early 90s to the present, interdisciplinary work in semantics/pragmatics, and philosophical uses of linguistic results have again flourished. Interdisciplinary work is more demanding than it was in the 70s, since a lot of sophisticated theory has been developed since then, and alternative frameworks have proliferated. But I have had a lot of help from the work of many linguists, and from discussion with them, including Angelika Kratzer, Paul Portner, Craige Roberts, Philippe Schlenker, Mandy Simons, and my MIT colleagues, Kai von Fintel, Danny Fox, Irene Heim, and Sabine Iatridou.

Among philosophers, my debts to Paul Grice, David Kaplan, David Lewis, John Perry, and Mark Richard will be evident from the discussion in the book of their work and ideas.

I and my colleagues in philosophy at MIT have been fortunate to have a really excellent group of graduate students over the past few decades, many of whom have made and are making important contributions to the fast moving interdisciplinary field of pragmatics. Their work, and discussion with them while they were students and since, have had a profound, and I hope positive, influence on the ideas that I develop in this book. This group, going back more than twenty years, includes Lenny Clapp, Andy Egan, Sarah Moss, Dilip Ninan, Alejandro Pérez Carballo, Agustín Rayo, Paolo Santorio, Jason Stanley, Eric Swanson, Zoltan Gendler Szabó, and Seth Yalcin.

Craige Roberts read a complete draft of the manuscript, and gave me extremely helpful comments that led to major revision and reorganization. The ideas developed in Chapters 6 and 7 were strongly influenced by Seth Yalcin's work on epistemic modals, and extensive correspondence and discussion with him about these issues led to significant corrections and (I hope) improvements. Thanks to both Craige and Seth for their help.

A version of Chapter 5 was previously published as Stalnaker 2011a. Thanks to Oxford University Press for permission to include parts of that paper in this book.

Thanks to my editor, Peter Momtchiloff for advice, support, and patience. Thanks also to Jan Chamier for meticulous copy editing, and to Jack Marley-Payne for editorial help at the last stage of the process, including compiling the index.

Introduction

This book is an exploration of the contexts in which speech takes place, of the ways we represent them, and of the roles they play in explaining the interpretation and dynamics of speech. In this introductory overview, my aim is to provide a sketch of the general line of argument of the book, the narrative, as they say. Or perhaps I should say that my aim is to set the argument of the book in context.

The central thesis that guides the exploration is that it is possible and fruitful to theorize about the structure and function of discourse independently of specific theory about the mechanisms that languages use to serve those functions. This rough statement of the thesis (which I will dub *the autonomy of pragmatics*) needs to be refined and qualified, which I will try to do in the course of the book. I will defend the thesis mainly by developing some pragmatic theory that I hope will illustrate it, and by applying that theory to the explanation of a range of specific linguistic phenomena. The thesis needs qualification since the data to be explained by such a theory are always data concerning the uses of particular expressions of particular languages, and interpreting the data requires making some assumptions about the semantics of the expressions involved, but the hope is that one can sometimes defend and apply purely pragmatic principles while making only relatively uncontroversial assumptions about the semantics. Even though the focus will be on pragmatic explanation, the interaction of context with semantic interpretation will be a central concern of the book.

The thesis of the autonomy of pragmatics is inspired by the work of Paul Grice whose profound influence on my thinking about all the issues I will discuss will be clear. Grice wrote at a time when semantic theory, as applied to natural language, was at a much more primitive level than it is today, so the issues about the relation between semantics and pragmatics at that time were simpler, but I think the general Gricean strategy of explaining fundamental pragmatic concepts independently of language remains a fruitful one, and is perhaps made all the more urgent by the need to explain the complex interaction between context and the interpretation of speech that contemporary semantic theorizing reveals.

The fundamental concept in Grice's project was *speaker meaning*. His starting point was an attempt to identify the features of an action in virtue of which that action counts as an act of meaning, in one sense of that term. The idea was to give an analysis of this type of action in terms of the beliefs and intentions of the agent, and to explain it independently of any conventional rule-governed practice, and of the particular linguistic devices that are the most important means that rational agents use to mean things. This project contrasts with projects that take language or the practice of speech as a model for thought, aiming to explain the intentionality of beliefs, desires and intentions in terms of the intentionality of the languages in which they are expressed. It was essential to the success of Grice's project, and it is essential to the defense of my thesis of the autonomy of pragmatics, that one be able to understand propositional attitudes and to represent the content of propositional attitudes in a way that is independent of the vehicles that rational agents use, in either speech or thought, to encode or to articulate what they are thinking. A nonlinguistic conception of propositional content is important for understanding the cognitive activity of prelinguistic creatures, and of the knowledge of rational agents that is manifested in nonlinguistic action, but what is most relevant to Grice's project, and to the project of this book, is that a language-independent account of attitudes and their contents is also important for an adequate understanding of discourse.

The most important concept of the pragmatic framework that I have used for many years, and will further develop here, is the concept of *common ground*, which is a body of information that is presumed to be shared by the parties to a discourse. The course of a discourse and the interpretation of what is said in it are guided by that body of information, and by the way that it evolves in response to what is said. To understand that dynamic process, we need an understanding of information states of this kind and of the content of what is said in the contexts defined by such states, that does not itself rest on a linguistic account of informational content.[1]

---

[1] See Chapter 2 of Stalnaker 1984 for a discussion of what I called "the linguistic picture" of intentionality, and the contrasting "pragmatic picture" which I favor.

This exploration of the notion of context will mainly be a development of the notion of context as common ground. In fact, one way to see the narrative of the book is as a succession of refinements and applications of this notion. Since this theoretical notion has played a prominent part in my own theorizing about pragmatics over the past forty years, I will here throw in a brief digression about the relation between the ideas I will be defending in this book and my earlier work.

I first discussed the general idea of common ground in a paper published in 1970, and I then applied it in several other papers on presupposition and assertion published in the 1970s.[2] I did not use the label "common ground" until much later, talking instead about *speaker presupposition*, which is a propositional attitude that was explained informally as follows: "To presuppose a proposition in the pragmatic sense is to take its truth for granted and to assume that others involved in the context do the same."[3] The notion of "taking for granted" was not given any detailed characterization, but what was said about it in those early papers was perhaps more behavioristic and more tightly tied to linguistic action than I now think it should have been. What was important about the informal characterization of the notion given in those early papers was the suggestion that speaker presupposition has an iterative structure: one presupposes something only if one presupposes that others are presupposing it as well. But this structure remained in the informal commentary. A speaker's presuppositions were modeled formally, in those early papers, just by a set of possible worlds (those compatible with what is being presupposed), labeled the "context set". I made the iterative structure of common ground explicit, following the pattern of the notions of common knowledge and mutual belief,[4] only in a paper published in 2002.[5] Common ground, like common knowledge and mutual belief, is not an individual propositional attitude, but a concept defined in terms of the propositional attitudes of the members

---

[2] See Stalnaker 1970, 1974, 1975, and 1978, all reprinted in the first section of Stalnaker 1999.

[3] Stalnaker 1970, reprinted in Stalnaker 1999, 38.

[4] See Lewis 1969 for common knowledge and Schiffer 1972 for mutual belief. The pattern of the definitions is this: it is common knowledge that φ between the members of a group if and only if all in the group know that φ, all know that all know it, all know that all know that all know it, etc. One can substitute belief or some notion of acceptance for knowledge to get notions of mutual belief, or common ground.

[5] Stalnaker 2002.

of a group. The relation between common ground and speaker presupposition is this: a participant in a context *presupposes* that ϕ if and only if she accepts that it is common ground that ϕ, where "accept" is the attitude that is iterated in the definition of common ground.[6] Speaker presupposition and common ground will coincide in any context that is *nondefective*, where a nondefective context is one in which none of the participants in the context is mistaken about what is common ground. The basic propositional attitude that is the basis for the iterative definitions of common ground and speaker presupposition is not given a formal analysis, but is to be understood as something like "acceptance for the purposes of the conversation." In simple straightforward serious conversations, what is accepted will coincide with what is believed, but some conversations will involve some mutually recognized pretense about what is believed, or some tacit suppositions that are made in order to further the mutual aims of the conversation.[7]

Context as common ground, or something like it, has played a role in lots of semantic and pragmatic theorizing since the 1970s, particularly in the dynamic semantic tradition, but there is a second contrasting notion of context that has also played a prominent role, and that is perhaps what most theorists have in mind when they talk of context. Chapter 1 of this book will focus mainly on the representation of context developed and used by David Kaplan and David Lewis, and on the relation between this notion, which I label "K-context", and the notion of context as common ground (CG-context). The two notions are complementary—semantic/pragmatic theory has room for both—but there are some tensions between them that I will discuss, and some potential confusion if one equivocates between them in one's use of the term "context". This first chapter traces some of the early history of the development of formal pragmatics beginning with a quick look at what Richard Montague called "pragmatics", and followed by a discussion of David Kaplan's refinement of Montague's framework. Kaplan's modifications of the Montague framework were motivated by two very different concerns. One was a

---

[6] The definition of common ground that I give in this book is slightly different, and simpler, than the definition given in Stalnaker 2002. I now think that the more complex definition was a mistake.

[7] See Stalnaker 1984 for a discussion of a generic notion of acceptance—a family of belief-like attitudes.

language-internal semantic consideration: he argued that we needed a notion of *semantic value* for sentences that was more complex than the one used in Montague's theory in order to get the compositional semantics for context-dependent expressions to work in a smooth way. The second motivation was a language-external *pragmatic* consideration—one that concerned the functions that language serves rather than the semantic mechanisms that particular languages use to serve them. We needed a more complex semantic value than Montague's framework offered in order to distinguish the two different roles that facts may play in determining the truth-value of an utterance: first, facts about the context determine *what is said* in the utterance; second, different facts determine whether what was said is true or false. Kaplan's notion of *character* (a function from context to content) was intended to recover this distinction. These two very different motivations seemed to point in the same direction, and the two different problems with Montague's framework seemed to be solved by the same fix, which involved a two-dimensional semantic framework that yielded a more complex semantic value for sentences. But David Lewis argued that the more complex notion of semantic value that was needed for the purposes of compositional semantics did not yield a theoretically useful or intuitively plausible notion of *what is said*—of propositional content. Lewis's further refinement of Kaplan's semantics is guided just by the compositional considerations, and the pragmatic motivation drops out. But I will argue that even if the two problems don't have one solution, there remains a reason to look to semantics to yield, as its ultimate output for the interpretation of a sentence in context, a *proposition*: something that can play a central role in an account of the use of language to exchange information and to engage in rational deliberation and debate. The tasks of finding an adequate compositional semantics, and of characterizing the kinds of semantic values that are appropriate to it, will not be completely independent of the tasks of finding an adequate account of the exchange of information and of the representation of the items of information exchanged, but the tasks need to be separated, and that is what an autonomous pragmatics tries to do. This chapter will conclude with a discussion of some of the tensions between the Lewis/Kaplan notion of context and the notion of context as common ground. Some of these tensions will get more detailed treatment in later chapters, and the interaction between the two notions of context will be a recurring theme throughout the book.

The autonomy thesis gets its most explicit defense in the second chapter. David Lewis, in an influential paper published in 1979,[8] developed a pragmatic framework in which the dynamic process of discourse was modeled as a game with constitutive rules that define the way the score of the game evolves as it is played. Common ground, in Lewis's account, was one of the elements of the score, and he took one of the constitutive rules of the language game to be a *rule of accommodation*, according to which propositions automatically come to be presupposed (to be part of the common ground) when they are required by what is said. My main argument in this chapter is that common ground and speaker presupposition can and should be understood independently of the conventional rules of language, and that the process of accommodation that Lewis identified is not the application of a rule, but is the result of rational responses to events that take place in the course of a conversation. Any cooperative joint project will be carried out in a situation in which certain information is taken to be shared by the participants in the project, and will be guided by that body of information. Accommodation is just the adjustment of what the common ground is taken to be in response to evidence that becomes manifest as the project proceeds. I will look closely, in this chapter, at the dynamic process, and at the role of the iterative structure in the explanation of context change.

So the main theses defended in this second chapter are, first, that common-ground context should be characterized independently of particular conventional linguistic practices, second, that it will play a guiding role in any cooperative project, whether it involves a language or not, and third, that accommodation is a response to evidence of any kind that becomes manifest as the joint project is carried out. But of course we are most interested in cases where the cooperative project involves a language and conventional rules governing the performance of speech acts. In this case, shared information about the semantics of particular expressions, and about the conventional force of speech acts, will be central to the process, and the evidence that generates changes in common ground by accommodation will include the evidence that certain words are used with certain meanings, and that certain speech acts are performed. In the last part of this chapter, I will look briefly at the interaction of

[8] Lewis 1979b.

assumptions about a conventional practice of assertion with the pragmatic process of accommodation.

One reason to put such emphasis on the fact that accommodation is a pervasive and inevitable feature of any kind of cooperative activity is it that provides a different perspective on the status of a range of specific linguistic phenomena involving presupposition, and on the debates in the linguistics literature about presupposition. So part of the motivation for the arguments of Chapter 2 is to set up the discussion, in Chapter 3, of presuppositional phenomena more narrowly conceived, and of the way I think the problems about these phenomena should be described and explained. The main thesis of Chapter 3 is that the concept of pragmatic presupposition, applied to sentences or utterances, is not an explanatory concept of semantics, but a concept (like *felicitousness* or *appropriateness*) for characterizing surface phenomena to be explained. To say that a certain expression "triggers" a presupposition φ is to say something like this: the data suggest that the expression is normally inappropriate or infelicitous when used in contexts in which the speaker is not presupposing (taking it to be common ground) that φ. According to this rough and ready characterization, the notion of a presupposition trigger is a notion used to describe some data that need to be explained, and not a concept in any theory used to explain the data. There are more theoretical notions of sentence presupposition in the vicinity such as the notion, going back to Frege, of *semantic* presupposition: a sentence S semantically presupposes that φ if and only if S has a truth-value only if φ. A particular semantic theory may stipulate that certain sentences get a semantic value only under certain conditions, and those conditions will be semantic presuppositions of the sentence. More theoretical notions of presupposition of this kind may play a role in the explanation for the phenomena, since appropriate speech will normally require that speakers presuppose that their utterances have truth-values. But this is just one way that presuppositional phenomena might be explained, and so it is important to distinguish the descriptive concept by which one identifies the data from theoretical concepts that are in some cases involved in the explanation of the data. This third chapter spends some time on the more general distinction between descriptive and theoretical concepts, and on the fallacy (when the two kinds of concepts are confused) of inferring uncritically from a descriptive fact about the data to a conclusion about its theoretical explanation. I argue that some arguments in the linguistics literature seem to commit this fallacy. The chapter concludes with a look at the diversity of presupposition triggers, and more generally at the diversity of the phenomena that are grouped together in a category of presuppositional phenomena. This diversity, which is well brought out in the linguistics literature, supports the idea that it is a mistake to look for a uniform explanation, or even a uniform theoretical description, of the phenomena.

The most prominent specific problem about presupposition in the linguistics literature is the so-called *projection problem*: the problem of identifying and explaining the relation between what is presupposed in the use of certain complex sentences and what is presupposed when the sentential constituents of those sentences are used alone. The projection problem was originally seen, and is still sometimes seen, as a problem of compositional semantics, but I (among others) argued, in early work on pragmatic presupposition in the 1970s, that the problem should be seen as a problem not about compositional structure, but about conversational dynamics. The relation between compositional structure and conversational dynamics is, however, complicated, and the explanation of discourse phenomena involves the interaction of semantic and pragmatic processes. Chapter 4 is a discussion of this interaction, beginning with an examination of the pattern of pragmatic explanation that Paul Grice used to derive what he called "conversational implicatures". In discussions of conversational implicature it is often assumed that semantics first determines what is said (or, to use a chraracteristic Gricean expression) what the speaker "makes as if to say", and then pragmatic reasoning of the kind that Grice made famous is used to explain how additional or different information may be conveyed indirectly (conversationally implicated). But I will argue that Gricean reasoning is much more pervasive, and is involved at all stages of the process of interpretation.

After a general discussion of the interaction of Gricean reasoning with compositional interpretation, I look, in the rest of this fourth chapter, at some specific kinds of interaction between the evolving common ground and the interpretation of complex expressions. I discuss the idea of a *subordinate context*, or what is sometimes called, in the dynamic semantic literature, a *local context*, which plays a role in the interpretation of speech, and in the explanation of presuppositional phenomena. Continuing the theme of the autonomy of pragmatics, I will argue that the notion of a subordinate context is a pragmatic notion, and that while subordinate contexts play a role in the explanation of semantic phenomena, and are made relevant by conventional speech acts, they are wholly derivative from the basic context, which, I argue, is intelligible independently of the conventional rules of any language, or language game. Chapter 4 will conclude with a discussion of the projection problem, and of the strategy of describing and explaining the projection phenomena in pragmatic terms.

Both in the discussion of accommodation in Chapters 2 and 3, and in the discussion of subordinate contexts in Chapter 4, the iterative structure of common ground plays a prominent role. What this kind of structure implies is that the information in the common ground is not just information about the subject matter of the discourse, but also information about the discourse itself, and about the attitudes of the parties to the discourse—information about who and where they all are, what they know about who and where they are, what they accept about what others accept, and so what they agree and disagree about. The last four chapters of the book focus on this kind of information, and its role in the dynamics of discourse.

Information shared by the participants in a discourse that is about the participants and their discourse is essentially *self-locating* information. Chapter 5 is about the distinctive character of self-locating information—not just a single individual's knowledge and beliefs about who and where he or she is, but the knowledge and beliefs of the members of a group about themselves and each other. David Lewis gave us an elegant way of modeling self-locating attitudes that built on the possible-worlds representation of information, but replaced possible worlds with *centered worlds*—the same abstract objects that (as will be discussed in Chapter 1) were used by Lewis and Kaplan to represent context. (A centered world is a possible world plus a designated center, consisting of a time and place, or a time and an agent.) The idea was that if we represent the informational content of a belief by a set of centered worlds we can represent not only what the world is like in itself, according to the believer, but also where she locates herself in the world, and which person in that world she takes herself to be. The problem with Lewis's theory was that it made it difficult to compare the attitudes of different agents, or the attitudes of a single agent at different times. For this reason, Lewis's theory as it stands is not suitable for a project that is centrally concerned, first with the relations between the attitudes of different agents, and second with the way in which their attitudes evolve over time. The main constructive task of Chapter 5 is to develop a way of modeling information states that allows for self-locating information, but that is also able to account for one person's attitudes toward the attitudes of another, for agreement and disagreement, and for changes of what is known or accepted over time. The models will follow Lewis in using centered possible worlds to represent information states, but I will argue that with a small modification of the way these abstract objects are used we can recover the benefits of the classical Hintikka models that, as will be discussed in Chapter 2, extend naturally to models for multiple agents, and straightforwardly yield analyses of common knowledge, mutual belief, and common ground. The upshot will be a modified model for common ground in which the points in the space that represents the shared information will be, not simple possible worlds, but multiply-centered worlds—worlds centered on a time and a sequence of individuals (the participants in the conversation). So the context set will represent the information about where they locate themselves and each other in the worlds they mutually take to be compatible with their shared information. One side benefit of this representation of common ground is that it helps to clarify the relation between the two notions of context discussed in Chapter 1. Because the possibilities that are the elements of the context set (the CG-context) will be centered, they will be something like contexts in the sense defined by Kaplan and Lewis (the K-context).

Self-locating information, in this broad sense, includes information about what the parties to a conversation know and accept about what they themselves know and accept—about where their attitudes agree, and where they disagree. It is crucial to the smooth running of a discourse that as the discourse evolves the participants stay on the same page about such information, and the main focus of Chapters 6 and 7 is on some of the devices that languages have for helping them do this. Modal expressions ("may", "might", "must", "probably", among others) and the conditional "if" have received a lot of attention in the linguistic and philosophical literature recently, and there remains some puzzlement and controversy about exactly how they work. I will argue in these chapters that the pragmatic framework we are developing helps to account for their behavior, and their role in the negotiation about how a discourse should evolve.

Getting clear about epistemic modals and conditionals requires sorting out the pragmatic and semantic dimension of the problem. Chapter 6 begins with a consideration of the relation between speech act force and semantic content. Should we understand an utterance of something of the form "It must be that ϕ" or "It might be that ϕ" as having the content ϕ, but expressing it with a distinctive kind of speech act force, different from assertion, or should we understand it as expressing a distinctive kind of modal proposition asserted with the standard assertive force? There is a parallel question about indicative conditional assertions that has long been a topic of controversy: should we understand "if ϕ, then ψ" as a qualified assertion of ψ, with ϕ providing the qualification of the assertive force, or should we understand it as expressing, with ordinary categorical assertive force, of a proposition that is a function of the propositions expressed by ϕ and ψ? I will approach this question indirectly, at the beginning of Chapter 6, by considering an artificial language game invented by David Lewis with deontic modal operators that involves both a distinctive kind of deontic content and a distinctive kind of speech act force. Because of the simplicity of Lewis's artificial model, the pattern of interaction between content and force in the dynamics of the game is crystal clear. Things are messier in a more realistic account of modal expressions, but I will argue that some of the features of the simple game are present in defensible accounts of epistemic modals and indicative conditionals, and that the analogy with the game helps to clarify the relation between the pragmatic function of such expressions and their compositional semantics.

The account of epistemic modals and indicative conditionals developed in Chapter 6 is in a sense a kind of *expressivism* about such constructions, but it gives a truth-conditional formulation of their semantics. Part of the advantage of the truth-conditional formulation is that it helps to give a perspicuous representation of the relation between the uses of modal expressions and conditionals that express epistemic attitudes and those that aim to state objective facts about the world. This formulation of the expressivist account brings out the continuity between the different uses, and allows for disagreement, uncertainty and debate, not only about which modal statements to accept, but also about whether those statements state facts, or only express epistemic policies and priorities. Chapter 7 is about these continuities and relations. Much of the chapter focuses on the contrast between so-called indicative and subjunctive conditionals, and on the pragmatic role of the grammatical devices that mark this distinction. The main idea is that the tense, mood and aspect properties of the conditional sentences called "subjunctive" serve to signal that, in the subordinate context relevant to interpreting the conditional, some presuppositions made in the basic context are being suspended.

The overall picture of the dynamics of discourse that I try to paint in the book shows it as an enterprise of negotiating over the way that a body of information—the common ground—should evolve. The process involves the pooling of information, but also debate and disagreement about what the common ground should be—about what the parties to the negotiation are in a position to jointly accept. The points in the space that define this evolving information state are individuated in whatever way is necessary to represent all the distinctions that may be relevant to what is at issue in the negotiation, including not just distinctions of objective fact about what the world is like, but also distinctions between different hypotheses about where in the world the parties to the discourse are, and distinctions between the epistemic policies and priorities the parties should have. Because the information that defines a context, and the informational content of what is expressed in a context, may be individuated more finely than what there is a fact of the matter about, the account I wind up with might be thought of as a version of the kind of semantic relativism that has been a focus of controversy in recent semantic and pragmatic theorizing. The last chapter of the book is a discussion of some versions of semantic relativism, and of the relation of relativism to contextualism and to expressivism. I will express some skepticism about John MacFarlane's notion of assessment sensitivity, and about the idea of faultless disagreement, according to which two people may both be right even though they disagree. On the other hand, the framework I am developing and defending is friendly to some aspects of the project of semantic relativism, and I will argue that it can account for some of the phenomena that motivate that project. I will compare some examples used in defense of relativist theses with some of the examples that I discuss in Chapter 7, arguing that they point in the same direction.

1

Three Notions of Context

There was, in the philosophy of language in the 1970s, a lot of ink spilled in debating just what pragmatics was, and where the line was to be drawn between semantics and pragmatics. As is usual with such border disputes, it was often unclear what the question was, but there seemed to be some substantive issues in the vicinity, perhaps a tangle of issues about the nature of linguistic competence, its role in communicative practices, and the relation between language and thought mixed in with methodological questions about the most fruitful direction for linguistic research to take. In the thirty years since then, the terrain has changed a lot, in many ways. Sophisticated theories of indexical semantics have provided formal models of a certain kind of context sensitivity. Context and context change, presupposition and Gricean implicature have been incorporated into a range of different formal semantic/pragmatic theories that model whole discourses and the way they evolve. The general account of discourse took a dynamic turn, and this complicated the questions about the relation between semantics and pragmatics. Should the way contexts evolve in a conversation be incorporated into semantics? Detailed theories about the way the semantic properties of expressions interact with what the users of those expressions bring to the situations in which they are used have proliferated, but despite all of the progress, the border disputes are as heated, and the underlying foundational questions are as unclear, as they were when theorizing about context was just beginning. In a way, this is not surprising, since as theories are developed and applied to a widening range of linguistic phenomena, the basis for drawing lines keeps changing, and as theories are developed in increasing detail, it is easy for fundamental questions about the relation between languages and what they are used to do to get lost in the details.

Part of the problem is that there are several different notions of context involved in current pragmatic theorizing, notions that have their origins in the early attempts to think systematically about pragmatics. My main aim in this first chapter is to get clearer about the relations between two different theoretical notions of context that have played a role in pragmatic theory, and to bring out some tensions between them.

My title says *three* notions of context, but the first is the informal target notion, the intuitive idea of a context: the thing one gets quoted out of, or that one provides some of when one sets the stage for a report, a discussion or a deliberation ("let me give you some context"). It is worth taking a quick look at the intuitive notion or notions of context before looking at the formal objects that theory uses to explain some of the phenomena that we describe in terms of these intuitive notions.

It is natural to think of a speech context as the concrete situation in which a conversation takes place, a situation with a more or less definite group of participants with certain beliefs, including beliefs about what the others know and believe, and certain interests and purposes, both common interests and purposes, and interests and purposes that are recognized to diverge. Contexts, in the ordinary sense, evolve in the course of a conversational exchange, but retain their identity. We are, in a sense, in the same context when I ask you a question as when you give the answer, even though a different person is speaking, and even though beliefs about each other and about the subject matter of the conversation are changing as we speak.

It seems reasonable to take a context, in the ordinary sense, as a situation that is intelligible independently of any institutional linguistic practice. A context is not defined by the constitutive rules of some language game; it is enough that a group of people is in some common setting, with some recognition of each other's presence. The constitutive rules of an institutional linguistic practice may appeal to facts about the setting in which speech takes place, and the beliefs of the members of the group in terms of which the context is defined may include beliefs about the rules of a linguistic practice. But the notion of a context does not seem to involve essentially any rules or conventions. It is not just linguistic actions, but actions of any kind that take place in a context.

Features of a context might be relevant in at least two different ways to the understanding of what is going on in a conversation: first, the context is a resource that the participants might use to achieve their communicative purposes: they can make what they say or mean depend on features of the context, so long as the relevant information is available to the addressee. Second, the context, since it includes the beliefs, plans and purposes of the participants, is what speech acts act upon; it is their point to change certain features of the context. To account for the first of these two roles, a theoretical notion of context should identify the features of the setting in which speech takes place that semantic rules exploit. To account for the second of the roles, a theoretical notion should help to sharpen our understanding of the intended effects of speech acts. A notion of context playing these two roles will be involved both in an account of what language is used to do, and in an account of the mechanisms it uses to do it.

1.1 Intensional semantics and formal pragmatics, first version

To get at the two more theoretical notions of context that I will consider, I am going to trace some of the history, starting with the prehistory, of formal pragmatics. Richard Montague might be regarded as the founding father of the field, or at least of one very influential strand of it. Linguistic semantics, as it is practiced today, began with Montague grammar, the application of formal semantics (model theory) to natural language.[1] But Montague was also the first to apply these tools to what he called pragmatics. The kind of semantic theory that Montague applied was *intensional* semantics. Let me say a bit about the intensional generalization of extensional semantics before looking at the further generalization that Montague called "pragmatics".

Formal semantics, in general, is supposed to be compositional: the semantic value of any complex expression must be a function of the semantic values of its immediate constituents. In extensional semantics, the values are extensions, and in the case of sentences, truth-values. Since modal operators are not truth functional, we need a finer grained notion of semantic value to do compositional semantics for a modal language. Possible worlds semantics provides a way to define a finer grained

---

[1] See the papers collected in Montague 1974, and particularly, Montague 1973.

semantic value that smoothly generalizes any extensional semantics. An *intension*, generally, is a function from possible worlds to extensions. Since the extension of a one-place predicate is a subset of the domain of discourse, the intension of such a predicate will be a function taking a possible world to a subset of the domain of that world. And since the extension of a sentence is a truth-value, the intension will be a function from possible worlds to truth-values. With this notion of a semantic value, all of the extensional rules and operators automatically generalize to intensional rules and operators, and one also has the resources to interpret a new range of intensional operators—not just the traditional modal operators, but also, for example, adverbs and adjectives, that operate on predicates in a nonextensional way.[2]

Intensional semantics not only made it possible to apply compositional semantics to a richer range of expressions by providing a finer grained notion of *semantic value*. It also brought a fringe benefit: the theory yielded an autonomous notion of *informational content* which made it possible to represent one thing that language aims to do (to express a thought with a certain content) independently of the means that the language uses to do it. The *intension* of a sentence, in modal semantics, is a function from possible worlds to truth-values, and so is a representation of *truth conditions*. The information conveyed in a statement is represented by the possibilities that the statement excludes. This fringe benefit is relevant to pragmatics in a broad sense—to the use of language to convey information—since it provides a formal representation of an item of information.

So the intensional generalization had two benefits, giving us two motivations for the move from extensional to intensional semantics. One of the motivations is language-internal (getting the compositional semantics to work); the other is external to the mechanisms of any particular language: it concerns the clarification of what a language is used to do.

---

[2] See Stalnaker and Thomason 1973, for a formal semantic analysis of adverbs. Adverbs such as "slowly" are (as analyzed there) operators taking predicates to predicates. They are non-extensional operators, since the extension of a complex predicate is not a function of the extension of the part. For example, even in a domain where the walkers are all and only the talkers, it might be that the set of those who walk slowly is different from the set of those who talk slowly.

This was such an elegant theory that Montague generalized it further, and it is here where we have the first incarnation of one of the two abstract, formal notions of context: the notion of an *index*.[3] Modal semantics said that a truth-value is dependent on (sensitive to) a possible world. Context-sensitive expressions are dependent on (sensitive to) other things as well: a person (the speaker), a time of utterance, a place of utterance, etc. So Montague generalized the notion of an intension to a function from an *index* to a truth-value (or more generally, from an index to an extension) where an index is a sequence of items, a sequence that should include whatever the extension of any expression might be dependent on. For example, to interpret a language containing tenses and personal pronouns, the index will contain (in addition to a possible world) a time (the time of utterance) and a sequence of individuals, defined by their roles (speaker and addressee).

There are two problems with this generalization, and the problems provided two reasons to modify the theory. The two reasons seemed to point in the same direction—to the same kind of required modification. The first problem is that the fringe benefit is lost. A function from indices to truth-values is not a candidate for an item of information that might be an object of belief, the content of a thought, or of a statement. The second, quite different problem is a language-internal problem. We need (it was argued) a theory that is more complex than the simple index theory to get the compositional semantics right. First, let me sketch the modification, and then the two problems, and the way the modification addressed them.

1.2 Character and content: formal pragmatics, second version

The idea of the modification was to divide Montague's index into two parts. The Montague index consisted of a possible world, plus some other parameters on which the truth-value of the sentence might depend. On the modified theory that David Kaplan proposed,[4] the move from sentence meaning to truth-value was made in two stages: the meaning

---

[3] See Montague 1968 and 1970.
[4] Kaplan 1989. This monograph dates from the 1970s and was widely circulated for many years before it was published.

(*character*, to use the technical term that Kaplan adopted) of a sentence is a function from a *context* to a *content*. A *context*, for Kaplan, was something like Montague's index: a sequence of items on which the content of the sentence might depend. The *content* is also a function, one that takes *possible circumstances* (a possible world, or perhaps a possible world plus a time) to a truth-value. So in the Kaplan theory, the move from sentence meaning to truth-value was made in two steps: first from meaning to content, and then from content to truth-value.

The first of the two reasons to complicate the story in this way is a language-external reason concerning the function of semantics rather than its details: We need to make the distinction between meaning and content in order to recover the fringe benefit of intensional semantics—to have a representation of the information that a speech act intends to communicate. The Montagovian index represents all of the facts on which the truth-value of a sentence might depend, but the problem is that the facts are playing two very different roles in determining a truth-value. I will illustrate this with an old example that I used to motivate the two-step procedure in my original paper on pragmatics about 40 years ago:[5] I say to O'Leary, "You are a fool." The truth-value of this utterance depends on two things: (1) who the addressee is, and (2) whether that person is a fool. Daniels might think that what I said was false in either of two ways: (1) he knows O'Leary is a fool, but mistakenly thinks that I was talking to him (Daniels), and he believes he (himself) is not a fool; (2) he knows I was talking to O'Leary, but disagrees with me about whether O'Leary is a fool. It is important to distinguish these two ways that an utterance might be false. Only in the second case do we have a genuine disagreement. The first case is a case of miscommunication. Kaplan made this point by putting weight on the notion of "what is said": he argued that we must distinguish the meaning of a sentence from what the sentence is used to say.[6]

The second, more technical motivation for dividing the index into two parts was to get the compositional semantics right. The technical problem and its solution were developed by Hans Kamp and Frank Vlach, who were at UCLA at the time Montague and Kaplan were developing their theories.[7] Consider the sentence: "Once, everyone now alive hadn't

---

[5] Stalnaker 1970.   [6] Kaplan 1989, 500.   [7] Kamp 1971 and Vlach 1973.

yet been born." The quantifier must be inside the scope of the temporal operator, since the quantified sentence is said to be true, not now, but at some past time. The restriction "now alive" must be inside the scope of the quantifier, since it restricts the quantifier. But the "now" takes what it modifies *outside* of the scope of the temporal modifier, since the restriction is to people who are alive at the time of the context of utterance, and not those who are alive at the "shifted" past time. In the simple compositional theory, these constraints are inconsistent, but if we separate the world and time of the context of utterance (which remain fixed) from the world and time of the index (which may shift in the scope of a modal or temporal operator), we can give general compositional rules that get it right. The rule for "now" will say that it picks out the time of the context of utterance, even when it occurs within the scope of a temporal operator. There will be an analogous rule for the modifier "actually", which takes you back to the actual world of the context of utterance, even if it occurs within the scope of a modal operator. So one can interpret a sentence like, "If Florence had twice as much money as she actually has, she would quit her job." By separating the context of utterance from the possible circumstances, one can use the context as a resource to appeal to, even from within the scope of an operator that takes one to a different world or time. A time and world parameter will be represented twice: as part of the context, but also in the "shiftable" part of the circumstances.

1.3 The context/index (CI) framework: formal pragmatics, third version

David Lewis gave an elegant formulation of a modified version of the Kaplanian theory.[8] He agreed that the compositional semantics motivates dividing the Montagovian index into two parts, one that is determined by the concrete situation in which the utterance takes place and that is held fixed through the process of compositional interpretation, and the other that can shift or change within the scope of some operator. Lewis called the unshiftable component "the context", and the collection of shiftable components "the index". But he went on to argue that there is no reason to think of the process taking place in two stages; it is just a

[8] Lewis 1980.

dependence on two different parameters. Think of the meaning, or character, of a sentence as a function taking a context-index pair to a truth-value. A function from an A to a function from a B to a C is just a notational variant of a function from a pair of an A and a B to a C. In Lewis's equivalent picture, the intermediate semantic value (the function from index to truth-value) drops out, but Lewis argued that the separating out of this intermediate semantic value ("what is said") was unmotivated.

Lewis's CI framework addresses only the first motivation for the two-step procedure: his argument was that the intermediate semantic value played no role in the compositional semantics, but he ignored the second consideration, which is what I want to emphasize.[9] Let us step back and look, not at the internal workings of the compositional semantics for the language, but at what one is using the language, in context, to do.

1.4 The background pragmatic story

Start with a very general question about what a grammar is supposed to tell us. An utterance event takes place; certain sounds are produced. The sounds constitute the utterance, in a particular situation, of a sentence of a language with a certain semantics. The job of the semantics is to define a function that delivers a certain output, where the input is the sentence that was uttered, plus whatever features of the situation may be relevant to determining the output.

On the Lewis picture, the output is a *truth-value*, and Lewis's background story of what is going on when one engages in the activity of assertive speech is something like this: It is presumed that speakers aim to say things that are true, and so the addressee uses her knowledge of the semantics plus other facts on which the truth-value of the utterance depends to figure out what the world must be like in order for that utterance to be true, and then infers that the world is that way. Here is Lewis's summary of the background story:

---

[9] In the paper in which I first argued for the two-step procedure (Stalnaker 1970), I was motivated entirely by the pragmatic, language-external considerations. The compositional issues were not, at that time, on my radar screen at all.

I know, and you need to know, whether A or B or . . . ; so I say a sentence that I take to be true-in-English, in its context, and that depends for its truth on whether A or B or . . . ; and thereby, if all goes well, you find out what you needed to know.[10]

The speaker and addressee, on Lewis's story, are both conforming to *conventions* of truth and trust (in some specific language).[11] The convention (if the conversation is in English) is that the speaker will utter only sentences that are truth-in-English (in context), and that the addressee will trust the speaker to be aiming to do so.

But this story misses the important distinction between the different roles that information plays in determining a truth-value—the difference illustrated above with the contrast between the two reasons that Daniels might have had for believing that my statement about O'Leary was false. To get at this difference, the output should be, not a truth-value, but a *proposition*—a piece of information, represented by a function from possible worlds to truth-values. I would rather put the background story this way:

I know, and you need to know, whether A or B or . . . ; so I produce a sentence that I take to *say* in its context, whether A or B or . . . ; and thereby, if all goes well, you find out what you needed to know.

Lewis's argument against the significance of the two stages is that the notion of "what is said" can't bear the weight that Kaplan put on it. Kaplan motivated the distinction between character and content with examples where we individuate "what is said" differently from the way we individuate sentence meanings. (You say, "I am hungry". I say *the same thing* by saying of you, "he is hungry". But when I say, "I am hungry", I say something different from what you said, even though my sentence has the same meaning (character) as yours. But Lewis responds: "I put it to you that not one of these examples carries conviction. In every case, the proper naïve response is that in some sense what is said is the same . . . whereas in another – equally legitimate – sense, what is said is not the same."[12] Lewis is perhaps right, but the important issue is not the role in natural language of the locution "what is said," but a theoretical

---

[10] Lewis 1980, 37.
[11] Lewis's account of conventions of truth and trust was developed in Lewis 1969. See also Lewis 1975a.
[12] Lewis 1980, 41.

account of the function of speech. Behind intuitions about the use of the expression "what is said" is the distinction between two contrasting roles of factual information in determining a truth-value, a distinction that plays an important role in the explanation of the dynamics of speech. The moral of Lewis's argument should be that the two motivations for complicating the Montague story come apart. We need to separate the language-internal compositional considerations from the language-external pragmatic considerations. The problem that Lewis brings out is that even in the more complicated story that separates context from index in order to get the compositional semantic to work, we need to include in the index (and not just in the context) features that are not appropriate for defining a notion of informational content. So we don't recapture after all the fringe benefit that came with the original move to intensional semantics, since there are contextual features that can be shifted in the compositional process, and so that need to be included in the index, but that are not features that belong in the ultimate output of the compositional process—the piece of information that the speaker is aiming to communicate. Both times and places, for example, are elements determined by context that can be shifted in the compositional process, and so must be included in the index. This implies that the abstract object that the compositional semantics delivers (a function from index to truth-value) is not the same as the abstract object that represents the information that a speech act aims to convey.

The proper response to the problem that Lewis raises is not (as Lewis suggests) to give up the idea that the road from sentence meaning to truth-value takes place in two stages, but rather to give up the idea that the two very different problems that motivate the more complex semantics have a common solution.[13] What we want from our semantic theory is a mechanism that takes as its input a sentence with a certain meaning together with a context and delivers, as its output, a proposition—the content that is asserted or expressed with some other force. A theory of the mechanism for getting from input to output should include whatever

[13] Jeffrey King, in King 2003, offers a different response to the problem Lewis raises. He argues that we can retain the unified approach to the two problems if we limit the index simply to a possible world, and he argues that we can do this if we explain tenses and locative expressions in terms of covert object language quantifiers. I think there are several reasons why this attempt won't work. See the Appendix, section 3, for further discussion of this issue.

is needed to give a smooth account of the compositional process. If indices with multiple coordinates are required to accomplish this, then they should be part of the semantic machinery, but whatever the necessary machinery turns out to be, the end result should be, not a function from indices to truth-values, but a proposition. One can extract a proposition (a function from possible worlds to truth-values) from the output of the compositional process postulated by Lewis's context/index framework, but as Lewis notes, one can do so in different ways; a full account of the semantic framework should say what the propositional output is.

The main reason it is important that the output of our semantic theory be a proposition, and not just a truth-value, is (as I have argued) that our semantics is supposed to be a part of a more general theory of communication. Our general background story says that language is a device for conveying information. Speakers exploit information (both information about the semantic properties of the conventional device that is used to facilitate communication, and information about the situation, or context, in which that device is used) in order to communicate, and we need to distinguish the role of information in determining what is communicated from the information (or misinformation) that is the content that the speaker intends to communicate. The lesson of Lewis's arguments, I have suggested, should be that the semantic value that a sentence must have to get the compositional semantics right when sentences are constituents of more complex sentences may come apart from the final output that is the information the speaker is expressing. To use terminology that Michael Dummett introduced for the two different roles that a semantic value may play, we need to distinguish the *ingredient sense* of an expression—the semantic value that is needed for compositionality—from the *assertoric content* of a complete sentence, used to perform a speech act.[14] But the problem is not just with the *output* of the semantic mechanism: our background story, with its distinction between the two different roles of informational content in determining a truth-value also points to a problem with the *input* to the compositional process—the

---

[14] Dummett 1991, 47–50. See also Ninan 2010, which develops the point that the semantic values for sentences that are needed for compositional semantics are different from the values needed for the role of sentences in speech acts. See also Stanley 1997 for an earlier discussion of the role of Dummett's distinction.

context. What a context must be to get the compositional semantics right is not the same as what is needed for the explanation of the role of contextual information in determining what a speaker intends to communicate, and this gives us reason to consider our second theoretical notion of context.

1.5 Context as common ground

A K-context (as I will call the Kaplan/Lewis notion of context) can be identified with a centered possible world—a possible world plus a designated time and a subject (the speaker). A centered possible world, since it includes all that is the case, will obviously include any information that is relevant to determining what is said in an utterance, but the notion of a K-context does not isolate the relevant information. If communication is to be successful, the contextual information on which the content of a speech act depends must be information that is *available* to the addressee. When I said to O'Leary, "You are a fool", the content of my speech act depended on the fact that O'Leary was my addressee, a fact that (like all facts) is determined by the K-context in which I am speaking. But if O'Leary does not realize that I am talking to him, then communication will not be successful.

The truth of my statement depends on a different fact—that O'Leary is a fool—but successful communication does not require *that* fact to be available (in fact the utterance will have a point only if the information communicated is not available, prior to the speech act). So the account of context we need for our background story must distinguish a body of information that is available, or presumed to be available, as a resource for communication. The development of this point is part of what led to the second notion of context, context as a body of available information: the common ground. This notion of context, like any notion of a body of information, can be modeled by a set of possible worlds, labeled "the context set"—the set of possible worlds that is compatible with the presumed common knowledge of the participants. The information that a context set models includes all the information that is a resource for the interpretation of context-dependent expressions, but it is also a representation of the live options that participants take themselves to be distinguishing between in the discourse. The same notion of context plays the role of providing the information relative to which context-dependent expressions are interpreted and the role of representing the possibilities that speech acts aim to discriminate between, and it is this fact that allows for a perspicuous representation of the dynamic interaction of context and content.

The notion of common ground is a propositional attitude concept. Since the body of information that we are calling "common ground" is what is presumed to be *common* knowledge among the participants in a conversation, it is a concept with an iterative structure: a proposition is common ground between you and me if we both accept it (for the purposes of the conversation), we both accept that we both accept it, we both accept that we both accept that we both accept it, and so on. While this concept is modeled on common knowledge, it is not a factive concept. False propositions may be *presumed* to be common knowledge, and false propositions may be part of the common ground either because of error, or by pretense. Common ground, like common knowledge, is definable in terms of the propositional attitudes of the members of some group, but is not itself an individual propositional attitude. We can, however, define the individual propositional attitude of *speaker presupposition* in terms of common ground: An agent A presupposes that ϕ if and only if A accepts (for purposes of the conversation) that it is common ground that ϕ.

Our context—what is common ground between us—is constantly changing as we speak, and the iterative structure of common ground helps to explain exactly how it changes. I will say more about the iterative structure of common ground, and about its role in the dynamics, in later chapters.

1.6 Connections and tensions between the two notions

These two notions of context (K-context and common ground, or CG-context) exist side by side: From the Kaplan-Lewis theory, we have a *centered possible world*, which determines a sequence of elements (agent, time of utterance, world of utterance, suitably related so that the agent exists at the time of utterance in the world). From the common ground theory we have a *context set* of possible worlds, representing the background information available to the participants, and the possibilities among which their speech acts aim to distinguish. These notions are complementary, rather than alternative theories of the same thing, and both have been developed and applied by linguistic semanticists. But while they are not in conflict, the relations between them are unclear and there are some tensions that arise when one is not careful to distinguish these two notions of context. Here are two different ways to think about the relation between the two notions: First, one might think of common ground (or speaker presupposition) as something determined by a K-context, and so in a sense a part of it. A K-context is a concrete situation that includes a whole possible world along with a designated agent and time, and it will be a fact about the individual in the world at the time that he or she is presupposing certain propositions, and that certain propositions are common ground in the conversation that the individual is participating in at the time. But second, one might think of the common ground as something like a set of K-contexts, rather than a set of possible worlds. A propositional attitude such as belief or acceptance for the purposes of the conversation can be represented by a set of *centered* possible worlds, since the subject of the attitude will locate herself in the world as she takes it to be. An iterated attitude concept, such as common knowledge or common ground might be represented by a set of possible worlds with multiple centers, one for each of the members of the relevant group. (We will develop this idea in detail in Chapter 5.) These two ways of relating K-contexts and CG-contexts are not incompatible, but we need to be clear about just which notion of context, and what relation between them, we are considering. Claims about context, context-dependence, and truth in a context are sometimes made without making clear what notion of context one intends, and equivocation between them may occur. To conclude this chapter I will point to three places where tensions between the two notions of context emerge, each raising questions that require further discussion: first, I will look at the Kaplanian notion of a *monster*, and at Kaplan's thesis that there are no monsters. Second, I will consider a problem raised by one of the operators that motivate the context-index semantics: the actuality operator. Third, I will look briefly at problems with the role of essentially indexical or self-locating information, problems that will get more detailed discussion in Chapter 5.

First, here is what Kaplan said about "monsters begat by elegance":

> My liberality with respect to operators on content, i.e. intensional operators (any feature of the circumstances of evaluation that can be well defined and isolated) does not extend to operators which attempt to operate on character.... Indexicals always take primary scope. If this is true—and it is—then no operator can control the character of indexicals within its scope, because they will simply leap out of its scope to the front of the operator. I am not saying we could not construct a language with such operators, just that English is not one. *And such operators could not be added to it.*[15]

Kaplan is somewhat equivocal about the modal status of his prohibition of monsters. His claim is explicitly about English (is the claim supposed to apply to natural languages more generally?), and he allows that there could be languages with monsters. But it is said to be a *necessary* feature of English that it have no monsters. If there could be languages with them, what prevents English from changing to become one of them? I think there is a sense in which monsters are impossible, but it has nothing to do with English, or natural language: it is an essential feature of the semantic framework. On the other hand, there may be ways of understanding the notion of a monster according to which monsters are not only possible, but actual.

In the Lewis context-index theory, the semantic value of a sentence is a function taking a context-index pair to a truth-value. Any compositional rule for a sentence operator will give the value of the complex sentence for an arbitrary pair $\langle c,i \rangle$ as a function of the value of the inner sentence relative to a related pair $\langle c,i^* \rangle$, where i^* varies from i in some specified way. (For example, *Once* ϕ is true relative to $\langle c,i \rangle$ iff ϕ is true relative to $\langle c,i^* \rangle$, for some i^* that differs from i in its time parameter; the time parameter of i^* must be before the time parameter of i.) But in all such rules, the c parameter remains the same. One may ask why there couldn't be, for example, an operator "C" with a rule like this: Cϕ is true relative to $\langle c,i \rangle$ if and only if ϕ is true relative to $\langle c^*,i \rangle$ for some context c^*, which shifts the context component. The answer is that this restriction is no substantive constraint at all, since the general abstract theory puts no limit on what can go in the index. The idea is that the index should include all of the "shiftable" elements. If one wanted to use a Lewisian

---

[15] Kaplan 1989, 510.

context-index semantics to account for a language that shifted something that looked a lot like the abstract object that we use to represent context, then all we need to do is to put an object of this kind into the index.

The question, "Could there be monsters?" is like the question, "Could one quantify over things other than those in the domain of the quantifier?" In one sense, yes (assuming that the quantifier is a restricted one, so that there are things that are not in its domain). In such a case, one can always expand the domain to include things that were not in the original domain. But in another sense no, since if one changes the semantics in this way, it is no longer true that what one is quantifying over is not in the domain of one's quantifier. With quantifiers, the point is a trivial one, but I think the prohibition of monsters should be understood in an analogous way. There may be features of context that are not (also) elements of the index, and if there are, one cannot (in the Kaplan/Lewis semantics) have operators that "shift" those features. But one can always change the semantics by adding to the index features corresponding to them.

I think this is the right answer to the question, why are monsters forbidden, within the context of Lewis's particular semantic framework, but one has to be careful with the metaphor of *shifting*. K-contexts do not, by definition, shift in a compositional sense, but of course contexts (both the common ground, and the K-context) are changing (and so in a sense "shifting") all the time. Furthermore, as we will discuss in later chapters, our general account will allow for the creation of subordinate contexts (for example by conditional suppositions) that shift the CG-context temporarily. The issue about monsters may become more complicated when shifting contexts interact with the compositional rules, for example when the compositional rules for conditional constructions interact with the context shifts that are involved when one makes a supposition. Complications will also arise when we modify the Lewis semantics so that the output of the process is a proposition (the assertoric content) rather than just a truth-value. As noted above, there are different ways of extracting a propositional output, and as we will see, something like monsters might emerge in this process.[16] Some of

---

[16] See the Appendix, section 2, for more discussion of this issue.

these complications are illustrated by puzzles about the sentence modifier, "actually".

A related place where a tension between the two conceptions of context arises is in the semantics and pragmatics of the modifier "actually", which is one of the words that, along with "now", motivated Kaplan's move to two-dimensional semantics. Examples such as, "I thought that your yacht was larger than it actually is"[17] seem to show that "actually" is an operator that allows one to talk about what is true in the actual world, even when it occurs within the scope of a modal operator or a propositional attitude verb. In the Kaplan-Lewis framework the rule for such a modifier will be something like this: "actually ϕ" is true, relative to an index $\langle c, i \rangle$ if and only if ϕ is true relative to index $\langle c, i^* \rangle$, where i^* is like i, except with its world component replaced by the world of the context, c. It is because of operators of this kind that (to get the compositional semantics right) the K-context must include a complete possible world. But the information about what specific possible world we are in cannot be part of the information represented by the context set—the information that is presumed to be available, in common, to the participants in the conversation. (If it were, context sets would all be unit sets, and communication would be unnecessary.) When a statement is made in possible world x, the world of the context (in the Kaplan/Lewis sense) is world x, whatever the speaker may believe, and whatever may be the presumed common knowledge that defines the context in the other sense. The context set that defines the common ground for the speaker in a given K-context will not even include the world of the context, if the participants happen to be presupposing something that is in fact false. How are we to interpret "actually" in such a case? Let's consider an example: Our speaker, Alice, makes the following statement:

(1) Florence would quit her job if she had twice as much money in the bank as she actually has.

The facts (in the actual world, α, where the statement was made) are these: Florence has $150G in the bank, but it is mistakenly presupposed

---

[17] This famous example was Russell's. See Russell 1905. The original example does not contain the word "actually", illustrating that the work done by this operator is sometimes implicit, or accomplished by grammatical rather than lexical means.

by Alice (and common ground in the conversation in which she makes the statement) that Florence has $200G in the bank. Now let world β be a world that is compatible with the common ground, and with Alice's beliefs. So in world β, Florence has $200G in the bank. Let's suppose that it is also true in world β that she *would* quit her job if she had $400G, but would *not* quit her job if she had less than that. The question is, what is the truth-value of Alice's claim *relative to possible world β*? (We are not asking about the *actual* truth of the statement (made in world α)—just whether it is true in world β, which is the way Alice believes the world to be.) Now it is intuitively clear that given Alice's beliefs, her statement (1) is a sincere one, which implies that it is true in the worlds compatible with her beliefs, and so true in world β. But in order to get this result from our semantic rules, given the facts as we have described them, we must treat world β, and not world α, as the actual world when we evaluate the sentence at world β. That is, when we are evaluating the statement (made in world α) at world β, the "actually" in statement (1) shifts the index, not back (from the counterfactual world) to α (the actual world in which Alice is speaking), but rather to world β.

The "contexts" that are relevant to interpreting what Alice said are the K-contexts that are compatible with the common ground, and not the actual K-context in which the statement is made.

A further aspect of the problem of interpreting "actually" is brought out in an argument given by Timothy Williamson that concerns the interaction of the rigidifying operator with indicative conditionals. Williamson contrasts

(2i) if Jim is two meters tall, Jim is actually two meters tall

with

(2s) if Jim had been two meters tall, Jim would have actually been two meters tall

claiming that while (2s) is false if John is not in fact two meters tall, (2i) is trivially true. He then argues that "the danger for a possible worlds account of *indicative* conditionals such as Stalnaker's is that it delivers the same result for them [as it does for the subjunctive case] falsely predicting that (2i) is false if John is not two meters tall."[18]

---

[18] Williamson 2009, 136. The numbering of the example is changed to fit with the numbering of examples in this chapter.

I think there is a real puzzle in the vicinity of Williamson's argument, but there are some distracting problems with the argument that need to be cleared up before we get to it. First, Williamson is explicit that he is talking about a rigidifying operator with a stipulated semantics, and not making claims about natural language:

> Our concern here is not primarily to investigate subtleties of the use of 'actually' operators in natural languages. Rather, we will take for granted an operator in a formal language with the evidently intelligible rigidifying reading in order to investigate formally some ways in which it constrains the space of available semantic options for other constructions in the language, such as indicative and subjunctive conditionals.[19]

But the problem he raises (for the possible-worlds analysis of indicative conditionals) is that there is a conflict between the intuitive judgment about the content of a natural language sentence and the results of a theoretical semantic analysis. Unless one assumes that the English "actually" is a rigidifying operator with a semantics like the one in the formal language that Williamson is using, the intuitive judgment about the natural language sentence is not relevant. Williamson's argument asks us to fix by stipulation the semantics for one of the expressions in a certain sentence (the "actually"), and then to use our intuitions about natural language to pass judgment on the right semantics for another of the expressions (the indicative "if"). He is right that if we stipulate *both* the simple rigidifying semantics for "@" (the actuality operator) and the possible worlds analysis for the conditional "→", the result will be that a sentence of the form ($\phi \rightarrow @\phi$) will not be trivially true, but will be true if and only if ϕ is true. Since it seems reasonable to judge that a natural language sentence of the form "if ϕ, then actually ϕ" is trivially true, the conclusion should be only that one or the other of our stipulations must not be right for the interpretation of the natural language sentence. Once this is acknowledged, I think it will be clear that the main problem is with the interpretation of "actually", though there will also be problems with the "if".

A related problem with Williamson's argument is that his intuitive judgment about the contrasting (2s) is wrong. It seems to me clear (assuming we are talking about the natural language sentence) that (2s) is just as

---

[19] Williamson 2009, 137.

trivial as (2i). To get the contrast Williamson wants, (2s) should be replaced with the following:

(3s) If John had been two meters tall, then John *is* actually two meters tall.

To get the rigidifying interpretation of the modifier "actually", one must use the indicative in the clause containing it. (3s) is distinctly odd, since it seems to be presupposing that John is not in fact two meters tall, while asserting that he is, but it is not, in any case, trivially true. But the fact that the original (2s) *is* trivially true is an indication that Williamson's solution to the problem of the triviality of (2i) will not generalize. Williamson shows that the only way to ensure the triviality of (2i) is to interpret the indicative conditional as a material conditional, but one cannot make a similar move to explain the triviality of (2s). No one thinks that (so-called) *subjunctive* conditionals can be interpreted as material conditionals. The material conditional analysis is not a plausible explanation of the natural language sentence, (2i), in any case, for familiar reasons—all of the usual paradoxes of the material conditional. For example, while (2i) comes out trivially true on this analysis, (4i) also comes out (nontrivially) true, on the assumption that John is not in fact at most two meters tall:

(4i) If John is at most two meters tall, then he is actually four meters tall.

One might think that (4i) should come out trivially false, rather than factually true.

David Lewis, who was one of the first to spell out the rigidifying interpretation of "actually", observed that the word does not always have this interpretation:

"actual" and its cognates are like "present": sometimes rigidified, sometimes not. What if I'd had an elder sister? Then there would have been someone who doesn't actually exist. (Rigidified.) Then she would have been actual, though in fact she is not. (Unrigidified.) Then someone would have been actual who actually isn't actual. (Both together.)[20]

The subjunctive/indicative contrast plays an essential role in determining when the "actually" gets a rigidifying interpretation. For example, compare

---

[20] Lewis 1986, 94.

Lewis's case of an unrigidified use, "then she would have been actual, though in fact she is not" with this variation: "then she would have been actual, though in fact she would not have been." The variation, unlike the original, is a contradiction.

The uses of "actually" in Williamson's (2i) seems to be a non-rigidifying use, and so the triviality of the natural language (2i) does not pose an immediate problem for the possible-worlds analysis of indicative conditionals. But there are examples where the use of "actually" in the consequent of an indicative is clearly rigifidying, and these examples point to a problem with the standard semantics. Consider this variation on our earlier example of Florence and her bank account:

(5) If Florence has $200G in the bank, then if she had twice as much money as she actually has, she would have $400G.

For this example, assume that it is *not* presupposed that she has $200G in the bank. (If it were, the indicative supposition would be unnecessary, and so inappropriate.) So assume it is an open question how much money Florence in fact has, and that the actual α of our original example (in which Florence has only $150G in the bank) is for this example compatible with the context. Is (5) true in α? It seems intuitively that (5) is true in virtue of the arithmetic fact that 400 is twice 200, so it should be true in α. But when we do the compositional semantics in the straightforward way, using the possible-worlds semantics for the indicative conditional, and the Lewis rule for "actually", we get the result that (5) is false in α. Our problem is that we have a subjunctive conditional nested in an indicative conditional, so there will be two "shifts" in the computational process: the indicative antecedent shifts the world from α to the "nearest" world in which that antecedent is true, and then the antecedent of the inner counterfactual shifts *that* world to the "nearest" world to *it* in which the antecedent of the inner counterfactual is true. But the counterfactual antecedent has an "actually" in it, which takes the relevant clause back to the world of the context (the K-context), which is α. So the rule says that she would have only $300G if she had twice as much money in the bank as she actually has. To get the right result, the "actually" in the inner counterfactual antecedent must take us back, not all the way to the world α where the complete statement is being evaluated, but only part way, to the intermediate world in which the antecedent of the indicative conditional is true. If this is right (and to echo Kaplan, *mutatis mutandis*, it is) then it appears that something monstrous, in Kaplan's sense, is going on. We will say more about this problem in later chapters, when we look at conditionals and subordinate contexts, and in the appendix.

I will conclude this chapter with a brief remark about a third example of a tension in the relationship between the two notions of context, a problem that will be discussed in more detail in Chapter 5. The issue concerns self-locating, or essentially indexical information. The original idea, implicit in the motivation for the character-content distinction, was that indexicality is a part of the means used to communicate, and is not involved in the content of the information that one is communicating. When I say, "I was born in New Jersey," the content of what I say is the same as the content of your utterance of "Stalnaker was born in New Jersey." You might in fact just be passing along the information that my statement gave you. But the phenomenon of essentially indexical belief complicates the story. My beliefs about who I am, and what time it is, seem to have the indexical element in the content of what is believed, and not just in the means used to express it and this threatens to blur the line that I have emphasized between the two roles of information in the determination of the truth-value of an utterance.

David Kaplan's response to the problem was to suggest that while the *content* of a propositional attitude was an ordinary objective proposition, the *cognitive significance* of the thought was a *character*, which in the Lewis formulation of the semantic framework is a function from a context-index pair to a truth-value.[21] But this move undercuts the motivation for giving a distinctive pragmatic role to propositional content, and it also implies that if we are able, in our attitude ascription, to make claims about the cognitive significance of the subject's thoughts, we will need to violate the Kaplanian ban on monsters, since the referent of a that clause will depend on the character, and not just the content, of the clause. I think this is the wrong response, and I will develop an alternative to it in Chapter 5. In the next chapter, we will look more closely at the notion of context as common ground.

---

[21] In Kaplan 1989, 530, the following two principles are stated:
    E. Principle 1 Objects of thought (Thoughts)= Contents
    E. Principle 2 Cognitive significance of a Thought= Character

2

Common Ground and Keeping Score

The main concern of Chapter 1 was the Kaplan/Lewis notion of context, its different roles in the explanation of semantic and pragmatic phenomena, and some tensions between it and a contrasting notion of context as common ground. In this chapter, I will look more closely at this contrasting notion: of how it should be characterized and modeled, and how it evolves in the course of a discourse. I will be particularly concerned with the relation between common ground and the rules of a conventional practice of using a language in a discourse or a conversation. My argument will be that we should explain this notion of context independently of any language or institutional practice of using a language. (This argument is part of a general defense of what, in the introduction, I called the thesis of the autonomy of pragmatics.) In section 2.1 I will sketch two contrasting strategies for relating the notion of common ground to a linguistic practice, and connect this contrast with an old debate in the philosophy of language. In section 2.2 I will review the general Gricean strategy for explaining communicative action and argue that it supports the idea that a notion of common ground is an essential feature of any communicative practice. In section 2.3, I will say more about the structure of common ground, and the role of the structure in explaining the dynamics of discourse. I will argue that the process of *accommodation* is an inevitable part of any cooperative activity. The chapter will conclude, in section 2.4, with a brief look at the role of the rules of a language, and of a conventional practice of using that language, in the dynamic process.

2.1 Mutual attitudes and constitutive rules

I will start by reminding you of the general idea—the common ground about what common ground is. The common ground is an information state that we represent with the set of possible worlds (the context set) that is compatible with the information. The rough idea is that the information is the presumed common background knowledge shared by the participants in a conversation (or perhaps more generally the participants in some cooperative activity). This body of information plays two roles: first, it provides a resource that speakers may exploit in determining how to say what they want to say; second, it identifies the possibilities between which the participants aim to distinguish in their speech, and so provides a resource for the explanation of speech acts in terms of the way the act is intended to change the context. The two roles lead to a dynamic interaction: context constrains content, since what is said may be context-dependent, and content (expressed with a certain force) affects subsequent context. It is important for explaining this interaction that the information in a context includes both information about the subject matter of the discourse, and information about the discourse itself (about who knows what about the subject matter, and about what is going on in the conversation).

So common ground is an information state determined by a group engaged in a conversation at a particular time, but what is it about the attitudes or behavior of the individuals in the group at that time that determines the content of that information state? How is the set of possibilities that defines the context for a conversation (at a given time) determined by the facts about that conversation? There are two contrasting strategies for answering these questions: First, one might think of a context set (the set of possibilities compatible with the relevant informational state) as a component, perhaps the central component, of the score of a language game. The game analogy is a familiar one that has played a central role in discussions of the philosophy of language at least since Wittgenstein's discussions of language games, and it is a rich metaphor with many dimensions. The aspect of the analogy that is relevant to the first strategy for explaining common ground is the idea that a game is something defined by constitutive rules. The crucial idea of this strategy is to think of communication in terms of a conventional, institutional practice, one that involves types of actions that are intelligible only in the context of a practice governed by the constitutive rules of that practice. On this kind of account, the common ground is the body of information that plays a certain role in such a conventional practice, and that evolves in response to the rules of the practice.

The second strategy is to think of the common ground as a propositional attitude, or as a complex state definable in terms of the propositional attitudes of the participants of the conversation. The notion of the knowledge or belief that is common to a group is intelligible independently of any practice, and these notions are definable in terms of the individual knowledge or belief of the members of the group. Our notion of common ground is modeled on common belief, but more needs to be said about what the basic attitude is if we are to defend the idea that common ground is intelligible independently of a conventional practice.

The contrast between these two strategies reflects an old debate in the philosophy of language, with philosophers such as John Austin and John Searle on one side, and Paul Grice on the other.[1] All of these philosophers emphasized the way that speech was a kind of action, but Austin focused on actions that changed institutional relations in virtue of constitutive rules: his paradigm speech acts were cases where, for example, one becomes married, or comes to own a piece of property in virtue of someone saying something in the right setting. Searle argued that we could make sense of acts of meaning only in the context of conventional practices. Grice, in contrast, wanted to explain communicative practices, ultimately, in terms of the intentions and beliefs of the participants, attitudes that can be understood apart from any convention. The difference between the two approaches is the focus of a classic paper by P. F. Strawson, where he contrasts "cases where the overt intention is simply to forward a definite and convention-governed practice (for example a game) in a definite way provided for by the conventions or rules of the practice and those cases in which in which the overt intention includes that of securing a definite response (cognitive or practical) in an audience over and above that which is necessarily secured if uptake is secured."[2]

---

[1] See Austin 1962, Searle 1965, and Grice 1989.   [2] Strawson 1964, 460.

David Lewis sketched these two strategies, as applied to his notion of "conversational score", and then suggested a compromise. Here is his way of putting the contrast:

> To the extent that conversational score is determined, given the history of the conversation and the rules that specify its kinematics, these rules can be regarded as constitutive rules akin to definitions.... Alternatively, conversational score might be operationally defined in terms of the mental scoreboards—some suitable attitudes—of the parties to the conversation. The rules specifying the kinematics of the conversational score then become empirical generalizations, subject to exceptions, about the causal dependence of what the scoreboards register on the history of the conversation.[3]

Lewis thought that both strategies were problematic; on his suggested compromise, "conversational score is, by definition, whatever the mental scoreboards say that it is", but rather than specifying the relevant mental states, we hypothesize that there are mental states that play the role of a scoreboard in the following sense: "What they register depends on the history of the conversation in the way that score should according to the rules."[4] I am not completely clear what this means, but the rough idea seems to be that the relevant attitude is to be defined, or to have its reference fixed, functionally as the attitude of the participants that best fits what the rules say it should be. As I understand it, this is a version of the first strategy, since it implies that the rules of an institutional practice play a constitutive role in determining the relevant information state.

Max Kölbel also argues for a version of the first strategy, proposing that we should "define speaker presupposition in such a way that it is conceptually tied to certain rules and conventions. Thus a *social* or *conventional* notion of acceptance, rather than a psychological one, seems to be needed."[5] But I am going to argue for an uncompromising version of the first, Gricean, strategy for explaining common ground. I agree with Kölbel that common ground, and speaker presupposition, are social and public attitudes, but I want to explain the social, public character of the attitude in terms of the iterative structure, as in common knowledge and belief. I also want to concede that one can perhaps not identify the individual attitude that is iterated independently of the role of the public attitude. We have said that common ground is something

---

[3] Lewis 1979b, 420.   [4] Lewis 1979b, 420.   [5] Kölbel 2011, 60.

like mutual *acceptance*, in some sense. Acceptance generally, as I use the term, is acceptance for some purpose or other,[6] and in this case the relevant purposes are social and public. But it is a wholly different matter whether this public, social attitude is conceptually tied to the rules of some conventional practice. I will agree that the conventional practice of using a language to *say* things is defined in terms of the common ground: the illocutionary force of an assertion (on the kind of account I have promoted) is explained as a proposal to change the common ground in a certain way. But I will argue that common ground itself is intelligible independently of the particular rules of this kind of practice, and that we have strong reason to aim for an independent account of it.

To motivate and to clarify my uncompromising stance, I am going to review the general Gricean program, as I understand it, and then connect the notion of common ground to Grice's project of explaining speaker meaning.[7]

2.2 The Gricean program

Grice's general project was to reduce *semantic* concepts to *mental* intentional concepts such as belief and intention. This kind of project contrasts with the more familiar one of trying to give a naturalistic account of intentionality,[8] since it takes individual mental intentional concepts such as belief and intention as given, though it is not incompatible with that different project. The idea was to characterize a family of concepts that were essentially involved in communicative action. His fundamental concept was speaker meaning (meaning$_{NN}$). The overall project was to build on that concept to explain all other semantic notions. The main benefit of an autonomous account of speaker meaning—of a reduction of that notion to intentions and beliefs—was to make it possible to understand conventional linguistic practice as a practice whose function is to facilitate the activity of meaning things. Grice's assumption was that to explain how linguistic communication works, we would do better if we

---

[6] See Stalnaker 1984, 79-81.
[7] See the papers collected in Grice 1989, especially "Meaning", first published in 1957, and the William James lectures (Chapters 1-7 of the collection).
[8] See Stalnaker 1984, Chapters 1 and 2 for a discussion of this issue. Grice himself wanted to defend a functionalist account of intentionality, but this was a separate project.

separate means and ends. Questions about what a device (a language) is used to do are best separated from questions about the means language uses to do those things.

Here is Grice's initial analysis of speaker meaning (meaning$_{NN}$):

"A meant$_{NN}$ something by x" is roughly equivalent to "A uttered x with the intention of inducing a belief by means of the recognition of this intention."[9]

This approximation to an analysis, first presented in print in 1957, became the subject of an extensive literature in which ever more Byzantine counterexamples were proposed, followed by ever more Byzantine modifications and qualifications. I am going to ignore these complications, and the question whether genuine reduction can be accomplished. What I want to do is to draw out some of the significance of the general idea, and to argue that it is an illuminating idea that helps to understand linguistic communication.

Suppose that an agent A performed an action (by uttering U) that fits Grice's definition, and so that A meant$_{NN}$ something—say the proposition that ϕ.[10] The analysis focuses our attention on the following two questions about the act:

(1) Why should uttering U be a way to get the addressee to recognize the speaker's intention to induce in him the belief that ϕ?
(2) Why should getting the addressee to recognize the speaker's intention to induce in him the belief that ϕ be a way of inducing in him the belief that ϕ?

The first question might be answered in different ways in different cases. If one thinks of language as a device that links particular linguistic items (sentences) to propositions, then if A presumes that her addressee knows about the device—and more, that it is common knowledge that the device links sentences to propositions in the way that it does—then it will be easy and natural to have a *convention* to use utterance of the sentences to mean$_{NN}$ the propositions associated with them. (Here we assume that a convention is something like the pattern of beliefs and

---

[9] Grice 1989, 219.
[10] Grice's analysis is cautious, giving conditions only for the existential claim that A meant *something* by uttering U. But I am going to assume that the belief that A intended to induce was what A meant.

intentions that David Lewis used to define the notion of convention.)[11] The idea is that *saying* something in a language is a central way to *mean* what one is saying—one central way to answer the first of the two questions that are raised. But the constitutive conditions for meaning$_{NN}$ are independent of how this question is answered; one might mean things without using language at all, relying on ad hoc expectations about what actions will or might give rise the recognition of an intention. One can exploit natural gestures (smiles and frowns, pointing) that as a matter of empirical fact tend to occur in certain circumstances, or naturally to direct one's attention in a certain way. And once one has a conventional device such as a language, one can also use it to mean things different from what one says.

The second of our two questions arises since it is clear from the definition that even if it is known, and commonly known, *what* is meant, the action may not succeed in its aim. The second question can get a satisfactory answer only if there is a certain pattern of common interest. Only if the addressee believes that the speaker wants him to believe the truth (whatever it is), will the fact that she is manifestly trying to induce in him the belief that ϕ be a reason for him to believe that ϕ. And since an intention requires the belief that there is at least a reasonable chance of success, the definition implies that it is not even possible to mean$_{NN}$ that ϕ unless there is a mutual expectation that there is a pattern of common interest sufficient to ground the credibility of the act of meaning.[12]

In his development of the idea of conversational implicature, Grice stated a *cooperative principle*, which he took to be a general principle governing conversation:

Make your conversational contribution such as is required, at the stage at which it occurs, by the accepted purpose or direction of the talk exchange in which you are engaged.[13]

Our second question brings out the way that this principle is grounded in the definition of speaker meaning. The cooperative principle is compatible with lots of conflict. It can be satisfied in contentious debates and

---

[11] Lewis 1969.
[12] I attempt, in Stalnaker 2005, to spell out, in a game theoretic context, the kind of common interest that is necessary for credibility.
[13] Grice 1989, 26.

negotiations as well as in simple exchanges of information. But for communication (trying to get people to believe things by meaning them) to be possible, there must be a recognized common interest in sharing certain information.

In his discussion of conversational implicature, Grice emphasized that the cooperative principle was not just a rule of a game that might have been different. The presumption that it is being followed is necessary for the possibility of communicative action. The echo of Kant in this way of phrasing the point is appropriate: Grice thought of his project as Kantian in spirit.[14] He also emphasized a second feature that the structure of the Gricean analysis of speaker meaning brings out: once one has a conventional device designed to mean things, it is inevitable that the device will be capable of exploitation to mean things with expressions of the language other than what those expressions conventionally mean. Any way of getting one's intentions recognized can be a way to meaning$_{NN}$ something, and an elaborate set of conventions associating types of acts that are easy to perform and to identify (utterances of expressions of a language) with propositions will provide new ways of getting one's intentions recognized that go beyond those built into the semantics for the language. All of this is grounded in the basic idea of the Gricean account of speaker meaning.

The upshot for our purposes is that common interest and common knowledge are necessary for the possibility of communication. Only against a relatively rich background of common belief is it possible to get people to recognize the very specific intentions that must be recognized for successful acts of meaning, and only where there are mutually recognized common interests will the recognition of the intentions be effective in changing beliefs.

2.3 The iterative structure of common ground

I have argued that we should characterize the common ground of a conversation in terms of the propositional attitudes of the participants in the conversation, but we need to say more, first about what propositional attitudes of those participants are relevant, and second about how

---

[14] The allusion to the structure of the Kantian categories in Grice's organization of his maxims of conversation was playful, but there was a serious point behind it.

the common ground is related to those individual attitudes. I will use a standard formal semantic model for logics of knowledge and belief to help sharpen these questions. This kind of representation of knowledge, belief, and other attitudes is highly idealized, but it has proved useful for clarifying issues in epistemology, and will help to bring out some abstract features of the dynamics of discourse. I will first sketch the basic ideas of the theory, and then consider how common ground should be defined within that framework.

In the classical theory,[15] a belief or knowledge state is represented by a set of possible worlds. The intuitive idea is to represent a subject's cognitive situation by the set of possible states of a world that from the subject's perspective might be the way the actual world is. The point is not to provide a substantive analysis of knowledge and belief, but to represent their abstract structure in a revealing way. One does not say what it is to be a doxastic or epistemic alternative possible world; one simply assumes it by specifying, as a primitive component of the model, a binary relation between possible worlds that determines a set of alternative possible worlds as a function of each world. What is being modeled is the beliefs or knowledge that a given subject has (at a given time, which usually goes unmentioned) in a given possible world. The relation holds between possible worlds x and y if and only if the subject's state of knowledge in world x, at the relevant time, is compatible with possible world y being the actual world. That is, if xRy, then for all the subject knows or believes in world x, she is in world y. The theory will put various constraints on the relation of doxastic or epistemic accessibility, which will correspond to assumptions about the logic of knowledge or belief. For example, since knowledge is factive, the epistemic accessibility relation must be reflexive, which means that the state of knowledge that an agent is in (in a given possible world x) must be compatible with that state of knowledge. A standard semantics for a logic of belief will assume that the doxastic accessibility relation is both transitive and Euclidean,[16] which implies that the believer has access to her beliefs: if she believes

---

[15] The study of the logic of knowledge and belief in this kind of framework began with Hintikka 1962. It has been widely applied in theoretical computer science and game theory, as well as in epistemology. See Stalnaker 2006 for a general survey of semantics of epistemic logic, and Fagin et al. 1995 for a survey of some applications in computer science.

[16] A binary relation R is Euclidian if it satisfies the following condition: for all x, y, and z, if xRy and xRz, then yRz.

that ϕ, she believes that she believes it, and if she does not believe that ϕ, she believes that she does not believe it.

Hintikka focused on models of the attitudes of single subjects, but much of the interest in this kind of model comes from its account of the interaction of the attitudes of different subjects: what I know or don't know about what you know, including about what I know about what you know about what I know, etc. Even though Hintikka did not talk about the interaction of the attitudes of different subjects, his models generalize without further assumptions or problems: one just has an epistemic accessibility relation with the appropriate properties indexed to each knower. A model will yield, for each proposition ϕ and knower A, a proposition that A knows that ϕ, and that proposition will itself be something that may be known, or not, by A, or by another agent B. So claims about knowledge straightforwardly iterate, both for the same subject, and for different subjects. For any given proposition ϕ, we get, for example, the propositions that A knows that A knows that ϕ, that A knows that B does not know that ϕ, that A knows that either B knows that ϕ or else C does, but doesn't know which. And one can define a notion of common knowledge for a pair or group of knowers in terms of the epistemic accessibility relations for the different members of the pair or group. One does this by defining an accessibility relation for common knowledge as the relation that is the *transitive closure*[17] of the accessibility relations of the members of the group. Then the semantic rule for common knowledge will have the same form as the rule for individual knowledge: if R* is the accessibility relation for common knowledge, then it is common knowledge that ϕ in world x if and only if ϕ is true in all possible worlds y such that xR*y. Given the definition of R*, this will imply that it is common knowledge that ϕ in a group of knowers G if and only if all members of the group know that ϕ, all know that all know it, all know that all know that all know it, etc. ad infinitum.

It is common *knowledge* that has received the most attention, but an infinitely iterated extension of belief, or any acceptance concept can be defined in an exactly analogous way, with a semantics in terms of the

---

[17] The transitive closure, R* of a set of binary relations, $R_1, \ldots R_n$ is defined as follows: xR*y if and only if there is a sequence $z_1 \ldots z_m$ such that $z_1 = x$ and $z_m = y$, and for each pair, z_i, z_{i+1} there is a j such that $z_i R_j z_{i+1}$.

transitive closure of a set of accessibility relations of the appropriate kind for the members of the relevant group.

Since the transitive closure of a set of binary relations is itself a binary relation, the logic and semantics of common knowledge, common belief, or common acceptance will be like the logic of knowledge, belief, or acceptance. The properties of the derivative accessibility relation for the common notion will be determined by the properties of the relation for the individual notion, but the properties of the derived relation will not necessarily be the same. For example, if it is assumed that the accessibility relation for belief is transitive and Euclidean, this will not imply that the relation for common or mutual belief is Euclidean. Even if we assume that everyone believes what he himself believes (and so always believes that he does *not* believe that ϕ when he does not believe it), this will not imply that if something is *not* common belief, then it is common belief that it is not common belief. Suppose I fail to believe that ϕ, and so believe that it is not common belief that ϕ. You might believe that ϕ, and also mistakenly believe that this is a shared belief—that it *is* common belief that ϕ. In such a case, it is not common belief that it is not common belief that ϕ, and so the Euclidean condition on the accessibility relation for common belief is violated.

Common ground, in a formal model of this kind, will have the structure of common knowledge and belief, with an accessibility relation defied in terms of the transitive closure of the accessibility relations for a notion of *acceptance for the purposes of the conversation*. The notion of acceptance is modeled on the notion of belief, and I will assume that the relevant kind of acceptance has the same formal properties as belief, and so that the formal properties of common ground will be the same as those of common belief. That is, I assume that one has access to what one accepts, which means that one accepts that one accepts that ϕ when one accepts it, and accepts that one does not when one does not. And while acceptance in this sense may diverge from belief in ways we will discuss, I will assume that belief (and common belief) are the default settings for acceptance for the purpose of the conversation (and for common ground). That is, I assume that divergences between what is believed, and mutually believed, and what is accepted, or commonly accepted need to be explained. The common ground is what is *presumed* to be common knowledge, and normally one presumes that something is common knowledge when one believes that it is. But in some cases, it may serve the purposes of the conversation to engage in some mutually recognized pretense, or to carry on a conversation within the scope of some mutually recognized supposition. One principle that plays a critical role in the explanation for some of the ways in which common ground may diverge from common belief is what I will call a *norm of agreement* for common ground, a norm that is grounded in Grice's cooperative principle. In the next section, I will look at the role of this norm in the way that contexts evolve.

I have said that one may *accept* things, in the relevant sense, that one does not believe in cases where it facilitates the conversation to do so, which means that something may be part of the common ground even when it is not mutually believed. But as I have learned from the work of Elisabeth Camp, it is also important to allow for a divergence between belief and acceptance in the other direction. It might be that something is mutually believed, but not part of the common ground because one or another of the parties to the conversation is not prepared to acknowledge that it is mutually believed, and so not prepared to draw on this information in the conversation. Just as there can be a pretense that one has certain information that one does not have, so there can be a pretense that one lacks certain information that one does have.[18]

2.4 Accommodation

We can make sense of common knowledge and common belief even for a pair of agents who have no interaction with each other. In such a case, your beliefs about what beliefs we share may diverge from mine, and this is just a fact about the situation; there need be no pressure to change it, even if it is recognized by one or both of the agents that their beliefs about what is common belief diverge. But a conversation is presupposed to be a cooperative enterprise, and successful communication will depend on agreement about what the common ground is. So it is a norm of communication that the presuppositions of the participants—what they take the common ground to be—should be the same. There will inevitably

---

[18] Camp's fascinating work (as yet unpublished) concerns some of the conversational strategies in play in adversarial conversations in which one may want to communicate something while maintaining deniability, and so while not being prepared to publicly acknowledge that one is communicating what one is communicating.

be contexts in which there is a difference in what is presupposed by different parties to the conversation, but these will be *defective* contexts, and cooperative speakers who recognize a defect of this kind will take steps to ensure, in one way or another, that it does not persist. This norm, and the presumption that it is in effect, creates both a motive and a mechanism for adjustment in the context when a divergence comes to light.

Changes in the common ground, like changes in common knowledge and belief, will normally take place in response to what I will call a "manifest event". A manifest event is something that happens in the environment of the relevant parties that is obviously evident to all. A goat walks into the room, or all of the lights suddenly go out. In such a case, it immediately becomes common knowledge that the event has happened—that there is a goat in the room, or that the lights have gone out. Speech acts will themselves be manifest events (at least when all goes well): when one produces an utterance, it becomes common ground that it has been produced, and when the semantics of the language is common ground, it will be manifest that an utterance with a certain meaning has been produced. When a context is defective, the fact that it is defective may be revealed by a manifest event.

Suppose I recognize a defect in the context. Suppose, for example, that it becomes manifest that you are presupposing something that I don't, or didn't, believe. What do I do? Here are three possible cooperative responses.

First, I may accommodate by changing my belief so that what you are taking to be common ground is in fact common ground. In many cases, the fact that you apparently believe some proposition, and take it be common belief, may be a reason for me to believe it. Many of the standard examples of presupposition accommodation fit this pattern: you say "I have to pick up my cat at the veterinarian"; I didn't know, prior to your statement, that you had a cat, but the fact that you were presupposing that you did is a good reason for me to believe that you do.

In this kind of case, it is reasonable for me to accommodate by changing my beliefs in this way, but was it reasonable for *you* to have presupposed it in the first place? You, let us suppose, did not have any reason to believe that I knew about your cat. There is a delicate question of timing here, since presuppositions and common ground are constantly changing as we speak. It was reasonable for you to believe that

I *would* come to know that you had a cat, and that we were both presupposing that you had a cat *after* you made your statement. The (tacit) reasoning (to spell it out in tedious detail) might go something like this: you manifestly are presupposing that you have a cat, so I come to believe that you believe that it is common belief that you have a cat. Since I believe that you know whether or not you have a cat, and that you would not be presupposing that you did unless it were true, I also come to believe that you have a cat. So I (the addressee) have two premises of the form (1) B (the speaker) believes A (the addressee) believes that it is common belief that ϕ, and (2) ϕ. It is a valid inference in a logic for the iterated attitude from the premise that A believes (1) and (2), to the conclusion that A believes that it is common belief (between A and B) that ϕ, so I infer that this is common belief. The inference takes place *after* the manifest facts are recognized. We will come back to the question of timing after considering two other cooperative responses.

A second possible response is for me to try to change *your* presuppositions, rather than to change my own, by making manifest that I do not believe the proposition that you are presupposing, so that you will no longer mistakenly take it to be common belief. This will often be a more costly kind of repair, since it may require me to interrupt the flow of conversation, and comment on it. (To reject an assertion is to make a standard move in the language game, while to reject something that has been presupposed requires an explicit recognition that the game has gone off course.) There are, however, devices in the language for correcting presuppositions. I might, for example, make an assertion that manifestly presupposes something contrary to what you presuppose. (Alice says to Bert, who is holding his infant son, "How old is she?" Bert responds, "*He* is four months." In some cases, a "might" statement can be used to correct a defective context. (Alice says, "The butler didn't do it, so the gardener must be the guilty party," presupposing that they are the only two suspects. Bert replies, "It might have been the chauffeur.") I will discuss epistemic modals in Chapters 6 and 7.

A third cooperative response is a variation on the first: suppose the fact that you presuppose that ϕ is not, in the circumstances, a reason for me to believe that ϕ (perhaps I have independent reason to think that ϕ is false), but suppose the question whether ϕ is not particularly relevant to our communicative exchange. Your manifestly presupposing that ϕ may have played a role in your communicating some other proposition ψ, but the question whether ψ was more or less independent of whether ϕ. In this case, I might accommodate by *accepting* ϕ, for the purposes of the conversation, even though I don't come to believe it. Keith Donnellan's famous case of the man described as "the man drinking a martini" fits this pattern.[19] The man is in fact drinking something else in a martini glass, and the addressee knows this, but the point of the description was just to pick out the man. The claim about the man (perhaps that he was a philosopher) had nothing to do with his drinking habits. So it is reasonable for the addressee to go along, accepting the presupposition, though not coming to believe it. Compare this with the alternative second response, "You know, that is not really a martini. If you look closely, you'll see that it is Perrier in a martini glass." This would seem pedantic, and would divert the conversation in an irrelevant direction. As Donnellan noted in his discussion of referential uses of definite descriptions, the speaker need not believe what he is presupposing—he might use that description because he assumes that the *addressee* believes that the description applies. Or it could be a mutually recognized pretense, as in Donnellan's example of the pretender to the throne who we describe as "the king" even though it is common knowledge between us that he is not really the king.[20]

Now let's look back at the question of timing raised just above. In many cases, a speaker may say something that reveals that she *anticipates* that it will be common ground as a result of her saying it. This seems to be the case where the speaker was presupposing that she had a cat: the time at which the proposition becomes common ground (if all goes well) is the time at which the speech act in question is assessed, and this is what the speaker intends and expects. In an idealized model, we assume that there is a time *after* the speech act has been manifestly recognized, but *before* it has been accepted or rejected. This is of course an idealization. In simple cases of uncontroversial exchange of information, an assertion may be accepted at the point at which it is understood. Or suppose your reference to your cat was in a letter or an email, and you are unsure exactly when I will read it. In such cases, there may be a certain amount of pretense in the assumption that there is a single point in time at which the presuppositions of the parties to the conversation have been adjusted,

---

[19] Donnellan 1966, 287.   [20] Donnellan 1966, 291.

and coincide, prior to the assessment of the assertion. This is perhaps another way in which what is accepted for the purposes of the conversation may diverge from what is believed. But the theoretical question of timing is clearly not a problem for achieving the coordination that is required for mutual understanding, and it is important to recognize that this kind of anticipatory presupposition is the normal case. It is a very obvious and general requirement of cooperative communication that the speaker presuppose that the information needed to understand what she is saying be available to the addressee, but in most cases of context-dependent reference, the speaker will not presuppose that the addressee has the relevant information before she begins to speak. The manifest event that the speech act took place will frequently be the source of the relevant information. For example, when the shopkeeper says to the boy leaving the shop, "Hey, you in the purple T-shirt – you forgot your backpack", the utterance, using the pronoun "you", is appropriate only if the speaker can reasonably presume that the addressee knows that he is the addressee. (It must be common ground that he is the addressee.) But the point at which he must know this is of course only *after* the statement has been made.

I have argued that presupposition accommodation, and a divergence between acceptance and belief, are grounded in very general features of any communicative activity. We can make sense of notions of acceptance and of common acceptance for the purposes of a conversation independently of particular rule-governed institutions if we can make sense of the point and purpose of a communicative exchange, in accord with the Gricean project.

2.5 The language game of assertion

So far we have made no assumptions about a conventional language, with constitutive rules and rule-governed moves that change the context in the way that Austinian illocutionary acts alter an institutionally defined status. But now let us assume that we are playing a language game, in Lewis's sense, with a speech act of assertion as one of the possible moves. To make an assertion is to *say* something, and not just to *mean* something, in Grice's sense of speaker meaning discussed above. The moves in the game will involve a language that has a semantics (a grammar, in Lewis's terminology) that matches sentences with propositions as a function of the context. A move in the game will be the production of a sentence with a certain conventionally indicated force, where force is explained in terms of the way that the move is intended to change the context. So the game will be defined by rules of two kinds: lexical and compositional rules that determine the *content* of what is said, and rules that determine the *force* with which the content is said. Assume that the speech act of *assertion* is governed by the following rule: an assertion changes the context by adding the propositional content of the assertion to the common ground. That is the default rule, but it is a rule of the assertion game that the addressee has the option of rejecting the assertion, blocking this rule-governed change. Rejection is another of the possible rule-governed moves in the game. So the assertion is, in effect, a proposal to change the context (the common ground) in a certain way, a proposal that takes effect if it is not rejected. All of this is, of course, a highly idealized and simplified model of what goes on in real conversations, but it will help to clarify the interaction between the constitutive rules of a linguistic practice and the contexts in which those rules are applied.

Once we have a specific linguistic practice, with rules that are presumed to be common knowledge among the participants in some communicative exchange, we have a further basis for inferences from the manifest events that take place to changes in the common ground. When you say, "It is snowing in Budapest" (in a context in which it is common ground that we speak English) it becomes common belief, not only that you uttered certain sounds, but also that you said that it is snowing in Budapest. Or suppose you were to say something that would be appropriate (given the linguistic rules of our common language) only if you were presupposing (taking it to be common ground) that it was snowing in Budapest, and suppose further that I believe that you intended to speak appropriately; then it will become common belief that you were presupposing that it was snowing in Budapest. This adjustment, or accommodation, is an example of the simple and straightforward response to a manifest event: something becomes common belief because something happens that is obviously evident to the parties concerned.

In general, given the assumption that the semantics of the language and the rules of the game are common knowledge among the players, we can conclude that when an assertion is made, it will be a manifest event that an assertion with a particular content was made by the person who made it. So the assertion changes the context in a way that depends on the fact that we are playing a game with these particular constitutive rules, but the change will not itself be the result of the application of the rules. That is, it is because of the constitutive rules of the game that a certain act counts as an assertion (in English) that φ, and if it is common ground that the participants are speaking English, then the act will change the context by making it common ground that the speaker has just asserted that φ. But it is not a rule of the game that the context should change in this way. This change is just a mutual recognition that an act of a certain kind has been performed. In earlier work, I labeled the change in the context that *is* the result of the application of a rule of the assertion game "the essential effect". This is the change of adding the content of the assertion to the common ground. I distinguished the essential effect from the change that results simply from the manifest fact that the assertion was made. This connects with the point about timing discussed above. The context in which an assertion is evaluated (the point at which the addressee decides whether to accept or reject it) is the context as it is after the assertion has been made and mutually recognized.

In a game of this kind, an assertion might or might not be *appropriate* or *felicitous*. Appropriateness and felicity are not concepts that will occur in the constitutive rules of the language game, but the game is presumably being played for some purpose, and normally with some mutually recognized common purpose. Moves that fail to serve the purpose, in one way or another, are inappropriate. While inappropriateness will not appear in the constitutive rules of the game, generalizations about appropriateness may play a role in explaining the way the context changes in the course of play. If it is common ground (based on something like Grice's cooperative principle) that the players are speaking appropriately, and if some move in the game is appropriate only if it is presupposed that φ, then the manifest fact that the move is made may suffice to make it the case that it is common ground that φ. This particular way in which the context is adjusted in response to speech is independent of the reason why the move in question would be inappropriate if the speaker were not presupposing that φ. It might be that there is a rule of the semantics that stipulates that one should not assertively utter some sentence S unless it is presupposed that φ. But it also might be that there is some general Gricean explanation for the fact that the presupposition is required for the utterance to be appropriate. The simplest and most common case where a presupposition is required by the use of a sentence is a case where the addressee can apply the semantic rules to figure out what the speaker is saying only if he has certain information. In a case like this, the semantic rules help to explain why a presupposition is required, but the rules themselves need make no mention of presuppositions.

Much of the discussion in the literature on presupposition focuses on one very specific role of common ground: to analyze the linguistic notion of presupposition (an alleged relation between sentences and propositions). Part of my point in reviewing these Gricean ideas, and in arguing for a central role of the notion of accommodation in the explanation for the way contexts change, is to emphasize that common ground and speaker presupposition are not concepts developed or deployed to explain this narrow range of linguistic phenomena, but are central concepts in the characterization of any communicative practice. If Grice was even roughly right about what communicative action is, then it is clear that something like our notion of common ground must play a central role in any kind of communication, and something like our notion of accommodation will play a central role in any account of how contexts change. In the next chapter I will look at the dialectic of debate in the linguistic literature about presupposition in the light of these general considerations, arguing that they motivate a different perspective on that debate.

3

Presupposition Requirements

In the last chapter I discussed presupposition and accommodation in the setting of a pragmatic framework for representing context, but discussions by linguists of what they called "presupposition" predate the development of this framework, or of any systematic theory of context. In this chapter, my plan is to look at the way the problems about presuppositional phenomena were posed in these early discussions and since, and at the dialectic of argument in the linguistics literature about how those problems should be solved. I will start, in section 3.1, with the arguments given in the early 1970s for a pragmatic account of presupposition, and look at two different ways of developing the pragmatic account. There were some putative counterexamples that the pragmatic account was said to face, and in section 3.2 I will consider the response to those problems that invoked the notion of accommodation, and look at some criticisms of that response. My argument will be that this critical response to the pragmatic account of presupposition was based on a misunderstanding of the pragmatic account, at least of the pragmatic account as I think it should be understood. Specifically, I will argue that the criticisms confuse theoretical concepts with concepts for describing surface phenomena, and this will lead, in section 3.3, to a methodological digression about the contrast between these two kinds of concepts, and their roles in debates concerning linguistic data and the hypotheses that aim to explain them. After some remarks about this general issue, I will consider, in section 3.4, the interplay of theoretical notions of sentence presupposition with more descriptive notions, using some examples of specific debates about presupposition to illustrate the importance of being clear on the distinction. I will conclude, in section 3.5, with some remarks about the diversity of the phenomena that have been grouped together under the label "presupposition".

3.1 The pragmatic account of presupposition

Early discussions by linguists of presupposition began with a familiar collection of paradigm cases without any very clear account of what these were cases of. Certain words or grammatical constructions "gave rise to" presuppositions. For philosophers, definite descriptions had long been the central paradigm: the sentence, "The present king of France is wise" presupposes that France has a unique king. Other instances of the phenomenon that linguists were concerned with are factive verbs, change of state verbs, cleft constructions, words like "too" and "again". "Jacques regrets voting for Sarkozy", "Harry stopped smoking", "It was Lauri who solved the projection problem", "John is in trouble again" presuppose, respectively, that Jacques voted for Sarkozy, that Harry used to smoke, that some unique person solved the projection problem, and that John has been in trouble before. In the old days (pre-1970) the linguists followed the philosophers in taking for granted that presupposition should be defined in terms of truth-value gaps: it was assumed that what it means to say that sentence S presupposes that φ, is that S has a truth-value only if φ. Much of the discussion of presupposition, in this early work, focused on what was called "the projection problem": the problem of explaining how the presuppositions of complex sentences were a function of the presuppositions of their component parts. If one assumes that presupposition is to be analyzed in terms of truth-value gaps, then one should expect the projection problem for truth functional connectives to be a problem of extending the truth tables to three-valued truth tables, but when the problem was posed this way, the data suggested that the compositional rules would be complex in surprising ways. For example "and" and "or", symmetric in the two-valued case, seem to be nonsymmetric in the three-valued extension, and also not to be three-value truth-functional.

At this point it was proposed (by me, and independently by Lauri Karttunen) that the phenomenon of presupposition should be characterized in pragmatic terms. My suggestion (in a paper published in 1974)[1] was not that one should offer a new analysis of a presupposition relation between a sentence and a proposition, but rather that one should redescribe the phenomena to be explained in terms of a relation between

---

[1] Stalnaker 1974.

a *person*—the speaker—(rather than a sentence) and a proposition. What is to be explained is why a speaker tends to take certain propositions as common ground.[2] Lauri Karttunen agreed that we should describe the phenomena in a different way, as a constraint on contexts, rather than as a relation between a sentence and a proposition, but he proposed to formulate a pragmatic account as a definition of pragmatic *sentence* presupposition, roughly as follows: "Surface sentence A pragmatically presupposes a logical form L if and only if it is the case that A can be felicitously uttered only in contexts which entail L."[3] (Karttunen took a context to be "a set of logical forms that describe the set of background assumptions, that is, whatever the speaker chooses to regard as being shared by him and his audience." But the basic idea of his definition can be applied in a theory in which background information is represented by a set of possible worlds, rather than a set of logical forms.) Most semanticists have followed Karttunen in giving something like this kind of definition of pragmatic sentence presupposition.

On the pragmatic account, the data concerning the presuppositions of complex sentences were not seen as evidence for compositional rules, but rather as reflections of the way contexts are constrained by what is said. The idea was to *dissolve* the projection problem by showing it to be an artifact of a mistaken understanding of what presupposition is. "The best response to the projection problem," Karttunen wrote, "is to do away with it."[4]

It was immediately observed (by myself and Karttunen, as well as by others) that the pragmatic definition did not straightforwardly fit many of the paradigm examples of the linguistic phenomenon that had been identified. Grice noted, for example, that certain information might be given what he called "common ground status" by a certain speech act even though it was not common ground before the speech act occurred. Here is Grice's example:

It is quite natural to say to someone, when we are discussing some concert, *My aunt's cousin went to that concert* when we know perfectly well that the person we

---

[2] I did not use the term "common ground" until later. I believe the use of the term in the relevant sense has its origin in Grice's William James lectures, where he talks of propositions having "common ground status".
[3] Karttunen 1974, 181.   [4] Karttunen 1974, 190.

are talking to is very likely not to know that we have an aunt, let alone know that our aunt has a cousin.[5]

Karttunen gave the following list of examples of cases that seem to involve presupposition, but that also seem to be appropriate even if the addressee had no prior knowledge of the required presupposition:[6]

> We regret that children cannot accompany their parents to commencement excercises.
> There are almost no misprints in this book.
> I would like to introduce you to my wife.
> John lives in the third brick house down the street from the post office.
> It has been pointed out that there are counterexamples to my theory.

These examples show that the phenomenon of what in the last chapter I called "anticipatory presupposition" is common and natural. The first example is a case where the main point of the speech act is to convey what seems to be presupposed, and so to involve a kind of indirect communication, but the rhetorical reason for avoiding a blunt statement of prohibition is easily explained. This example is also a case of a conventionalized formula. In the other cases, what is presupposed is a bit of background information where the explanation for communicating indirectly is simply that it is a way of getting information across more efficiently. As Karttunen said about his examples:

People do make leaps and shortcuts by using sentences whose presuppositions are not satisfied in the conversational context. This is the rule rather than the exception, and we should not base our notion of presupposition on the false premiss that it does not happen. But granting that ordinary discourse is not always fully explicit..., I think we can maintain that a sentence is always taken to be an increment to a context that satisfies its presuppositions.[7]

David Lewis later introduced the term "accommodation" for the phenomenon of adjusting a context in this way: "Presupposition evolves according to a rule of accommodation specifying that any presuppositions that are required by what is said straightway come into existence, provided that nobody objects."[8] We have appropriated Lewis's label for

---

[5] Grice 1989, 274. [6] Karttunen 1974, 191.
[7] Karttunen 1974, 191. [8] Lewis 1979b, 240.

the phenomenon, but without his assumption that to accommodate is to apply a constitutive rule of a language game.

3.2 The accommodation response to counterexamples

Some critics of the pragmatic account thought of the accommodation move as a kind of ad hoc fix, a way of reconciling a definition with recalcitrant phenomena. As such, the move was too easy; it was a kind of all-purpose response to any possible counterexample: whenever presuppositions are not there to start with, we have a rule that automatically adds them. Even those sympathetic to the pragmatic approach worried that the accommodation move robs the theory of any substantive content. Rich Thomason, for example, is quoted in Saul Kripke's paper on presupposition as saying (in discussion) that "Stalnaker states conditions for the conversational notion of presupposition that, even according to him, hold except insofar as they don't."[9]

This critical response seems to me to be seriously confused. Perhaps Karttunen and I contributed to the confusion by giving what seems to me, in hindsight, an overly concessive response to the examples that require accommodation. As I argued in the last chapter, the time at which the information required for interpreting a speech act needs to be available is a time *after* the speech act takes place (but before it is accepted or rejected). We have independent reason to believe this. And it never should have been thought that accommodation was the application of a conventional rule, a rule that provides a response to putative counterexamples to some hypothesis about sentence presupposition. Accommodation is an essential feature of any communicative practice. If common ground is (at least close to) common belief, then it will adjust and change in the face of manifest events that take place, including events that are themselves speech acts. Accommodation is just an example of this kind of change.

The more serious problem with the critical response is that it misconstrues the fundamental idea of the pragmatic account, at least the account that I was trying to promote. The criticism seems to be

[9] Kripke 2009, 369 (footnote 3).

presupposing that the dialectical situation is something like this: we begin with a concept of *sentence presupposition*—a relation between a sentence and a proposition that we native speakers can somehow recognize, intuitively, independently of an account of its role in discourse. The pragmatic theorist then proposes an empirical hypothesis about the role of this relation: the hypothesis is that a sentence is felicitously used only in contexts in which its presuppositions are entailed by the information in the common ground. This hypothesis can then be tested against the data, and when it is, it is found that there are many counterexamples. A rule of accommodation is invoked to explain away the counterexamples. But (in my view) the dialectical situation is nothing like this. It is a mistake to think that we begin with notion of sentence presupposition. The idea of the pragmatic account was to begin with a notion of *speaker* presupposition, and to describe the phenomena to be explained in terms of it. I proposed no hypothesis of the kind described above, since I made no use of any notion of pragmatic sentence presupposition.

Kripke seems to be presupposing this kind of dialectical situation when he sums up the pragmatic account at the beginning of his discussion of presupposition this way:

The idea [of the pragmatic account of presupposition] roughly speaking, is that you shouldn't make an utterance involving a presupposition unless it is in the background assumptions of the participants in the conversation that the presupposition holds.[10]

But what is it for an utterance to "involve a presupposition"? Kripke answers the question this way:

We are all familiar with the intuitive concept of presupposition. Though there have been many conflicting attempts in the literature to capture what this concept means, to some degree Justice Stewart's comment about pornography holds here: we all recognize it when we see it, even if we can't say exactly what it is.[11]

Now I think Justice Stewart's comment is wrong about pornography: there are some paradigm cases, but it is highly controversial, not only how pornography should be defined, but also whether certain individual depictions or writings count as instances of it. So we don't all recognize it

---

[10] Kripke 2009, 369.   [11] Kripke 2009, 367.

when we see it. But whatever is to be said about pornography, I think it is a mistake to begin a discussion of so-called "presupposition projection" without first saying something about what it is that is being projected. A definition is not required, but one needs to say something about the kind of concept we are talking about. Specifically, is the relevant notion of sentence presupposition supposed to pick out a surface phenomenon—a kind of datum to be explained—or is it supposed to be a theoretical concept: perhaps something delivered, along with truth-conditional content or Kaplanian character, by a semantic theory for the language? There are concepts of both kinds that are related to the intuitive idea of presupposition. The traditional notion of *semantic* presupposition, explained in terms of truth-value gaps, is a theoretical concept of semantics. But what the Justice Stewart criterion, such as it is, identifies is a surface phenomenon, and so is akin to concepts like felicity and appropriateness. A lack of clarity about whether talk of presupposition concerns a surface notion or a more theoretical one is responsible for some of the confusion in the literature about presupposition, and it was part of the point of my early work on speaker presupposition to try to distinguish the two kinds of notions, and to clarify the relation between them.

3.3 Surface phenomena and theoretical concepts

There are some parallels between the early discussions of pragmatic presupposition and two older controversies in linguistic theorizing that concerned the relation between surface phenomena and theoretical hypotheses. Let me remind you of them, since I think they help to bring out some of the issues to which the pragmatic account of presupposition, as I understood and understand it, was responding.

First example: in the early days of the development of generative grammar, hypotheses about the syntax of a language such as English were tested against the intuitions of native speakers. But certain sentences were held to be grammatical, according to a proposed grammar, even though they were, according to native speakers, clearly deviant. Sentences like *"colorless green ideas sleep furiously"* and *"the man the dog my brother bought bit died"* were judged by some to be counterexamples to theories that implied that these sentences were grammatical. (Those critics might have appealed to the Justice Stewart criterion: we may not know how to characterize grammaticality in general, but we native speakers know it when we see it.) The defenders of the grammatical hypothesis respond that the intuitive datum is only that the putative counterexample sentences are deviant in some way. Ungrammaticality is one possible explanation for deviance, but there may be others. Grammatical sentences may, for example, be *semantically* deviant, or in other cases be too hard to interpret because of processing limitations. Noam Chomsky distinguished competence from performance, arguing that grammatical competence was a cognitive ability that was manifested in linguistic performance only when it interacted with other cognitive abilities and limitations. Critics complained that this kind of response made it too easy to defend a syntactic hypothesis against counterexamples. The reply was to acknowledge the need for independent motivation for the principles used to explain processing limitations and other sources of deviance. One must grant that testing hypotheses about grammaticality is more difficult than one might hope, but it is undeniable that one will need to distinguish surface judgments about whether sentences are acceptable from theoretical judgments about whether they are the output of an empirically adequate grammar.

The second example is closer to the issues we have been discussing. At the beginning of the William James lectures, Grice describes what he calls a "very natural maneuver which is of frequent occurrence in conceptual inquiries" that "proceeds as follows" (here I will give a simplified paraphrase of a typically convoluted Gricean characterization). One observes that a certain range of expressions E containing a term α is such that in situations that fail to meet some condition C, the use of the expressions would be odd or inappropriate. One then concludes that it is a feature of the meaning of α that E(α) is true only if condition C is satisfied. But the inference made in this maneuver, Grice argued, is not always justified. The theoretical judgment that a sentence *semantically entails* a certain proposition is one explanation, and perhaps the most straightforward one, for the surface fact that the sentence may be used to communicate the information, but there may be other explanations, and the theory of conversational implicature was the development of one contrasting kind of explanation. As in the case of the issue about grammaticality, it was acknowledged that we need independent tests for the alternative explanatory hypotheses so that it does not become too easy to defend a semantic analysis against counterexamples. Grice emphasized the need for constraints and empirical tests to distinguish implicatures from entailments. One must grant that evaluating semantic hypotheses against intuitive judgments is more difficult than one might hope, but it is undeniable that one will need to distinguish surface judgments about what is communicated in a speech act from theoretical judgments about the semantic properties of the sentences used to communicate it.

Both of these episodes in the history of linguistic theorizing are old and familiar news. My point is to bring out a common structure in the dialectic, and to suggest that the early debates about pragmatic presupposition have a similar structure. In both of the debates I have sketched, it is argued that it is a mistake to infer too quickly from a surface datum to a theoretical conclusion. The early discussions of pragmatic presupposition also involved the interaction of a more theoretical concept with a concept used to describe the surface phenomena. There was a theoretical notion—a property that semantic theory attributed to sentences—with which the phenomenon of presupposition had been identified: a sentence S semantically presupposes that ϕ if and only if the truth of ϕ is a necessary condition for S to have a truth-value. The main point of the development and defense of a pragmatic account of presupposition was to separate the surface data concerning presupposition from a theoretical property that might, in some cases, explain that data. The argument was that to treat all presuppositional phenomena as cases of truth-value gaps was to make a mistake that was similar to the kind of mistake that was made in these other cases: the mistake of inferring too quick from a surface phenomenon (a fact in need of explanation) to a theoretical conclusion about what explains it.

3.4 Semantic presupposition and presuppositional phenomena

So what, in the case of presupposition, is the phenomenon to be explained? My argument (in that early work) was that the relevant phenomena concern what speakers presuppose, where this is to be understood as what speakers take to be the shared common background. This hypothesis does involve a theoretical notion (of pragmatics), but not a theoretical judgment *about the semantic properties of sentences*. The theoretical notions (speaker presupposition and common ground) are notions used to describe a communicative situation—a context—and to clarify what the data about the use of language are that semantic/pragmatic theory needs to explain. I remarked, in one of those early papers, that one *could* define a notion of *pragmatic sentence presupposition*, and I suggested a number of distinct ways of doing so. But I remarked that "it would not be fruitful to refine them, or to choose one over the others."[12] One reason why I thought (and still think) that it is not fruitful to define such a notion is that it tends to blur the line between an explanatory concept and a concept used to describe phenomena to be explained. (Suppose a linguist were to spend time and energy trying to give precise necessary and sufficient conditions for the application of the concepts expressed by the asterisks, hash marks, question marks and double question marks used by linguists to label sentences that are anomalous in one way or another. Wouldn't that show a misunderstanding of the role of such labels? All the worse if the linguist were to try to state projection rules spelling out how the asterisks on complex sentences were related to the asterisks on their parts.) Attempts to characterize a notion of pragmatic sentence presupposition usually make use of a notion of *felicity* (as Karttunen's definition did) or *appropriateness*—notions whose use is to describe surface phenomena. I think it is a mistake to think of pragmatic presuppositions as something that semantic theory should generate, along with propositional content, for the sentences it interprets.

The original notion of *semantic* presupposition, explained in terms of truth-value gaps, *is* a theoretical notion of semantics, and it has never been my aim to argue against the applicability of this notion, or against its relevance to explaining some phenomena concerning what speakers must presuppose in order to speak felicitously. The aim was only to block too quick an inference from the datum that a certain presupposition seemed to be required for the felicitous use of a sentence to the theoretical conclusion that the relevant sentence was neither true nor false in cases where the presupposition is not met.

Let me say a little more about semantic presuppositions and their relation to constraints on common-ground contexts. In a Kaplanian

---

[12] Stalnaker 1974, 50.

semantic theory, there are potentially two kinds of truth-value gaps. First, the *character* of a sentence is a function from context to content, and it might be a partial function: for some contexts, the feature of context relevant to determining content might be undetermined, and in this case an utterance of the sentence will fail to have a truth-value because it fails to express any proposition at all. Second, content is itself a function (from possible worlds to truth-values), and these functions might also be, in some cases, partial functions—undefined for some possible-world arguments.

It seems reasonable to assume that it would be normally be inappropriate to make an assertion (or more generally, to perform some speech act that requires the expression of a proposition) with a sentence that had a truth-value gap of either kind, relative to possible worlds that are compatible with the common ground. Since one essential aim of the speech act is to express a proposition, it is easy to explain why it would be inappropriate for a speaker to use a sentence that fails to do so, relative to the context he or she is in. And since the aim of expressing the proposition is to distinguish in an unambiguous way between the possibilities compatible with the context, the speaker would not achieve the aim by expressing a partial proposition that failed to decide whether some possible situation compatible with the context should be included or excluded. So we have a straightforward way, grounded not in some conventional rule, but in general Gricean norms of rational communication, of connecting the semantic presuppositions of a sentence with a pragmatic constraint on the contexts in which the sentence is felicitously used. But the connection goes only one way: this is only one possible explanation for the fact that a certain pragmatic presupposition may seem to be required.

A dynamic semantic theory of the kind developed by Irene Heim draws a tighter connection between semantic presupposition and pragmatic constraints on context. According to this theory, what a semantics for the language delivers for a sentence is not (as in the Kaplanian theory) a content, as a function of context, but instead a context change potential, which is a function taking a prior context to a posterior context. Content and force are merged in this theory: the output of the semantics for a sentence is a direct specification of the way that an assertive utterance of the sentence changes the context in which it takes place. The context change potential that the semantics delivers may be a partial function, and the constraints on the contexts for which it is defined are the (semantic) presuppositions of the sentence. This kind of semantics does yield, as a byproduct, a partial proposition for any given context that meets the definedness conditions: the proposition that is true in possible worlds compatible with the posterior context, false in possible worlds that are excluded from the prior context, and undefined for possible worlds that are not in the prior context. So while this theory's notion of semantic presupposition is stated as a constraint on contexts, it has the consequence that sentences are neither true nor false in any possible world not satisfying the contextual constraint that is its semantic presupposition.

I think this way of semanticizing the pragmatic story is a mistake for at least two reasons which I will just mention here, and say more about later. First, I think it is important to maintain the distinction between content and force, a distinction that is lost by merging the effect of an assertion with the semantic content of the sentence used to make it. Second, I think it is important that (at least in some cases) the truth-value of what is said be defined for possible worlds that are incompatible with the specific context in which they are made. If informative conversation is to have any lasting effect, conversational participants must be able to take information away from the contexts in which they acquired the information. But while in general I prefer a dynamic pragmatics to the dynamic semantic story, the point I want to make here is that even in the context of a semantic account of the kind developed by Heim, one needs to distinguish surface phenomena about what seems to be pragmatically presupposed from theoretical judgments about definedness conditions for the interpretation of a sentence. Even on the dynamic semantic theory, there may be cases where a presupposition is required for felicitous use, or can be inferred in a normal context, even though the relevant proposition is not entailed by the definedness conditions built into the semantics.

Let me give two examples where distinguishing surface presuppositional phenomena from a theoretical notion of presupposition helps to clarify what is at issue. First, a quick look at an example that Kripke discusses; second, a remark about what has come to be called the proviso problem.

In a footnote in his paper on presupposition, Kripke expresses skepticism about a generalization about presupposition accommodation, giving the following example:[13]

---

[13] Kripke 2009, 369 (note 3). I don't want to make too much of this example, since it is just a side remark in a footnote, but I think it is instructive.

A problem for me is that a French monarchist might belligerently say to a republican, "No matter what you republicans say, I met the king of France last week." Here it isn't taken to be uncontroversial or expected to be uncontroversial that there is a king of France.

Kripke is certainly right that his king of France example, unlike Grice's and Karttunen's examples mentioned above, is *not* a case of accommodation. As his description of the case makes clear, it is explicitly recognized in the context that the question whether France has a king is in dispute; the monarchist's statement is made to give a reason to support a positive answer to that question. But why is it a problem that this is not a case of presupposition accommodation? Why should one think that presupposition, in any sense, is involved in this case? I am not suggesting that the example does not raise a problem. The point is that it is not made clear what problem it raises. The question what the problem is might be answered in either of two contrasting ways: first, one might agree that the relevant facts concerning presupposition are surface data, but take it to be a datum that definite descriptions require pragmatic presuppositions, whatever that means. The example is then a counterexample to the claims I and others made about how the surface data are to be characterized. But how then should they be characterized? The Justice Stewart criterion is no help here; one does not know what could count as an explanation for the datum unless one has some story to tell about what the relevant datum is. Alternatively, the problem might be a more theoretical one: one might think that well-motivated semantic theory yields the conclusion that statements containing definite descriptions are neither true nor false in possible worlds in which there is no uniquely salient semantic referent of the description. If this is the problem, then it is not a problem for the pragmatic characterization of presupposition accommodation, but instead a prima facie counterexample to the alleged truism that it is not felicitous or appropriate to utter sentences that are neither true nor false in possible worlds compatible with the context. Or perhaps it is a prima facie counterexample to the semantic hypothesis, since it seems at least intuitively plausible to take the monarchist's statement (assuming that the republican's views are correct) to be straightforwardly false. It would be perfectly natural for the republican to reply, "You couldn't have met the king of France last week, since there is no such person."[14] But even if the linguists convince us that the semantic hypothesis is sufficiently well motivated by systematic semantic considerations,[15] that would still not raise a problem for the pragmatic characterization of presupposition and presupposition accommodation. What it would show is that, sometimes, one can manifestly intend to exclude a possibility from the context by using a sentence that, strictly speaking, is neither true nor false in the possible situation that is to be excluded.[16]

My second example concerns what has been called "the proviso problem", an alleged problem first raised by Bart Geurts for the projection rules implied by what he calls "the satisfaction theory". The satisfaction theory is an approach to presupposition that he takes to include both Heim's dynamic semantics and the pragmatic account that I have defended. I will say more about projection rules in the next chapter, but at this point I just want to use Geurts's argument to make a point about the relation between theoretical hypotheses and surface phenomena. Since the projection rules are explicitly spelled out as semantic hypotheses in Heim's theory, I will focus on that version of the problem.

The proviso problem is that the satisfaction theory makes the wrong predictions about the presuppositions of complex sentences. Specifically,

---

[14] There is some irony in Kripke giving this example, since in another paper (Kripke 1979) he argues that Russell's analysis of definite descriptions can be defended against certain criticisms by giving a pragmatic explanation for the apparent presupposition that the description has a unique denotation. Grice gave a less qualified defense of the Russellian analysis. Even Strawson, who of course argued against the Russellian analysis and for an analysis that allowed for truth-value gaps, thought that in some cases, statements involving definite descriptions were straightforwardly false when nothing fit the description. Strawson's account would say that the monarchist's statement was false, and so involved no semantic presupposition.

[15] Kai von Fintel has argued for an account of definite descriptions according to which they are always truth-valueless when there is no referent for the description (von Fintel 2004). The main focus of his argument is on the problem of explaining away the falsity intuitions for cases, like Kripke's, where the relevant sentence seems intuitively to be false rather than truth-valueless. I agree with von Fintel that intuitions about truth-value should not be assumed to be reliable (another case involving the interaction of surface judgments with theoretical conclusions). But what needs explaining is not a simple intuition about truth-value, but the fact that an utterance that is deemed neither true nor false in a given possible situation can nevertheless be used to exclude that possible situation.

[16] Michael Dummett 1959, argued that even if we need truth-value gaps (or more than two truth-values) for compositional reasons, in the end we will need to distinguish "bad" truth-value gaps (where the possibilities in which the sentence is neither true nor false are to be excluded) from "good" gaps, where the truth-valueless cases are not excluded.

"The satisfaction theory often predicts presuppositions of the form $\phi \to \psi$ where the intuitively perceived presupposition is simple ψ."[17] Here is the example that Geurts first used to pose the problem:

Theo hates sonnets, and his wife does too.

Since the definedness conditions for the second conjunct require the presupposition that Theo has a wife, the projection rules imply that the whole sentence require only the presupposition that *either Theo does not hate sonnets, or he has a wife*, whereas the "intuitively perceived" presupposition, in this case, is that the whole sentence requires the stronger presupposition that Theo has a wife.

Now what is "intuitively perceived" does not concern a theoretical claim about the definedness conditions for certain sentences, but a fact about what it seems reasonable to assume is taken to be common ground in a plausible context for the sentence. As we noted above, even in the semantic version of the satisfaction theory, one cannot straightforwardly infer from an intuitive datum about what presuppositions seem to be made to a theoretical conclusion about the output of a semantic theory (in this case, concerning the definedness conditions on a context). Geurts's example would not even be a prima facie problem unless one could describe a plausible context that meets the following two conditions: (I) the weaker but not the stronger proposition was common ground, and (II) the conjunctive sentence ("Theo hates sonnets and his wife does too") is inappropriate. It is very difficult, for obvious reasons, to imagine a plausible context meeting condition (I), a context in which it is common ground that Theo either didn't hate sonnets, or else was married, but in which neither disjunct is itself taken to be common ground. But without such a context, and an intuitive judgment about it that conflicts with what is predicted by the dynamic semantic hypothesis, no datum has been presented that conflicts with the theory, and so no problem has been raised. One might respond that the fact that there is no plausible context meeting these conditions is just a feature of this particular example, and that there might be a different example that does raise a proviso problem by meeting both conditions (I) and (II). There are other examples for which there are plausible contexts meeting

---

[17] Geurts 1996, 260. The arrow here represents the material conditional.

condition (I), some of which Geurts and others have discussed, but the most straightforward of these are also examples that fail to meet condition (II).[18] I know of no examples meeting both conditions. There may be some, and if there are, then there is a problem to be addressed, but even so, the immediate conclusion would be only that the datum cannot be explained in the most direct way. One has to look at the example to see whether there is a plausible explanation for the data that is compatible with the received semantic hypothesis about the projection rules for definedness conditions.

What about cases where neither the weaker nor the stronger proposition is part of what the common ground was before the speech act took place, and so where accommodation is required? With the sonnet example, the data suggest that one will accommodate by adding the stronger proposition to the common ground, and not just the weaker one. That is, if one were told "Theo hates sonnets and his wife does too" in a context in which one did not know or presume, prior to hearing the statement, that Theo was married, one would accommodate by inferring that Theo was married, and that the speaker was presupposing this (and not only the weaker presupposition that Theo either didn't hate sonnets, or was married). This datum is evidence against the hypothesis that in cases of accommodation, one always makes the minimal adjustment required to satisfy the definedness conditions. But why should one expect such a minimal adjustment? Accommodation (I have argued) is not the application of a semantic rule, but an adjustment of the presumed common ground in response to the manifest event that a certain speech act took place. In a case like the example of Theo, the addressee asks what the speaker must be presupposing (that is, what the speaker must be taking to be common ground after the manifest event has taken place) in order for the event to be a cooperative contribution to the conversation.[19] It would be absurdly implausible for the addressee to hypothesize that the speaker must have been presupposing that either Theo doesn't hate sonnets or is married, but not presupposing either of the disjuncts. It would

---

[18] An example much discussed in the literature, "If Theo is a scuba diver, he will bring his wetsuit", first appeared in Geurts 1996, 272. He attributes it to an anonymous referee.

[19] I am of course over intellectualizing the process of accommodation. One need not assume that the addressee goes through any conscious reasoning process.

therefore be completely implausible to take the speaker to be presupposing this.

I want to emphasize that the point is not that a proponent of the satisfaction theory has a way of responding to a problem that has been raised—of explaining away an apparent counterexample; the point is that there is no problem to respond to, at least no problem raised by the initial example. The assumption that there is one seems to be a striking example of the mistake of confusing surface data with theoretical judgments, and inferring too quickly from one to the other. There are no doubt problems in the vicinity of the so-called proviso problem, but it has not been made clear exactly what they are.

3.5 The diversity of presuppositional phenomena

Distinguishing descriptive from explanatory concepts helps us to see, first, that presupposition requirements may have diverse explanations, and second, that the phenomena involving presupposition are broader than simply data about what can be inferred from the use of a sentence about what the speaker must be presupposing. The use of a sentence or a construction of a certain kind may, for example, require that the speaker *not* be presupposing a certain proposition. A sentence might require that one of a certain set of propositions be presupposed without requiring a specific one of them. And presupposition requirements may be defeasible, or may hold on some conditions, but not others. Let me conclude this chapter with a brief look at some examples of the diverse phenomena.

(1) "Too": Kripke criticizes at some length what he takes to be the received view that "the" presupposition of a sentence such as "Billy is guilty too" (with the focus on "Billy") is that someone other than Billy is guilty. The problem is not that it is false that this must be presupposed, but rather that more must be presupposed as well. I am not sure who holds the view that this is all that needs to be said about the presuppositional phenomena concerning "too", but Kripke is certainly right that what he treats as the received view is insufficient. The main problem here is that the required presupposition is not just the existential claim that someone other than Billy is guilty, but the stronger claim that some specific person or group, other than Billy, is guilty. This

presupposition requirement will follow from a standard semantic analysis of the word "too", together with the simple pragmatic truism that the information needed to determine the content of an utterance must be available to the addressee. As Irene Heim has observed, "too" means something like "in addition to x", with the x to be determined by context.[20] On this analysis, one does not know what has been said unless one knows the value of x. The semantic analysis need make no mention of presupposition, semantic or pragmatic, but given this kind of analysis, together with the truism that cooperative speech requires that one's utterances express propositions that are accessible to the addressee, there is a straightforward explanation for the fact that it must be presupposed of some specific person or group other than Billy is he or she is, or they are, both salient and guilty.

(2) Definite descriptions and other referring expressions: lots of presupposition requirements will be explained by the fact that it must be presupposed that the speaker's singular referring expressions succeed in picking out a unique individual in each of the possible worlds compatible with the context. As we saw with the case of the monarchist and the king of France, it may be plausible to take *some* statements involving definite descriptions to be false in possible situations where reference fails, and not to require a presupposition. But "the King of France" (despite being a philosopher's paradigm) is an atypical example of a definite description, since in this case the conditions for referential success seem to be clear and independent of the speaker's beliefs and intentions. If the description were instead "the dog", or "the beer", for example, the rules for determining reference would make more demands on what must be presupposed. We would be talking about a particular dog or some particular beer that is somehow determined by the context, and if the speaker had no particular dog or beer in mind, no proposition would be determined. What must be presupposed in such cases is that there be a unique referent for the description or other referring expression in each of the possible worlds compatible with the common ground, but not necessarily that it be the same referent in each of those possible worlds. In some cases it is presupposed that the speaker have a particular

---

[20] See Heim 1992, 189. The x must be an alternative to the focused element. If the sentence were "Billy is *guilty* too" then the claim would be that Billy is guilty as well as having some other specific salient property.

individual in mind, and that is enough to understand what is being said, even if the addressee does not know, and is not expected to know, who it is. This fact is relevant to some of the examples of presupposition accommodation we have discussed. When Karttunen says "I want to introduce you to my wife", it suffices (in our monogamous culture) to accommodate the presupposition that he is married. Given that, uniqueness comes for free. But when Grice refers to his aunt's cousin, it is not enough simply to infer that he has at least one aunt who has at least one cousin; we take Grice to have a particular cousin of a particular aunt in mind, and to be referring to her. Suppose Grice is mistaken about the cousin of the aunt that he had in mind—she did not go to that concert. But it happens that a cousin of a different aunt—one he knows nothing about—did attend the concert. In this case, I think we should say that Grice's statement is false, since his claim was about the particular cousin of the particular aunt to whom he was referring. If he had said instead, "I have an aunt who has a cousin who went to that concert", his statement would have been accidentally true.[21]

I should emphasize that these remarks do not presuppose any particular account of singular definite descriptions—any account of what it is that determines the referent of the descriptive phrase. All I am assuming is that these descriptions purport to refer to a single individual. This is enough to explain why speakers normally presuppose that the context plus the facts will determine a unique referent.

(3) Factives and clefts: presupposition requirements in these cases can be seen as special cases of the requirement imposed by conditions for reference. To say that it was (or was not) Lauri who solved the problem is to say that the person who solved the problem was (or was not) Lauri. To say that Chloe regrets or does not regret, realizes or does not realize, was surprised or not surprised, that Sam voted for Obama is to state that Chloe stands (or does not stand) in a certain relation to a fact. It is reasonable to assume in general that referential success is presupposed: one presupposes that there exists the fact that Sam voted for Obama, or that there exists the person who solved the problem. But this presumption does not by itself answer the question, what to say about the truth-value of the statement when reference fails. Like the case of "the

---

[21] Related phenomena are discussed in Stalnaker 1998.

king of France", and unlike the cases of "the dog", "my sister", and "my aunt's cousin", the conditions for reference in these cases are independent of local conditions, or of what the speaker had in mind, and it seems not unreasonable to say that even if the presupposition requirement is robust and indefeasible, the statement that Chloe was surprised that Sam voted for Obama, or that it was Lauri who solved the problem, should be judged false if it turns out that the presupposition that Sam voted for Obama, or that someone solved the problem, is false. Chloe fails to stand in the relation to the fact because there is no such fact, and it was not Lauri who solve the problem, because no one did.

There is some diversity in the presupposition requirements imposed by different factives.[22] "Chloe was surprised that Sam voted for Obama" requires the presupposition, not only that he did, but also that Chloe knows that he did. (Kai von Fintel's "hey, wait a minute" test supports this judgment. In response to the statement that Chloe was surprised that Sam voted for Obama, one might respond, "Hey wait a minute – I didn't know that Chloe knew about Sam's vote." Or consider the negation: "Chloe was not surprised that Sam voted for Obama." It would be distinctly odd, even if perhaps true, to say this in a situation where the reason she was not surprised was that she did not know about it.) But "Chloe realizes that Sam voted for Obama" requires that the stronger presupposition *not* be made. That is, if it is common ground that Chloe knows that Sam voted for Obama, it would be redundant to say, "Chloe realizes that Sam voted for Obama". The word "know" is of course itself a factive, and linguists usually assume that "Chloe knows that Sam voted for Obama" requires the presupposition that he did. But with "know", in contrast with "realize", the presumption of a presupposition can be defeated, for example by focal stress: one can suggest skepticism about whether Sam really did vote for Obama by saying "Chloe doesn't *know* that Sam voted for Obama", but one cannot express skepticism about this by saying "Chloe doesn't *realize* that Sam voted for Obama." The fact that the presumptive requirement of a presupposition can be defeated, in

---

[22] One puzzling verb that has something in common with factives is "tell". It is grammatically like "know", since it can take indirect questions, and with indirect questions, it seems to be factive: it is not correct that I told you who won the election unless I gave you the correct answer to the question. But it could be true that I told you that Romney won, even if he did not.

the case of "know", lends some support to the hypothesis that knowledge claims are false, and so their denials true, when the putative fact does not exist.

(4) Change of state verbs: the cliché paradigm of a presupposition requirement is of course the question, "Have you stopped beating your wife?"[23] To say that x has stopped ϕing is (normally) to assert that x does not now ϕ, while presupposing that x used to ϕ. But as Mandy Simons has persuasively argued,[24] the presupposition is defeasible, and it seems reasonable to give a Gricean conversational explanation for the fact that the presupposition is normally required. That is, it seems reasonable to say, for example, that "Sam stopped smoking" is false in possible situations in which he has never smoked, and so "Sam did not (or has not) stop smoking" is true in such situations, even though it would be misleading to say so. Normally, a context in which the question whether Sam has stopped smoking arises is a context in which it is presupposed that he has been a smoker, but there are contexts in which the question is appropriate, even though this is not being presupposed. To use one of Simons's examples, suppose Sam is nervously chewing on a pencil, and he is asked, "Have you recently stopped smoking?" "No," he replies. "That's not my problem. I am nervous because I have an important interview this afternoon." This conversational exchange will be appropriate, whether the reason that Sam has not stopped smoking is that he still smokes, or whether it is because he never did. The defeasibility of the presumption of a presupposition will be relevant to the so-called

---

[23] When discussing the presuppositions of questions, we will need to make a distinction, as we do with the presuppositions of statements, between a theoretical concept of semantics and a notion for describing the surface fact that the question is for some reason inappropriate unless the speaker asking the question is making a particular presupposition. The semantic presuppositions of a question are the conditions that must hold in order for the question to have an answer. If the semantic content of a question is defined as the set of its (complete) answers, then the semantic presuppositions of the question will be the entailments of the disjunction of those possible answers. But one cannot assume that the conditions for the appropriateness of a question are the same as the conditions under which it has a correct answer. One could argue (and I will) that the question, "Have you stopped beating your wife?" has a literally correct answer (no) in the case where the addressee has never beaten his wife, even if one agrees that the question is appropriate only when the speaker is presupposing that the addressee had previously beaten his wife.

[24] Simons 2001b.

presupposition projection phenomena that we will consider in the next chapter.

(5) Dedicated presupposition triggers: many presupposition requirements will be explained by the conditions for successful reference; others can be explained by general conversational principles. In both of these kinds of cases, there will be no need for a notion of presupposition to play a role in the semantics of particular lexical items or grammatical constructions, but a language might contain what Mandy Simons has called "dedicated presupposition triggers"—"lexical items whose sole function appears to be the triggering of a presupposition. These items can be omitted without affecting the assertoric content of the utterance." She gives four examples: "*even, yet, again,* and *too*",[25] I am dubious about three of the examples, for different reasons: It seems to me that "again" *does* affect truth conditions: I would think that "Jane has failed her driver's test again" is false if Jane failed it only once, but this judgment might be questioned. As von Fintel has persuasively argued, truth-value intuitions are not particularly reliable. The case of "too", as discussed above, involves an anaphoric element that I think is involved in the truth conditions. I agree that "yet" is a word that can be omitted without affecting the truth conditions, but I am not sure that its role is to be a presupposition trigger. Consider the minimal pair: "I haven't read *Infinite Jest*" and "I haven't read *Infinite Jest* yet". Both, I take it, are true if and only if the speaker has not read the book at the time of utterance, while with the latter, the speaker implicates that he or she at least may be planning to read it in the future. But I don't see the implicature as a case of presupposition, or of accommodation.[26] But what about "even"? If I say, "Even Bush has admitted that global warming is real" (to use Simons's example), I implicate, or perhaps presuppose, that it is particularly surprising or unexpected that *Bush* should admit this. Simons thinks that such examples raise a problem for the explanation of speaker

---

[25] Simons 2005c, 347.
[26] Even though inserting the word does not change the truth conditions, the explanation for the implicature may still be conversational. Note that the implicature is cancelable: I could say, "I haven't read it yet, and I have no intention of ever doing so." It seems that what the "yet" does is to make explicit that my claim is noncommittal about the future, similar to what would be done if I added a "right now" to a present tense claim to suggest the impermanence of my situation. (I am not employed right now.) One needs some explanation for why the speaker goes out of his way to emphasize that a present tense claim is restricted to the present.

presupposition in terms of common ground. Suppose it is part of the common ground that Bush is a particularly unlikely person to be expected to admit that global warming is real. "In this case, then, what point do presupposition triggers serve? Why should the speaker include them when the presupposition is already in the common ground?" Simons argues that her descriptive account of the phenomenon of presupposition ("the presuppositions of an utterance are the propositions which the hearer must accept in order for the utterance to be relevant to her")[27] puts her in a better position to answer these questions. Just to spell it out: the problem, as I understand it, is that (1) even if it is already common ground that it is more surprising that *Bush* should accept the reality of global warming than that most other people do, it is still perfectly appropriate to insert the "even" into the statement. But (2) since what is asserted is the same with or without the "even", and what might be implicated is already common ground, it seems (on the hypothesis that the role of the "even" is to be a presupposition trigger) that the insertion of that word should be gratuitous, and so inappropriate.

Now I find little to disagree with in Simons's explanation of the job that the "even" is doing in this kind of case.[28] She cites and endorses a general proposal, by Diane Blakemore, for how to explain the role of expressions that do not seem to be explicable in terms of their contribution to truth conditions, words such as *therefore, so, however, although*. Simons writes, "Her [Blakemore's] general claim is that the semantic contribution of certain expressions is to constrain, in one way or another the contexts (in the relevance theoretic sense) in which utterances are

[27] Simons 2005c, 333.
[28] And I am a little puzzled why she thinks we have a disagreement here. We agree that the issue is about how to describe the phenomena, and that the explanation for the phenomena may be diverse. I am not clear what is at issue when one is arguing about how to describe the phenomenon of presupposition. There are facts about what must or must not be taken to be common ground in order for a speech act to be appropriate, and there are facts about the presumed relevance or irrelevance of an utterance to an addressee. Facts of both kinds need to be explained. Is the issue about which facts should, by the Justice Stewart criterion, be labeled *presuppositional* facts? The two kinds of fact are closely related: the cooperative principle requires that what the speaker says should be relevant to the addressee, and since we are assuming that it is common ground that conversational participants are aiming to be cooperative, it will in general be common ground that what the speaker says aims to be relevant. But relevance is not all that is required for appropriate speech. One thing that the pragmatic account emphasizes is that information required to understand what is being said must be presupposed.

interpreted." This seems to me exactly right (though I suggest replacing the parenthetical qualification with "in the common-ground sense"). The general Gricean story that I have been promoting emphasizes the importance of coordinating the presuppositions of the different parties to the conversation: of being sure that they are in agreement about what they take to be their shared information. Given the importance of this kind of agreement for successful communication, it is not surprising that the language should contain devices, not just for saying things, but for signaling, as the conversation proceeds, what is common ground, just to keep the conversation on track. If one says something that might be surprising or unexpected, or if one says something that might seem to contrast in some way with what one has said just before, there is a potential danger of misunderstanding which can be avoided by indicating (by using "even", for example) that one means to be saying something surprising, or (by using "although" or "however", for example) that one recognizes the contrast between what one is saying and what one has just said. I agree with Simons that one role of such words is to signal what is relevant to what, and why it is relevant, but I think a proponent of the account of speaker presupposition as common ground should find such explanations quite congenial.

Much of the discussion of presupposition in the linguistics literature has been on the projection problem, which concerns the relation between the presuppositions required by simpler sentences and the presuppositions required by complex sentences that have the simpler ones as component parts. In the next chapter I will look in more detail at this problem, and at the pragmatic respose to it, in the context of a general discussion of the interplay of compositional processes and discourse dynamics.

4
Context and Compositionality

My arguments thus far have been in support of the importance of separating, in several different ways, an account of the properties of a conventional device used to communicate from an account of the nature and structure of a communicative situation—of the functions that linguistic devices are used to serve. In Chapter 1, I argued that one should distinguish two different motivations for the Kaplanian conception of context, with its distinction between character and content, one a language-internal motivation concerning compositional structure and the other based on the communicative function of language, which requires that the output of a semantic theory, in context, be a piece of information. In Chapter 2 I sketched the Gricean motivation for characterizing meaning and communication independently of a conventional linguistic practice, arguing that the notions of common ground and presupposition should also be characterized independently of the rules of a language, This way of thinking about presupposition and accommodation, I argued in Chapter 3, motivates a perspective on the linguistic issues about presupposition that is different from the prevailing one. But while I want to emphasize a conceptual separation of language-internal and language-external considerations, and to defend the thesis of the autonomy of pragmatics, it is a mistake, in my view, to think that there are separable pragmatics and semantics *processes*. Lexical and compositional semantics interact with pragmatic reasoning throughout the evolving process of interpretation, and the focus of this chapter will be in that interaction.

Here is a conception of the relation between semantics and pragmatics that I think we should reject: context has pre-semantic and post-semantic roles. Its first role is to determine what *sentence* has been uttered by resolving lexical and syntactic ambiguities. The simple lexical items will have "standing meanings", which will be functions taking certain contextually determined parameters to referents or other semantic values. The second pre-semantic job of context is to determine those values. At this point, the pre-semantic job of context is finished, and semantics takes over, using the compositional rules, to determine a propositional content for the utterance, and the conventional force with which it is expressed. The job of semantics is now done, and pragmatics comes back, in its post-semantic role, to explain how what is said is used to further the purposes of the speaker, perhaps by meaning something different from what is said. What this description misses is that the context—the common ground—is changing throughout the process of interpretation, and that the evolving pragmatic information in the common ground interacts with the compositional semantic rules in determining what is said, as well as how what is said affects what is communicated. Gricean reasoning that exploits what is common ground will play a role throughout the process of interpretation, and the compositional structure of the language will interact at various points with the dynamic structure of the communicative situation. Part of the point of insisting on a conceptual distinction between semantic/pragmatic means and communicative function is to help explain the interaction.

It is often assumed that the Gricean project and accounts of presupposition that are inspired by Grice involve this kind of sharp separation of semantics and pragmatics. Rob van der Sandt, for example, describes the pragmatic approach this way:

The basic tenet of this view is that semantic and pragmatic information constitute two different types of content. Propositional content captures only part of what is intuitively conceived as the meaning of an utterance. Presuppositions and implicatures equally contribute to our understanding of natural language sentences. But the latter are computed in a different way. They are not *part* of the truth-conditional content, but computed *on the basis* of the propositional content of the sentence uttered, contextual information, and pragmatic principles of a Gricean nature. They are thus computed and represented separately and merged only afterwards into a more substantial proposition. Contextual update will take place both with respect to the propositional content and information, which is conveyed by other means. It is the sum of both which will be incremented into the next context.

The general picture derives from Stalnaker's work: utterances are construed as context-sentence pairs. A discourse is conceived as a sequence of utterances.

Given an utterance of a sentence ϕ in a context c we first compute $[\phi]_c$, the proposition expressed by ϕ in c. Only then is further pragmatic information computed on the basis of contextual information and the propositional content of the sentence uttered.... [This view] implies that in processing a sentence ϕ its semantic content should be determined *before* any pragmatic information can be computed and this in turn implies that pragmatic information is to be represented separately from semantic content.[1]

Van der Sandt goes on to argue that these two alleged implications of the pragmatic approach are mistaken, and I agree. But it is a mistake to attribute this kind of separation, either to me or to Grice. It is true that Grice emphasized the difference between what is said and what is implicated, and at least in most cases, the implicature can be computed only on the basis of what is said (together with information about how it is said). But the same kind of Gricean reasoning by which implicatures are derived also plays a role, for Grice, in determining what is said. I am not sure what van der Sandt means by the computation or representation of pragmatic information, but I don't recognize the two consequences he draws as consequences of the kind of pragmatic account that I have advocated.

My main concern in this chapter will be with the interaction of context with the compositional process, but before getting to that I will say what I mean by Gricean reasoning, the kind of reasoning that I claim is involved at all stages of the process of interpretation.

4.1 Gricean reasoning

Begin, first, with the reasoning of an interpreter trying to figure out what a speaker means, says, or presupposes when she produces a certain utterance. We assume that the interpreter is presupposing that the speaker intends to make a cooperative contribution to the conversational exchange, and that there is some mutual agreement about what the purposes of that exchange are. The interpreter asks, what must the speaker have meant (or said, or presupposed, or more generally, what must she believe or intend) in order for the particular utterance she produced to have been a reasonable thing to have produced? Now consider the situation from the perspective of the speaker. She asks herself, what

[1] Van der Sandt 1992, 336–7.

information do I want to communicate, and given that, what means should I use to do it? Assuming she is also taking it to be common ground that she intends to make a cooperative contribution, she will choose her means of accomplishing her purpose on the assumption that the addressee—the interpreter—will reason in the way just sketched.[2]

The talk of "reasoning" here may be misleading if it suggests that the speaker and interpreter are engaged in a process of explicitly rehearsing arguments. Speakers and interpreters can engage in rational discourse without having any theoretical grasp of the way they are using information about the attitudes, intentions and strategies of one's interlocutors. They can respond to what is meant or implied, and can base their speech on what they take to be the common ground without having the capacity to articulate the information that they are using. Normal human beings, including children and unsophisticated and unreflective adults, are adept at responding appropriately to social cues, and this involves picking up information about the intentions and expectations of others, including information about their expectations about one's own beliefs and intentions.[3] One can act for reasons, even if one is unable to articulate those reasons, and one can have higher-order attitudes (for example, beliefs about what someone believes about what you believe about what they believe) even when those attitudes remain tacit. Such attitudes can play a role in guiding one's action even if one is unable to put their content into words.

The sketch I gave of what I called Gricean reasoning—the reasoning involved in speech and interpretation—is perfectly general, including the implicit reasoning involved in straightforward, boring cases of literal communication. For example, if a speaker utters "according to the weather report, it is going to rain all day" in a context in which it is common ground that the relevant parties speak English, then the addressee will recognize that a cooperative speaker would not say that unless she knew (or at least took herself to know) that the weather report said that it was going to rain all day, and wanted to communicate that information. In the processes of determining what to say, how to say it, and how to interpret

---

[2] See Neale 2005. This interesting paper is mainly about syntactic binding, but it has a nice discussion of Gricean reasoning.

[3] See Railton 2003 for an illuminating and empirically informed discussion of fluent tacit reasoning.

what is said, the speaker and interpreter are making use of two different kinds of information: (1) information about the syntax and semantics of a particular language, and (2) information about the expectations and intentions of the participants in the conversation. They are exploiting two different kinds of cognitive competence—linguistic and social competence—both of which are presumably innate. These cognitive capacities facilitate the fluent, tacit use of the two kinds of information. The two kinds of information interact in the process of interpretation, and the semantic/pragmatic theorist needs to separate them out: to determine what must be assumed about the syntactic and semantic properties of a particular language in order to explain the apparent facts about the way speakers communicate, and the way hearers interpret them. The interesting cases of meaning and interpretation—the ones that were of particular interest to Grice—are the cases where what is said or meant cannot be determined simply by applying the conventional rules of the language.

"Implicature" is a technical term that Grice introduced for thing that are *meant*, but not *said*.[4] What is *said* by a speaker, in the intended sense, is "closely related to the conventional meaning of the words (the sentence) he has uttered," though as we will see, some of Grice's retrospective remarks suggest that he thought (at least on later reflection) that the relation between what is determined by conventional meaning and what is said is a little more complicated. *Conversational* implicatures were, according to Grice's theory, a subclass of implicatures—those that are explained in a particular way, in terms of the cooperative principle and the maxims of conversation that fall under it. The rough idea was this: a speaker conversationally implicates that q if (a) the supposition that the speaker believes that q is required in order for her saying what she says to be in accord with the conversational maxims, and (b) this supposition is sufficiently obvious so that the addressee can infer that the speaker intended him to conclude that she had this belief. That is, to be a

---

[4] Grice did not put it this way. He introduced "implicature" as a "term of art" for a general concept common to an unspecified class of verbs of which "imply" is the only example given. The main thing that is said in specifying what "implicate" means is that it contrasts with "say", though he acknowledged that he is relying on an intuitive understanding of the relevant sense of "say", and that more needs to be said about that concept. But I think the explanation presupposes that implicating is a way of meaning, in Grice's favored sense.

conversational implicature, the supposition must be obvious enough for the speech act to count as a case of the speaker *meaning* that q, in Grice's favored sense. The cases of conversational implicature that were of particular interest to Grice were cases in which a maxim is *flouted*: the speaker manifestly violates a maxim, causing the interpreter to ask (perhaps implicitly), "How can his saying what he did say be reconciled with the supposition that he is observing the overall Cooperative Principle?" The fact that the prima facie violation was blatant rules out the possibility that the speaker was trying to be misleading, so the hearer is forced to reinterpret the speech act—to take the speaker to have meant something different from what was said.

To count as a case of conversationally implicating that q, according to Grice, the inference to the conclusion that the speaker meant that q "must be capable of being worked out; for even if it can in fact be intuitively grasped, unless the intuition is replaceable by an argument, the implicature (if present at all) will not count as a conversational implicature; it will be a conventional implicature".[5] I am not sure exactly what this means. What is it for the argument that is the basis of a conversational implicature to be "worked out", and who must be capable of working it out? If this condition requires that that the hearer must be capable of articulating the argument, or that the speaker must expect the hearer to be able to articulate the argument, then the requirement is too strong to be plausible. It should be sufficient that an argument of the kind that Grice sketches (appealing to the prima facie flouting of the conversational maxims) be a correct reconstruction of the tacit reasoning of the speaker. If the condition is given a stronger, more restrictive interpretation, excluding cases where the speaker or hearer is not capable of spelling out the explanation for the "intuitive grasp" that they have of the implicature, then it can't be right to claim that the excluded cases are

---

[5] Grice 1989, 31. François Recanati (Recanati 2003) discusses this necessary condition for Gricean conversational implicatures, arguing that it is not satisfied in some of Grice's paradigm cases of conversational implicature, and not in cases of scalar implicatures that have been a focus of attention in the linguistics literature. Whether this is right depends on how the condition is interpreted, and I suspect there are a number of different distinctions involved here. Recanati distinguishes inferences that take place at a personal, as contrasted with a subpersonal level, but I would argue that attitudes and inferences may be at the personal level even if they are tacit, and such that the subject is incapable of expressing them in linguistic form, or even of recognizing any linguistic expression of the content of the attitude or inference.

thereby *conventional* implicatures. It could be that something is *meant*, in Grice's sense, and that the correct explanation for the speaker's (tacit) expectation that the hearer (tacitly) recognize her intentions be given by a Gricean conversational argument, even if the participants are not capable of articulating the argument. One might exclude such cases from the category of conversational implicature by fiat, but they will not thereby be conventional implicatures, since for an implicature to be conventional, the explanation would have to be in terms of linguistic convention.

The crucial question for the theorist is this: what must be assumed about the conventional, language-specific meanings and rules (about what speaker and interpreter know and presuppose in virtue of their distinctively linguistic competence) in order to explain the fact that a certain utterance (in a certain situation) manifestly communicated a certain proposition? For this purpose, we need a notion of conversational implicature that allows for tacit conversational reasoning, and I will understand the notion in this way.

It has been generally assumed that the process of deriving implicatures is (to use François Recanati's term) *post-propositional*. "Implicatures are," Recanati claims, "generated via an inference *whose input is the fact that the speaker has said that p*. Hence no implicature can be computed unless something has been said."[6] This feature is suggested by Grice's account, since his explicit characterization of conversational implicature says what it is to implicate that *q* "*by (in,when) saying (or making as if to say) that p.*"[7] But I think Recanati's characterization is not quite right. Any fact about a speech act may be the basis for a conversational implicature, and the speech act need not be the assertion of a proposition. One might implicate something by asking a question or making a request, and perhaps by performing a speech act that has no propositional content at all. (A speaker might, for example, implicate that the interlocutor is saying what is irrelevant, or going on too long, by saying "yadda yadda yadda" but I don't think it would be plausible to say that such a speaker was *saying* that, or saying anything, in the sense of "saying" that requires the expression of a proposition.) In some of Grice's examples (such as the letter of recommendation example, where the

---

[6] Recanati 2003, p. 300.   [7] Grice 1989, p. 30. My italics.

writer comments only on the candidate's command of English and regular attendance at tutorials), the implicature is carried by what is *not* said. In another of Grice's examples, nothing at all is, strictly speaking, said: "At a Department meeting, one of my colleagues provides a sustained exhibition of temperamental perversity and caprice. At the close of the meeting... I usher him through the door with an elaborate courtly bow. It might be said that what... my bow convey[s] is that he has been behaving like a prima donna."[8] But the bow does not *say* anything. In this example there is at least a communicative action, but perhaps one could implicate something simply by remaining silent in a situation where to remain silent is to flout a conversational maxim.

Whether or not one can implicate something without saying anything, it is clear that the conversational maxims, and the presumption that they are being followed will play a role in the process of determining what is said, and not just what is implicated. If a statement made with a syntactically ambiguous sentence would be irrelevant or manifestly false on one of the readings, then that reading will be excluded, and the reason for excluding it will be that a conversational maxim would be violated if that were the intended reading. If a statement would be appropriate only on one of a number of linguistically possible ways of interpreting a pronoun, then the pronoun will be understood in that way. Even the specific kind of strategic conversational reasoning that Grice argued was involved in the derivation of one kind of conversational implicature (the speaker manifestly flouts the cooperative principle, forcing reinterpretation) can be involved in the process of determining what is said. Consider the familiar phenomenon of nouns used as verbs. In innovative cases (here is one of many examples from the classic paper on this phenomenon by E. Clark and H. Clark, "the paper carrier porched the newspaper"[9]), the sentence is (on an attempt at literal interpretation) ungrammatical, and so is a prima facie violation of cooperative speech. "Porch" is not a verb of English,[10] but it must be a verb for the morphology and syntax of the sentence to be right, so the charitable interpreter takes it to be a verb. Clark and Clark argue (on the

---

[8] Grice 1989, 362. [9] Clark and Clark 1979.
[10] My spell checker said "not in the dictionary", and suggested "perched", "parched", or "poached".

basis of the diversity of cases) that there is no simple function that might be built into the semantics that takes the standing meaning of a noun and delivers a verbal meaning. Rather, the interpreter takes the speaker to be exploiting the standing meaning of the noun, presupposing that that meaning is common ground, along with enough other information to enable the hearer to figure out a verbal meaning that would make the content of the sentence an appropriate conversational contribution, and on this basis attributes that meaning to the speaker. The general phenomenon is widespread, and the cases range from innovative uses that depend on common knowledge that is local and short-lived,[11] to cases that began as innovations but became conventionalized, and acquired their own dictionary entry. The origin of the verb "to duck", in the name for the bird, for example, is recognizable, but (according to the OED) the verbal use (of an ancestor of the word "duck") probably goes back to Old English, or further to Germanic ancestors of the language. Another example: some who understand perfectly well what is meant when it is said that the lawyer was badgering the witness may never have heard of the animal whose name is the origin of that verb. There will be a continuum of cases between creative innovations and established uses. Gricean exploitation may gradually morph into etymology, with intermediate stages that are hard to categorize.[12]

The situation is similar with metaphors and idioms. It is often assumed that innovative metaphors are cases of conversational implicature, but Grice, surprisingly, suggests that at least some metaphorical uses are cases of *saying*—cases where what the speaker meant is what his words said, even though the metaphorical meaning was not part of the conventional meaning of the words used. Here is the example Grice used to make this point: "If one were to say 'He's just an evangelist,' he might mean, perhaps, 'He is a sanctimonious, hypocritical, racist, reactionary

---

[11] To give a current example of an ephemeral case that will probably be forgotten by the time the reader reads this: the quarterback of the Denver Broncos, Tim Tebow has a habit offering a prayer in the endzone after scoring a touchdown. The verb, "to tebow" was used to describe this kind of action.

[12] Consider the verb "to roof", which is manifestly recognizable as a noun used as a verb, but which does get a dictionary entry as a verb, meaning to install a roof. If, however, the word were used to describe the inaccurate paper carrier, who roofed the paper, rather than porching it, this would not count as a "standing meaning", even though the intended meaning is clear.

money-grubber.'[13] If... his meaning were as suggested, it might well be claimed that what he meant was in fact what his words said." In the context in which Grice gives this example he distinguished two independent criteria for the "instances of signification" that are *central* cases of speaker meaning; he labeled the two criteria "formality" and "dictiveness". An act of meaning meets the formality condition if "the relevant signification is part of the conventional meaning of the signifying expression." It meets the dictiveness condition if "the relevant signification is part of what the signifying expression says." Grice gave the evangelist example as a case of dictiveness without formality—a case where the distinctive kind of reasoning involved in the derivation of conversational implicatures is used to determine what is said. I think the examples of innovative uses of nouns as verbs are also cases of this kind.[14]

Grice's judgment about his evangelist example will not be universally shared, and it is not clear exactly what hangs on the question whether, in this case, "he is a sanctimonious, hypocritical, racist, reactionary money-grubber" is a paraphrase of what the speaker *said*, or only of what he *meant* by conversationally implicating it. Whatever one thinks of this particular example, the main point is that the distinction between what is said and what is implicated is different from and independent of distinctions between different kinds of explanation for the fact that some particular utterance is a way of conveying some particular item of information. Recall the question, discussed in Chapter 2, that one might ask about a particular act of speaker meaning: "Why should uttering U (in this situation) be a way of getting the addressee to recognize her intention to get the addressee to believe that P?" In some cases, this will be answered entirely in terms of the conventional meanings of the expressions of the language used; in other cases the explanation will appeal to extra-linguistic facts about the intentions, purposes and shared information of the participants in the conversation, and the shared assumption that they are rational agents engaged in a cooperative enterprise. While Grice's use of his apparatus to derive conversational implicatures is what has gotten most of the attention, this is just one application of the more general project of developing tools for

---

[13] I confess that I myself would find it hard to extract this metaphorical meaning from the word, but Grice's community must have been different from mine.
[14] All of the quotations in this paragraph are from Grice 1989, 361–2.

characterizing the contexts in which communication takes place in order to help determine what needs to be assumed about the semantic features of particular languages, in order to explain how the expressions of those languages are used to communicate.

There is a tendency in the post-Grice literature to assume that if an explanation for some fact about usage appeals to relevance, informativeness, or the cooperative principle, it must be a case of conversational implicature, but this is a mistake. "Conversational implicature" is Grice's technical term, and perhaps a case can be made for Recanati's claim that conversational implicatures are essentially post-propositional, but there is no case to be made for a more general claim that pragmatic reasoning, exploiting the maxims governing rational communication and appealing to the shared information and purposes of speakers and hearers, takes place only after it is determined, what is literally said. Nor is there a case to be made for the claim that Grice held such a view.

4.2 Shifting contexts and derived contexts

In the remainder of this chapter, I will consider some of the ways that the notions of context we have been using help to clarify the dynamic process of interpretation. In particular, we want to consider the relation between compositional structure and the evolving structure of a discourse. Recall Lewis's formulation of the context-index semantics. His distinction between index and context (what we called K-context) was a distinction between parameters of interpretation that were, in a sense "shiftable" and those that were not. The elements of the index could be shifted; those in the context remain fixed. But of course contexts, in another sense, shift all the time. I have emphasized the ways in which common ground is constantly changing, but it is also clear that K-contexts (since they include parameters that indicate the time of utterance and speaker) shift and change, as time passes. Part of our job will be to sort out the relation between context shifts and the kind of shifting that indices undergo in the process of compositional interpretation. This problem is further complicated (or so I will suggest) by the fact that there are different kinds of context shifting. The basic common-ground context is constantly changing, but there are also what I will call *subordinate contexts*, or sometimes *derived contexts*,[15] that may play a role in interpretation. So on the one hand, the basic (common-ground) context changes, and on the other hand one may shift back and forth between basic and subordinate contexts, which are themselves changing.

In Chapter 2, I contrasted two different ways that the basic common-ground context changes: (1) to incorporate information that is implicit in manifest events that take place in the course of the conversation, and (2) as a result of a conventional speech act governed by rules that are explained (in part) in terms of the way they are designed to change the context. On the account of the speech act of *assertion* that I have been using, an assertion is something like a proposal to change the context by adding the content expressed in the assertion to the common ground. I should emphasize that I am not claiming that one can *define* assertion in terms of a context-change rule, since that rule will govern speech acts that fall under a more generic concept. A full characterization of what an assertion is would also involve norms and commitments. And whether an indicative speech act counts as an assertion or not will be partly a matter of what kind of discourse it is—what its common purposes are taken to be.[16] A more general kind of speech, still governed by the same context-change rule, will include conjectures and other less committal conversational moves. Just as what is mutually accepted for purposes of the conversation may in some cases involve a mutually recognized pretense, so in the right kind of context, the speech act itself made may be a proposal to accept something only in a sense of acceptance that diverges from belief.

I should also emphasize that the model of the speech act of assertion is highly idealized and oversimplified, best regarded as an artificial game

---

[15] A remark on terminology: the label "subordinate context" alludes to Craige Roberts's classic work on modal subordination (Roberts 1989). The label "derived context" underscores the fact that this kind of context is derivative from the basic context. I avoid the term "local context" that has been used in dynamic semantics for something like this kind of context, since basic, non-subordinate contexts may be either more robust and general, defined by common knowledge that is widely shared and relatively stable, or more fragile and "local" in the sense that they are defined by information shared only for the moment by a specific group of conversational parties. I want to avoid confusion between the subordinate/basic distinction and this other (vaguer) distinction between different kinds of basic contexts.

[16] Seth Yalcin's notion of "conversational tone" is one useful way to distinguish different kinds of assertion-like speech acts. See Yalcin 2007, 1008.

designed to model some of the features of the structure of a discourse. One specific way that the model is oversimplified is this: the context-change rule is a default rule. Although it is part of the assertion game that the interlocutors have the opportunity to reject the assertion, it is a rule of the game that the content of the assertion becomes part of the common ground if it is not rejected. But of course in any realistic situation, it cannot be assumed that the addressees accept every assertion that they do not explicitly reject. Consider a lecture, or even a case where in a conversation a speaker makes a point that takes several sentences to develop. It is not expected that hearers will interrupt at each point where they are unwilling to accept the speaker's claim. (In a notorious incident during a state of the union address by Barack Obama, a congressman shouted "You lie!" at a certain point, but this rejection of the President's assertion was not regarded as good form, even by those who did not accept as true everything that the President said.) Even at the end of a speech or lecture, one is not obliged to express all one's disagreements. A second, more general oversimplification: most speech acts have multiple hearers (or readers), and the line between addressees and over-hearers is sometimes hard to draw. Different presuppositions may be appropriate for different members of a larger audience, and speakers (and writers) need to take account of this in choosing what to say and how to say it in such situations.

But I will stay with the idealized picture of the assertion game for now, hoping that the complications and qualifications can be better understood if we first get clear about the basic dynamic structure of a simple kind of linguistic exchange. Things will get complicated enough as it is.

Even if we broaden the notion of assertion to a more general category that includes conjectures, and speech acts in a context that allows for pretense, we still need to distinguish the speech act of *supposition*. A supposition creates a subordinate context that, like the basic context, is represented by a set of possibilities. While assertions change the basic context in a rule-governed way, suppositions create a new context parallel to the basic context—one that is a function of the basic context. Discourse under the scope of a supposition exploits the information in the subordinate context in the same way that assertions and other speech acts exploit the information in the basic context, and the same principles and maxims that relate categorical speech to the common ground will relate speech under the scope of a supposition to the subordinate context.

For example, speech acts in general are appropriate only if the information necessary to determine the content of what is said is entailed by the common ground. Similarly, a conditional speech act, or speech under the scope of a supposition, is appropriate only if the information necessary to interpret the content is entailed by the subordinate context. And just as speech acts in general should express propositions that distinguish between the possibilities in the basic context, so speech acts made under the scope of a supposition should distinguish between the possibilities in the subordinate context. Suppositions are temporary—that is why one retains the basic context. But so long as the supposition is in force, its content is accepted by the participants in the conversation.

Fred Landman has argued that "the local context [what I am calling a subordinate context] isn't an actual speech context" and that "the notion of a local context is a **grammatical** notion." His reason for calling it a grammatical notion is that "the local context is derived from the actual speech context, following the semantic composition of the sentence."[17] It is true that *one* way to make a supposition is to use an "if" clause, and that sometimes the scope of the supposition will include just the main clause of the conditional statement. But a supposition is still a speech act—one that can be performed with a separate imperative sentence (Suppose that ϕ). And however the supposition is made, its scope may be go beyond a single sentence, including a sequence of statements, proposals, questions, perhaps involving different parties to the conversation. It is not clear why this is not an actual speech context, or what is at stake in denying that it is one. It is right that a subordinate context is distinct from, and derivative from the basic context. But it is a body of information[18] that, like the basic common-ground context, is available to the participants in the actual speech situation.

Even if derived contexts are not "real" speech contexts, it does not seem right to say that the notion of such a context is a *grammatical* notion. The grammar—the semantics—may appeal to such contexts, as it may exploit the basic common ground in determining what is said, and such concepts are of interest mainly because they can be used in this way.

---

[17] Landman 2000, 237.
[18] In a nonfactive sense of: "information". Strictly, perhaps "informational content" would be better.

But the subordinate contexts themselves are wholly definable independently of the semantic rules that may appeal to them.

If we restrict our attention for the moment to *indicative* suppositions, then the subordinate context that is created will be at least *like* a basic speech context in one important way: the possibilities compatible with the subordinate context will all be possible situations in which the conversation itself is taking place. As I have emphasized in characterizing the general notion, the information that defines the common ground includes both information about the subject matter of the discourse, and information about the discourse itself—about the participants and their evolving attitudes. When one speaks, one presupposes (takes it to be common ground) that one is speaking, and this means that the conversation is taking place, not only in the actual situation, but in each of the possible situations in the context set. This fact is reflected in the formal representation of the common ground by the iterative structure. The context set of the subordinate context created by an indicative supposition will be a subset of the basic context, and so will include all of the information that defines the basic context, plus more. It will thus have the same kind of structure, and will evolve in response to manifest events in the same way. Other kinds of subordinate contexts—both those created by *subjunctive* suppositions, and those that are relevant to the interpretation of attitude attributions—need not share this feature. If the supposition is counterfactual, then the conversation in which the supposition is made may not be taking place at all in the possible situations compatible with what is being supposed, and so the set of possibilities that models it will not have the same kind of structure. I will call subordinate contexts that are subsets of the basic context "*simple* subordinate contexts", and those that are not "*parallel* subordinate contexts".

I will have more to say about subjunctive suppositions in Chapters 6 and 7. Let me say a bit more now about the subordinate contexts that are relevant to propositional attitude attributions. Suppose that the beliefs of Charlie are part of the subject matter of a conversation between Alice and Bert. Then in each of the possible situations in the basic context set, Charlie will be in a certain particular total belief state, which we might represent (following the Hintikka strategy discussed in Chapter 2) by a set of possible situations—Charlie's doxastic alternatives, the possible situations compatible with what he believes in that possible world.

The union of the sets of doxastic alternatives determined by each of the possible worlds in the basic context will be the set of possible situations that, for all Alice and Bert are presupposing, might be compatible with Charlie's beliefs.[19] This set is a subordinate or derived context that is relevant to the interpretation of statements, questions, or other speech acts by Alice or Bert that are about Charlie's beliefs.

Is the notion of a derived (or local) context of this kind a *grammatical* notion, as Landman suggested? It is right that it is "derived from the actual speech context," and it is right that the *role* of this kind of derived context is to interpret a clause—a part of a sentence determined by the compositional structure of the sentence. But the derived context itself is defined wholly in terms of the basic context, and determined prior to the interpretation of any particular clause. Derived contexts of this kind evolve in the course of a conversation as the context sets they are defined in terms of are changing, and the information that they model will be used in the interpretation of clauses in the same way that the information in the basic context is used in the interpretation of speech acts. So just as a pronoun used in a simple statement requires a most salient relevant individual to be the referent in each of the possible situations in the basic context, so a pronoun in a clause attributing a belief to Charlie requires a most salient relevant individual in each of the possible situations compatible with the derived context. But since there are (at least) two parallel contexts in any conversation where that-clauses are being interpreted, there are two informational states that may play a role in the interpretation. Suppose Alice and Bert have been discussing Alice's new boyfriend, so he is salient in their basic context. Alice says, "Charlie doesn't know about him yet." Here a pronoun is used to pick out an individual in the basic context, and then Charlie's state of knowledge is described in terms of that individual. Cases of de re attitude attributions are like this. But one may also say things like this: "Hob thinks a witch blighted Bob's mare. He wonders whether she also killed Cob's cow." Here the "she" in the second statement picks up an individual who is salient in the derived context, but may not exist at all in the worlds of the basic context. And the individual became available in the derived context

---

[19] That is: if C is the basic context set, and R is the doxastic accessibility relation for Charlie, then the derived context set will be $\bigcup_{y \in C} \{x : yRx\}$.

only because of the way that context changed in response to the first statement.[20]

Charlie, of course, might have no knowledge of Alice and Bert's conversation about him, and so the conversation taking place in each of the possible situations in the basic context set may not be a part of any of the possible situations that define the derived context. But there is a special case where the attitude in question is what is accepted for purposes of the conversation, and where the subject of the attitude is one of the participants in the conversation. A derived context of this kind, like the derived contexts created by indicative suppositions, will be *simple* in the sense defined: represented by a subset of the basic context. I will suggest below that this kind of derived context has an important role to play in representing the dynamics of discourse, even when the relevant person's propositional attitudes are not the overt subject of the discourse. As a discourse evolves, speakers and hearers need to keep track, not just of the information they share, but also of the issues on which they differ.

4.3 Presupposition projection

In light of these general considerations about derived contexts, I want to take a look at the problem of (so-called) presupposition projection. I argued in Chapters 2 and 3 that the phenomena concerning presupposition should be described in terms of what speakers and other parties to a conversation presuppose, which means what they take to be common ground. Claims about what *sentences* presuppose should be understood as claims about what cooperative speakers can normally be expected to be presupposing when they use those sentences. A presupposition "trigger", on this way of thinking about the phenomena, is an expression or construction that signals, for one reason or another, that a certain presupposition is being made. Claims about presupposition requirements and triggers should, I have argued, be understood as descriptions of

---

[20] The example alludes to the puzzle about intentional identity first raised in Geach 1967. I have simplified the example to make a simpler point, but the derived context apparatus, suitably generalized, is relevant to the more general problem. Geach's puzzle concerns anaphora across different attitudes, and different subjects (as in "Hob thinks that a witch blighted Bob's mare, and Nob wonders whether she killed Cob's cow").

surface phenomena—claims about felicitous or appropriate speech. Such phenomena may have diverse explanations: it might, in some cases, be a semantic feature of a lexical item or a kind of construction that certain presuppositions are required (or forbidden), but it also might be that the explanation of a presupposition requirement is pragmatic. That is, the correct explanation might appeal only to general conversational principles together with the truth-conditions of the relevant expressions—conditions that do not themselves mention the notion of presupposition. And a pragmatic explanation for one case where a presupposition seems to be required may be different from the pragmatic explanation in another case. Furthermore, different theorists might agree in a particular case, about the phenomena concerning presupposition, while disagreeing about how the phenomena are to be explained.

The projection problem for presupposition was originally characterized as the problem of stating the right compositional rules for presupposition—of specifying how the presuppositions of complex sentences are a function of the presuppositions of their parts. This was an appropriate way to see the problem at a time when presupposition was assumed to be a semantic property explained wholly in terms of truth-conditions and truth-value gaps: sentence S presupposes that ϕ if and only if S has a truth value (true or false) only if ϕ. But it is not the right way to pose the problem on the pragmatic story that I have promoted, and am promoting. The projection problem (very roughly stated) is the problem of explaining some generalization about the relation between what speakers tend to presuppose (what they tend to take to be common ground) when they use certain complex sentences to make a statement and what they *would* be expected to be presupposing if they used a component part of the sentence, by itself, to make a statement.

Even after the phenomenon of pragmatic presupposition was distinguished from the semantic phenomenon of truth-value gaps, linguists continued to think of the projection problem as the problem of finding compositional rules. So, for example, in 1983, Irene Heim wrote, "The projection problem is the problem of predicting the presuppositions of complex sentences in a compositional fashion from the presuppositions of their parts."[21] And Philippe Schlenker recently described my attempts

---

[21] Heim 1983, 397.

to use the dynamic pragmatic apparatus to explain the phenomena as an account of "*how the presuppositions of complex sentences are computed from the meanings of their parts.*"[22] But even in the context of the kind of context-change semantics that Heim developed, it is a mistake to identify the explanation of projection phenomena with a problem of giving compositional rules. In Heim's dynamic semantic framework, there is a compositional question about how the admittance conditions of a complex sentence are derived from the admittance conditions of their parts, but not all facts about the pragmatic presuppositions that are required for felicitous speech are explained in terms of the admittance conditions. One should expect to find, and I think one does find, cases where the semantic rules yield a definite result for a given context (a proposition with a definite truth-value is determined), even though the assertive utterance of the sentence would (for purely pragmatic reasons) be inappropriate in that context.

So our problem is not to give compositional rules, but to explain certain generalizations about the phenomena. What Bart Geurts labeled "the satisfaction theory", in its original pragmatic form, aimed to explain these generalizations in terms of the way that contexts change in the course of a discourse. Consider first the simplest case of a generalization of the kind we want to explain, the case of "*and*" sentences, and my attempt, put forth in the early 1970s, to use this strategy to explain the generalization: The observation was that the presuppositions that are necessary for the felicitous assertion of a sentence of the form *A and B* are the presuppositions necessary for an assertion of *A* alone, plus the presuppositions that would be required by an assertion of *B* alone minus those entailed by *A*.[23] My proposed explanation for this generalization was this:

When a speaker says something of the form *A and B*, he may take it for granted that *A* (or at least that his audience recognizes that *he* accepts that *A*) after he has said it. The proposition that *A* will be added to the background of common assumptions before the speaker asserts that *B*. Now suppose that *B* expresses a proposition that would, for some reason, be inappropriate to assert except in a context where *A*, or something entailed by *A*, is presupposed. Even if *A* is *not* presupposed initially, one may still assert *A and B* since by the time

[22] Schlenker 2010, 117–18.   [23] See Karttunen 1973.

one gets to saying that B, the context has shifted, and it is by then presupposed that A.[24]

Philippe Schlenker rightly observed that this explanation cannot be quite right, since one cannot assume that the addressee will accept the assertion that A, and so cannot assume that A will be common ground by the time that the second clause is asserted.[25] Even in the simple idealized model of the assertion game, an assertion is something like a proposal to add the content of the assertion to the common ground. But it is a proposal that can be rejected, and so it cannot be assumed, midway through the speech act, that the content expressed in the first conjunct will be accepted. The parenthetical qualification in the above quotation shows a dim recognition of the problem, but the rest of the quotation ignores the fact that the qualification compromises the explanation.

The right response to the problem Schlenker raised, I want to suggest, is to appeal to a derived context of the kind defined above—specifically, to the derived context that represents the common ground *about what the speaker accepts*. Even if it remains an open question, midway through the speaker's statement, whether the addressee will accept her assertion that A, it will immediately become common ground *that the speaker accepts that A*. The hypothesis is that the information in this derived context is available for the interpretation of the speaker's subsequent speech acts.

Is this suggestion just an ad hoc fix that compromises the naturalness of the original pragmatic explanation? I don't think so, for the following two reasons: first, as noted above, these subordinate contexts for propositional attitudes are wholly derivative from the basic context. The hypothesis that there are such contexts depends only on the basic model of common ground, and on the Hintikka-style possible-worlds model for representing propositional attitudes. So while it is an empirical claim that contexts of this kind play a certain role in the interpretation of speech—that speakers and interpreters exploit the information in them in a way that parallels the use of information in the basic context—it is not a disputable claim (given the basic framework) that there are such bodies of information, and that they are available for the interpretation

---

[24] Stalnaker 1974, 90. Karttunen, independently, gave essentially the same explanation at about the same time.
[25] Schlenker 2010.

of what is said. Second, even aside from the specific use of such derived contexts to explain generalizations concerning presupposition projection, it is (I want to suggest) natural to hypothesize that speakers normally keep track, in real time, of the evolving information, not only about the attitudes they share, but also about the issues on which they differ. Parties to a conversation have a reason to keep track of such information, and I think the data about discourse will support the hypothesis that they do. We noted above that in the simple model of the assertion game, assertions are accepted as part of the common ground unless immediately rejected, but that in any realistic case, it cannot be assumed that the absence of dissent implies agreement. When a speaker makes an extended point, developed across a number of distinct speech acts, it is evident that interpreters make use of information about what has been said earlier in order to understand what is said later, and in doing that, they are exploiting the information in derived contexts of the kind we have described.

Schlenker also raised what he regarded as two more serious problems for the pragmatic strategy for explaining the projection phenomena: "The analysis failed to generalize to cases in which either (i) the beginning of a sentence does not have assertive force, or (ii) the presuppositional expression has predicative rather than propositional type."[26] Start with the first problem.

The examples Schlenker uses to illustrate the problem are disjunctive statements, and the problem is really just about disjunction. Conditional statements also fall under the general characterization, but the dynamic pragmatic explanation *does* naturally generalize to cases of this kind, since the notion of a subordinate context is straightforward when it is created by an explicit supposition. But Schlenker is right that the use of derived or subordinate contexts to explain disjunctive cases is not straightforward. The general strategy of a pragmatic account of presupposition projection is something like this: first, get clear about the relevant generalization—the facts about the relation between the presuppositions that seem to be required by an assertion expressed with the complex sentence and the presuppositions that *would* be required if sentences corresponding to the clauses were used to make separate

[26] Schlenker 2010, 118.

assertions. Second, try to explain these facts in terms of a semantic account for the relevant connective or construction (a semantics that makes no mention of pragmatic presupposition requirements), together with general discourse principles. The more specific *dynamic* pragmatic strategy is to explain why a presupposition that *would* be required by the separate assertion of one of the clauses is *not* required by the complex assertion by arguing that the relevant presupposition *is* made, not in the basic context, but in a subordinate context that is relevant to the interpretation of the complex sentences. Such subordinate contexts should be derivative from the basic context in light of the semantics for the word or construction. Now in the case of disjunction, the generalization to be explained is pretty clear, although the data are less robust than in the cases of "and" and "if". The presuppositions of a disjunctive statement (ϕ or ψ) seem to be those that would be required by an assertion of ϕ, together with those that would be required by an assertion of ψ, *except those entailed by the negation of ϕ*. This is illustrated by Barbara Partee's classic example: one can say

(1) Either this house doesn't have a bathroom or it's in a funny place.

The second clause, if used by itself, would requires the presupposition that there is a salient object to be the referent of the "it". If we added the negation of the first clause to the context, we would have one—the bathroom that the house would have if the first clause were false. But the asymmetry of the order of the clauses is less clear with "or" than it is with "and". One cannot easily reverse the disjuncts in (1), but if we vary the example by replacing the pronoun with a definite description, then the reversal is better; that is,

(2) Either it's in a funny place, or this house doesn't have a bathroom

is awkward at best, but

(3) Either the bathroom is in a funny place, or this house doesn't have one

is fine. The data seem to suggest that in cases where clause ϕ of a disjunction entails propositions that would be presupposed by the categorical assertion of the other clause ψ, there is a bias in favor of ϕ or ψ over ψ or ϕ, but the reverse order is often possible. The bias may be stronger or weaker, depending on the source of the presupposition, and the details of the case. In discussing the disjunction data, Schlenker suggests that "the linear bias is due to the fact that sentences are processed and comprehended in time," which supports the expectation that "the bias – just like other processing effects – could be overcome, though at some cost," as seems to be the case.[27] I agree with Schlenker's suggestion, and as he remarks, it lends support to a pragmatic explanation of the phenomena.

How might derived or subordinate contexts be relevant to explaining the phenomena? First, let me note that there remain questions about the *semantics* for disjunction. Despite the simple, truth-functional rule that seems, on first pass, to give the right truth-conditions for "or" statements, a correct semantic account of the word is probably more complex. It is well recognized that "or" interacts with modals and conditionals in surprising ways. There is some reason to think that the semantic value of a disjunctive sentence should be, not a proposition, but a set of propositions—something like the semantic value of a question.[28] But whatever the details turn out to be about the right semantic account of disjunction, it is clear that a disjunctive statement presents a set of alternatives. "φ or ψ" is often naturally paraphrased as "φ *or else* ψ", and "else" means something close to "if not". So it is not unnatural to think that what follows the first disjunct focuses on the alternatives to that disjunct—on the possible situation in which φ is false. That is, it is not unnatural to think that the *or else* clause is interpreted in a subordinate information state that includes only possibilities that are contrasting alternatives to the first disjunct.

In cases where the explanation for the expectation of a presupposition has a pragmatic, conversational explanation, the expectation will be defeasible, or "cancelable", in the right circumstances, and this will naturally make the generalizations about the projection phenomena more complicated—more dependent on the details of the example, and on the source of the expectation of the presupposition in the basic case. So for example, in Chapter 4, I followed Mandy Simons in arguing that the truth conditions for change of state verbs like "stop" imply that "John

---

[27] Schlenker 2010, 130. Schlenker cites Chemla and Schlenker 2009 for empirical support for this suggestion.
[28] Simons 2001a and 2005b.

stopped smoking" is true if John used to smoke and does so no longer, and false otherwise. So what is normally presupposed by such statements is *entailed* by them. The expectation that the first conjunct is presupposed has a conversational explanation that is defeasible: in the right conversational circumstances, one may appropriately deny that John has stopped smoking, or ask whether he has stopped smoking, without assuming anything about his prior smoking habits. Contexts in which a presupposition that is normally required is manifestly *not* required are sometimes described as cases where a presupposition is *canceled*, and one might describe cases where a disjunction does not presuppose what would be presupposed by one of the disjuncts alone in this way. That is, one might say that the second disjunct in

(4) John must have stopped smoking, or else he never smoked.

serves to cancel the presupposition that he used to smoke. "Cancellation" just means that the speaker makes manifest, in some way, that she is not presupposing what she might otherwise be expected to be presupposing.[29] In saying (4), the speaker is certainly making manifest that she is not presupposing that John used to smoke, since the second disjunct is incompatible with such a presupposition. Defeasible presupposition requirements will give rise to counterexamples to some generalizations about presupposition projection that have been proposed. One notorious example:

(5) John has either just started or just stopped smoking—I forget which.

This example is not a problem for the pragmatic strategy, though explaining such examples requires looking both at the explanation for

---

[29] The cancellation terminology has its origin in one of Grice's tests for conversational implicature: he claimed that unlike conventional implicatures, they are cancelable in just this sense. Successful cancellation of conversational implicatures requires two things: first, that the speaker make manifest that she is not implicating what she might otherwise be thought to be implicating, and second, that there is an alternative explanation for why the speaker is saying what she is saying in a way that would normally carry the implicature. Where the second condition is not met, the attempt at cancellation will not be credible. Consider Grice's famous letter of recommendation case, where the writer comments only on the candidate's attendance and command of English, implicating that he is no good at philosophy. One could not avoid this implication by adding: "Of course I don't mean to suggest anything, one way or the other, about the candidate's philosophical ability." That would just reinforce the implicature.

projection phenomena, and the explanation for the basic presupposition requirement or expectation.

The problem of presupposition projection is often discussed in isolation from assumptions about the nature or source of the presuppositions that are projected. We have already noted the way that Kripke used the Justice Stewart criterion to bypass questions about what the basic presupposition relation is, in order to focus on the claims that have been made about projection. Daniel Rothschild makes this separation strategy explicit as a methodological proposal: rather than aiming for a grand overall theory, which has thus far eluded us despite "thirty years of serious work on presupposition.... we ought to lower our sights a bit. We might try to make progress on one question while leaving others unanswered for the time being." Specifically, he proposes to "address the problem of presupposition projection while remaining silent about the triggering problem and ... about what presuppositions ultimately are."[30] This would be a natural strategy in cases where the problem is about compositional rules. It is, for example, uncontroversial that the compositional semantics for the operators and connectives of propositional calculus is independent of whatever makes the atomic sentences true or false. But if the projection problem is, as I have argued, the problem of explaining generalizations about the relations between what conversational participants are presupposing when they use different kinds of complex expressions, then I think the separation strategy is a mistake. One should expect to find, and one does find, variation in the projection phenomena that depend on the differences in the sources of the basic presuppositions, and on the interaction between the explanations of presuppositional phenomena in simple and complex cases. Perhaps one reason a more general theory of presupposition has eluded us over these thirty years is that we have been attacking problems piecemeal that need to be considered together.[31]

The second of the two problems that Schlenker raised concerns cases where "the presuppositional expression has predicative rather than propositional type." The "presuppositonal expression" is the trigger, which as I understand that notion is an expression or construction that

---

[30] Rothschild 2008, 447.
[31] cf. Simons 2013, which argues that the triggering problem and the projection problem for presupposition are not independent.

tends to suggest that, for one reason or another, a certain presupposition is being made. The cases he has in mind are cases where the trigger occurs in the scope of a quantifier. The question, framed in terms of the pragmatic strategy for explaining the projection phenomena that I have been promoting, is something like this: Suppose that affirming or denying that x has some attribute F tends to suggest that the speaker is presupposing that x has some other attribute G. What can we conclude from this about what is presupposed when one says that everything, most things, three things, few things, something, or nothing, in a given domain is (or are) F? In the case where the quantifier is positively or negatively universal (everything or nothing), the answer seems clear and unproblematic: so for example, it seems that when a speaker says of x that he regrets voting for Sarkozy, or does not regret voting for Sarkozy, she is normally presupposing that x voted for Sarkozy. Given this, it seems straightforward to conclude that if a speaker says that all of her friends, or that none of her friends, regret voting for Sarkozy, she will normally be presupposing that all of her friends voted for Sarkozy. It seems natural to describe the phenomena in terms of questions that are at issue in the context.[32] Normally, a statement that Pierre regrets voting for Sarkozy is made in a context in which a question at issue is what Pierre's attitude is toward the fact that he voted for Sarkozy. Similarly, it seems reasonable to think that in at least one standard context in which a speaker says that all or none of her friends voted for Sarkozy, a question at issue is what attitude each of her friends takes toward the fact that he or she voted for Sarkozy. The expectation of a presupposition (and the hypothesis about what questions are at issue in the context) may be defeasible in the individual attribution, and so may be defeasible in the quantified case as well. With this example, the positive ascription will *entail* that x voted for Sarkozy, so the negative attribution will be semantically compatible with the falsity of the presupposition. Suppose none of the friends who voted for Sarkozy regret doing so, but that some did not vote for Sarkozy. It will then (assuming the entailment hypothesis) be *true* that none of the friends regrets voting for Sarkozy. But it is a separate question whether it would be appropriate to say so—whether one would be implicating or suggesting that what is normally presupposed is true of all of them. The

---

[32] See Roberts et al. 2009 for discussion of the role of questions "at issue" in discourse.

expectation of a presupposition seems hard to defeat in the case of "regret" (in either singular or universal negative cases), but where it can be more easily defeated in singular cases (as in Simons's examples with "stop"), it can also be more easily defeated in universal negative cases. (A psychologist looking for subjects for an experiment about stress asks a colleague if any of the students in his class have recently stopped smoking. He inquires and reports back, "No, none of my students have recently stopped smoking." There is obviously no implication that all, or any, used to be smokers.)

The harder questions about quantified sentences arise with the nonuniversal quantifiers. If a speaker says that most, or some or a few, or only three people in some group have stopped smoking, or were surprised that they passed the exam, or were walking their dogs, can one infer that the speaker was presupposing that *all* of the people in the group used to smoke, passed the exam, or have dogs? I think the data show that it is hard to generalize. The expectation of such a presupposition will vary with the source of the expectation of a presupposition in the singular case, with the quantifier, and with the details of the example. To see that the variation is not simply a matter of the quantifier, consider these two contrasting cases:

(6) Most of the people who attended the caucus later regretted voting for Gingrich.
(7) Many people came into the park. Most of them were walking their dogs.

There is at least a suggestion, in (6), that all of the people at the caucus voted for Gingrich, but there seems to me to be no suggestion at all, in (7), that all of the people who came into the park have dogs. In any case, there are certainly many very natural examples where no universal presupposition can be inferred. Consider the following little monologue:

(8) My friends are a neurotic bunch. Each is discontent with her life in one way or another. One regrets that she didn't graduate from college; another feels guilty that she can't stop smoking, and several are always having problems with their boyfriends.

The speaker is clearly not presupposing that none of her friends graduated from college, that none of them can stop smoking, that all of them used to smoke, and that they all have boyfriends. But the absence of a universal presupposition raises a puzzling question. It is clear enough what the implied presupposition would be, if the presupposition were to be applied to *all* the members of the relevant domain, but if it is not, as in this example, then exactly what can the speaker be presupposing? It can't be that the speaker was presupposing, of those friends who quit smoking, that they used to smoke, of those who regret not graduating from college that they didn't graduate from college, etc., for the relevant friends have not been identified.[33] The speaker could have been making the weaker, merely existential presupposition that some of the friends used to smoke, that some did not graduate from college, etc., but it seems that not even this is suggested by the speaker's remark. The answer to the puzzling question, I think, is that despite the presence of the so-called "triggers" in the remark, those "presuppositional expressions" do not, in this case, give rise to presuppositions at all. Of course, in accepting the speaker's remark, the addressee *does* acquire the information that one of the friends used to smoke, that one didn't graduate from college, etc. In the "regret" case, the information is *entailed* by what is said. In the case of the friend who feels guilty that she is unable to stop smoking, the inference that this friend is a smoker will require a tacit background assumption, but it will be natural to take that assumption to be part of the common ground.[34]

Why should one think, in the case of the speaker's comment about her friends (or in other examples, such as (7)), that presuppositions are

---

[33] Heim 1983 raises what is essentially this problem, about indefinites, with the example:

(9) A fat man was pushing his bicycle.

She claims that the merely existential presupposition (that there is a fat man with a bicycle) seems too weak, while "a universal presupposition that every fat man had a bicycle would be too strong. What one would like to predict is, vaguely speaking, a presupposition to the effect that the same fat man that verifies the content of [(9)] had a bicycle. But it is [not]... clear exactly what this would mean." (p. 403). The problem arises, not just for indefinites (which Heim argues are not quantified expressions), but for any nonuniversal quantifier in cases where the universal presupposition is too strong.

[34] On the semantics that I take "stop" to have, it will be true that x didn't stop smoking if x never smoked, even if it would usually be misleading to say so in this circumstance. So, strictly, it is possible that the reason the friend can't stop smoking is that she is a nonsmoker. But it would surely be highly unusual to feel guilty about not being able to quit smoking because one never started, and so reasonable for the speaker and addressee to take for granted that this is not the explanation. This is not a case of presupposition accommodation, but simply a case where one ignores various bizarre but semantically possible ways that a statement might be true.

involved at all? Kai von Fintel has suggested the following rough and ready criterion for identifying presupposition requirements: If a speech act presupposes that ϕ, and the addressee was not presupposing that ϕ, he might respond by saying, "Hey, wait a minute, I didn't know that ϕ." But this test does not suggest the presence of a presupposition in these cases: ("Hey wait a minute, I didn't know one of your friends didn't graduate from college" "Hey wait a minute, I didn't know that any of the people who came into the park had dogs" These don't seem appropriate.) Does it seem plausible that *semantic* presuppositions are involved? Suppose that none of the speaker's friends have boyfriends, or that none of her friends smoke. Suppose none of the people who came into the park have dogs—those were their cats they were walking. In these circumstances, it seems to me, the statements would be flatly false (rather than lacking a truth-value). Is there more than the Justice Stewart criterion to tell us, in these cases, that presupposition must somehow be involved? Perhaps the reason it is assumed that presuppositions must be involved in these cases is that it is assumed that presupposition triggers are encoded in the lexical item (e.g. "regret", "stop") or the relevant construction, or perhaps the problem of presupposition projection is still seen as a problem about compositionality. Words like "regret" and "stop" are "presuppositional expressions", and the presuppositional properties of complex expressions must be a function of the presuppositional properties of their parts. Most of the puzzles about the presuppositions of quantified sentences depend on this way of framing the problem, which I have argued is a mistake.

I claimed above that it was hard to generalize about the relation between (a) what speakers tend to presuppose when making singular ascriptions with some predicate, and (b) what they tend to presuppose when making quantified statements with that predicate. The facts vary with the quantifier, the source of the presupposition in the singular ascription, and with the particular circumstances of the case. If the problem were to find a compositional rule, this would be a puzzle. There must be some general rule, and we should expect to find a relatively simple one. But I have argued that we should see the projection problem as the problem of explaining the generalizations about the data that we find. If there are no simple and robust generalizations, then one does not have the problem of explaining why such a generalization should hold. One has to explain the facts about the individual cases, but piecemeal explanations are a problem only if there are generalizations about the data that such case-by-case explanations miss.

I am not arguing that there are no robust generalizations about the projection phenomena to explain, generalizations that cut across the source of presupposition requirements ("triggers"), and that depend on the compositional structure of sentences, the dynamic structure of the discourse, and their interaction. I am arguing only that understanding the phenomena does not depend on finding such generalizations.

If my discussion of presuppositions and quantified statements is at all on the right track, it should help to explain why, even though questions about compositional structure interact with questions about discourse structure, it is important to distinguish the roles played by the two kinds of structure in describing and explaining the phenomena. The projection problem looks very different if one thinks of it, not as a problem of finding the right compositional rules, but as a problem of explaining what speakers and interpreters tend to presuppose when they use and understand various kinds of complex sentences. In the attempt to explain these phenomena, I have appealed to a number of kinds of subordinate context. As Fred Landman observed, subordinate (or local) contexts are not "real" speech contexts—not situations in which a discourse is taking place—and he concludes that the notion of a local context is therefore "a grammatical notion" (though it is not clear exactly what this label implies). Subordinate contexts can have a recursive structure (there can be subordinate contexts within a subordinate context), and they can be created by conventional speech acts (for example, by an act of supposition). So the problems of representing the evolving discourse, including the relevant subordinate contexts, can look a lot like a problem involving compositional rules. But I still think it is important to distinguish the grammatical structure of expressions from the complex structure of a discourse.

5
The Essential Contextual

In the last three chapters, we have been elaborating and applying the structure of an information state that contains the information that is presumed to be shared by the parties to a cooperative enterprise. In Chapter 2, I described an abstract model of the iterative structure of an information state of this kind, and discussed its role in explaining discourse dynamics. In Chapter 4, I discussed the subordinate contexts that can be derived from the information contained in an information state of this kind, including subordinate contexts for interpreting statements about the individual attitudes of the parties to the conversation. It is a central feature of a body of information with this kind of structure that the information in it includes information about the discourse itself, and about the beliefs, aims, intentions and other attitudes of the parties to the discourse. The information in the common ground is information that speakers and interpreters can draw on in deciding what to say and in interpreting what is said. But information can be drawn on by speakers and interpreters only if it is available, and so the information *that* certain information is available must itself be part of the information. So it is essential that speakers and interpreters represent themselves and each other—their place in the world, and their perspective on it—as well as information about the subject matter of their discourse, whatever that might be. This implies that our account of context must have a good way of representing such self-locating information—not just an individual's attitudes toward himself and his place in the world, but the information of the members of a group about themselves and each other. The question how to do this will be the focus of this chapter.

Discussions of self-locating propositional attitudes usually begin with the semantics for indexical expressions, and then extend it to a semantics for thought, but I think that this gets things the wrong way around. We should start by giving an account of self-location in thought, which will also give us a more general account of the complex iterated attitudes that define common ground (including the presumed common knowledge about who and where we are, and what time it is). When we have a notion of the common ground that can accommodate such information, the semantics for indexical pronouns will be a relatively straightforward matter. Given our general thesis of the autonomy of pragmatics, it is appropriate to begin with self-locating thought, since we are assuming that the idea of a context is not essentially tied to a conventional practice. Self-locating attitudes and presuppositions would play an essential role in a characterization of the context of a discourse even if the language being used in that discourse had no indexical expressions.

Here is my plan for this chapter. I will begin by reminding you of the classical possible-worlds representation of a state of belief or knowledge that we introduced in Chapter 2, a framework that provides a straightforward representation of iterated knowledge and belief, and of common knowledge and mutual belief, and so it provides the resources for the model of the notion of common ground that we have been using. But the classical model has a problem with self-locating belief, a problem that is particularly acute when the focus is on iterated attitudes. Our main task will be to explain how self-locating information, which seems to be essentially private, can be the content of what is expressed in a public communicative practice, and can be information that is mutually accepted by a group. After sketching the general problem of self-locating attitudes, I will describe David Lewis's modification of the classical analysis, a modification that remains within the possible worlds framework. Lewis's theory has the resources to represent essentially self-locating attitudes, but it is, in a sense, a static and solipsistic representation, and so does not provide for an account of change of belief over time, or of the interaction of the attitudes of different subjects. So I will suggest a modification of Lewis's analysis, one that uses formal tools from both the Lewis and the Hintikka frameworks, and show how this modified theory can represent the contexts in which exchange of self-locating information takes place. I will sketch a modified account of common ground that allows for shared background information about the location in the world of the parties to a conversation. I will conclude the chapter by applying this kind of model to a notorious puzzle case, Mark Richard's phone booth story. This is an example that involves multiple identity confusions, self-location, and context-dependence in a discourse situation.

5.1 Essentially indexical attitudes

I emphasized, when we introduced the classic semantic framework for the logics of knowledge and belief in Chapter 2, that the theory gives a smooth account of iterated knowledge and belief, for a single agent, or for a group of agents. Since the compositional semantic rules determine the proposition expressed by a sentence that says that Alice believes that Clara is a philosopher, it straightforwardly provides an account of a sentence that says that Alice believes that proposition, or that Bert does. That is, it provides a way to express and to interpret sentences like "Alice believes that Alice believes that Clara is a philosopher," ($B_A B_A F_C$) or "Alice knows that Bert knows that Clara is a philosopher" ($K_A K_B F_C$). We can have different knowledge and belief operators, indexed to the different knowers, and interpreted by different epistemic and doxastic accessibility relations, also indexed to the different knowers.

An agent's overall state of belief (in a given possible world) is represented in these models by a set of possible worlds each of which *is* the way that the agent takes the world to be. The "worlds" are more soberly described as states that a world might be in, or ways a world might be, but they are ways a world might be *in itself*, and not as seen or conceived from a certain point of view. What this kind of model seems to leave out is any representation, in an agent's cognitive state of the agent's perspective on the world, as he takes it to be: where in the world (as he takes it to be) he locates himself. Any possible world that is compatible with what Alice believes at some time *t* will be a world containing Alice (or whoever Alice takes herself to be), and it will be a world in which Alice (or the person she takes herself to be) is in a certain belief state at that time (or at whatever time she takes it to be). The classical models, in which the contents of knowledge and belief are represented by sets of possible worlds—worlds as they are in themselves—has no problem representing Alice's (or Bert's) beliefs about where Alice is in the world, but they don't have the resources to represent the link between Alice in the world in which she has the beliefs and Alice as the person in the world as she takes it to be, a link that is needed to distinguish Alice's first-personal beliefs about herself from beliefs about a person in the world who happens to be herself.

The point that there is sometimes an ineliminable indexical element in the content of belief goes back at least to Hector-Neri Casteñeda's work in the 1960s, but the issue was brought back onto the philosophical stage by John Perry's classic papers published in the late 1970s.[1] The thesis was that knowledge and belief about who one is, and what time it is *now* are not reducible to knowledge and belief about the impersonal and timeless features of the world. The point was made with a series of stories, some mundane, others fanciful: a person in a grocery store chasing a trail of sugar on the floor that was obviously leaking from a sack in someone's cart, only to discover that the sugar spiller was he himself; a man getting on a trolley who sees a "shabby pedagogue" at the other end, but then realizes that it is he himself in a mirror; an amnesiac, lost in the Stanford library, reading a biography that is in fact of himself, and so learning a lot about himself without knowing that what he is learning is about himself; two omniscient gods who know everything about what the world is like in itself, but that are each ignorant of who he himself is. These stories were all cases where objective knowledge about the knower came apart from the knower's first-personal knowledge, and they formed the basis for arguments that the one kind of knowledge could not be reduced to the other. There were also stories of a different kind that made the case for essentially indexical attitudes in a different way. These were stories in which two agents had all the same relevant (objective) beliefs and desires, but nevertheless were rationally motivated to act in different ways because of their different perspectives on the world. Here is John Perry's classic example: you are being chased by a bear; I run for help, while you curl up in a ball. We both have exactly the same beliefs about the situation, and about the most effective way for each of us to respond to it. We also have exactly the same motivation: to save you from the bear. The only differences in our attitudes that might explain our different actions are differences in self-locating attitudes.

Lewis's idea for modeling this distinctive kind of information was to use a different and more fine-grained object to represent the content of an attitude. Rather than *propositions*, represented by sets of possible

---

[1] Perry 1977 and 1979.

worlds (those in which the proposition is true), we are to use sets of *centered* possible worlds, which are pairs consisting of a possible world and a designated time and person within that world.[2] The world component of a centered world represents an objective possible situation that is compatible with the subject's conception of the way the objective world is. The person at the center represents the (objectively identified) person that the subject thinks she might be, in a world of that kind. The (objectively identified) time of the center represents a time that, for all the subject believes, might be the time she is in the belief state, in that possible world. So, for example, since the amnesiac Lingens knows (from reading a biography of himself) that Lingens was born in 1953, the possible worlds compatible with his beliefs will all be worlds in which Lingens was born in 1953. But since he does not know that he himself is Lingens, there will be *centered* worlds compatible with his beliefs that are centered on a different person than Lingens, perhaps one who was born at a different time. The possible worlds compatible with the knowledge of the person who knows that the meeting starts at noon, but not that it is starting *now* will all be worlds in which the meeting starts at noon, but the center component of some of his epistemic alternatives will be another time: in those possible scenarios, the time at which he is in the given belief state is some time before the noon meeting.

The Lewisian model of a state of belief is a straightforward generalization of the classical model, simply replacing the possible worlds with more fine-grained objects—centered possible worlds. They are more fine-grained in that a single possible world will correspond to multiple centered worlds. And as Lewis emphasized, his account is a generalization in the sense that contents of belief in the classical model (sets of uncentered worlds, representing timeless, impersonal information) will be a special case of contents of belief in his more fine-grained models: each timeless, impersonal proposition will determine a unique centered-worlds proposition, one in which the centers are irrelevant. Suppose X is a set of centered worlds meeting this condition: for all w and c,

---

[2] Lewis's theory is spelled out in detail in Lewis 1979a. In his formulation of the theory, it is *properties* that are the contents of belief, where properties are identified with sets of possible individuals. To account for the temporal dimension, it is assumed that it is not continuant individuals, but time-slices of individuals to which beliefs are ascribed. Given the assumptions of Lewis's general framework, there will be a one-one correspondence between properties in his sense and sets of centered possible worlds.

and c' $\langle c,w \rangle \in X$ if and only if $\langle c',w \rangle \in X$. Then X is a set of centered worlds that represents exactly the information represented by a simple set of possible worlds: the w such that for some (or all) c, $\langle c,w \rangle \in X$. So sets of centered worlds can represent objective information, as well as self-locating information, and it can represent the logical relations between objective and self-locating contents.

The Lewisian model is like the classical model in that belief states are abstracted from the believer who is in the state. It is the agent's cognitive situation that determines what belief state he is in, but the state itself is represented by a set of possible worlds (in the classical model) or a set of centered possible worlds (in Lewis's generalization) in which the believer plays no special role. I think this kind of representation misconstrues the real message of the phenomenon of self-locating information, which is that it is essential to an adequate representation of a state of knowledge or belief that the information that is the content of a state be linked to the knower or believer who is in the state, and to the situation in which she is in it. It is usually assumed that it is the more fine-grained distinctions between epistemic and doxastic alternatives that is doing the work in explaining the distinctive character of self-locating attitudes (the fact that a single possible world may correspond to distinct centered worlds), but this is a mistake; the real role that the centers play is to represent the links between a believer's actual situation (in the world in which he has the beliefs) and the possible worlds that are compatible with his beliefs. Using more fine-grained contents of belief does not help us to represent these links, and it is not necessary to use more fine-grained contents once we have added the structure to represent the links between a subject's situation and the possible worlds that represent his cognitive state in that situation.

The problem with Lewis's account of content is that it makes it difficult or impossible to compare beliefs across time, and across persons. One way to see the problem is to consider the representation of iterated knowledge and belief. Lewis does not formulate his theory explicitly in terms of doxastic and epistemic accessibility relations, but he might have, and if he had, it would provide a straightforward semantics for intrapersonal iteration: what any subject knows or believes about what he himself knows or believes. For any ϕ whose value is a set of centered worlds, "I believe that ϕ" will also have a value that is a set of centered worlds: those centered on a person who believes that ϕ at the time of the center. But in*ter*personal iteration: what A knows about what B knows—is a different matter. In order to make sense of interpersonal iteration, and more generally to make sense of the communication of information, we need an account of the contents of attitudes that is impersonal, or at least interpersonal, and this Lewis's account of content does not provide. Intuitively, it seems reasonable to say that if Daniels does not know the identity of Lingens, the famous Stanford amnesiac, then in a sense, he is ignorant of the same fact that Lingens is ignorant of. If he finds out, he can tell Lingens. When he says "You are Rudolf Lingens", he is giving him precisely the self-locating information that Lingens had previously lacked. But Daniels's knowledge of this fact is, of course, not self-locating knowledge. The property of being Lingens, or the set of centered worlds whose center is Lingens, cannot represent the information that *Daniels* acquires when he learns who Lingens is, and if this centered worlds proposition is not an adequate representation of what Daniels told Lingens, then it is equally not an adequate representation what Lingens learns. While Lewis's account succeeds in smoothly integrating one person's self-locating belief with that same person's impersonal beliefs, it fails to integrate the objective and self-locating attitudes of different agents, and that is what we need in order to explain communication.

As I noted, the Hintikka theory gives a straightforward account of iterated knowledge and belief, both intra- and interpersonal. Each knower has his or her own epistemic accessibility relation. A claim such as "A knows that B doesn't know that ϕ" can be formalized as $K_A \sim K_B \phi$, and the semantics will say that this iterated knowledge attribution is true in possible world x if and only if, for all worlds y such that xR_Ay, there is a world z such that yR_Bz and ϕ is false in z. (Where "R_A" and "R_B" are the epistemic accessibility relations for knowers A and B, respectively) But this representation is perhaps *too* straightforward, sweeping some problems under the rug. (Lewis's account makes iterated knowledge too hard, but Hintikka's makes it too easy.) We can compare the contents of belief and knowledge for different agents, but doing so is not always straightforward. The modified centered-worlds account that I will propose aims for a middle ground that allows for the interpersonal interaction of attitudes, but that also brings out the problems that arise for this kind of interaction.

5.2 A modified centered-worlds account

The modified account I will sketch[3] uses exactly the apparatus that Lewis introduced (centered possible worlds) to represent cognitive states, but it will be using them in a slightly different way. In particular, I will not appeal to the finer-grained distinctions between possibilities that the notion of a centered world permits, or at least not directly. Belief states will be modeled by sets of centered possible worlds, but the job of the center will be to link the believer as he is in the world in which he has the beliefs to the person he takes himself to be in the world as he takes it to be. It will be an assumption of the model that the centered worlds that are epistemic or doxastic alternatives will have different centers only if they are also different worlds. The assumption is that if you don't know where you are in the world, then (in all cases) you also do not know what world you are in. It is this assumption that will allow us to take ordinary impersonal and timeless propositions as the contents of belief, and so to allow for the comparison and communication of the information of different subjects, while at the same time accounting for self-location. But the assumption needs defense. I will use an extended example to motivate it.

It is Monday afternoon. After shopping in the mall, I take the elevator down to level B of the parking garage. I had gone up a different elevator, one in the center of the garage. The one I came down is either at the east or the west end, I am not sure which—there is an elevator at each end. I know my car is about in the middle along the northern edge, but is that to the right or to the left? I have a clear mental map of level B, but it has no "you are here" marker, so I don't know how to orient myself on it. The garage is pretty symmetrical, so it is hard to tell by looking around just where I am. I do know that there is a pale green Prius with Massachusetts license plate 374-BJ8 to my right as I come out of the elevator, but knowing that does not help, since of course my mental map of level B does not tell me what cars are parked in what places.

Clearly, it is self-locating knowledge that I lack: I don't know where to place myself in an environment of which I have a pretty clear objective mental representation. But the knowledge I lack is nevertheless knowledge

---

[3] The framework I will sketch and apply here was introduced in Chapter 3 of Stalnaker 2008a, and an appendix to that chapter has a few formal details.

of what possible world I am in. Presumably, there is not, in the *actual* world, a pale green Prius with Massachusetts license plate 374-BJ8 in the symmetrical place at the other end of level B of the garage, and there is actually no person, who might, for all either he or I know, be me, looking at it. Assume that I am actually at the east end. Then there is a *counterfactual* possible world in which I am (at the present time) at the west end. In that counterfactual world, the pale green Prius with that license number is parked at the west end, to my right as I emerge from the elevator. My car is to the north, in this counterfactual world, as it is in the actual world, but this means it is to my left, rather than to my right as it is in the actual world. My ignorance of where I am in the parking garage, and which way I should go to find my car, is represented by the fact that counterfactual worlds like this are compatible with my knowledge.

Now one might tell a science fiction story in which two events of the kind I have described take place, one on Monday at the east end, and one on Tuesday, at about the same time at the west end. The person (perhaps me) who emerges from the elevator at the west end on Tuesday glances at the same pale green Prius with the same license plate. On Tuesday, that car is parked at the west end, in the corresponding spot. The Tuesday person's experiences are, from the inside, indiscernible from mine. In fact all of that person's memories and experiences at the time are indiscernible from mine. (Perhaps we have led parallel lives, or perhaps we are both amnesiacs, or perhaps he *is* me, but was given a drug that snipped out all memory between today and tomorrow, without affecting the rest.) In this story, one might be tempted to say that these two *actual* scenarios, the one taking place at the east end on Monday, and the other taking place at the west end on Tuesday, are each epistemic alternatives for both me and for my counterpart. Even if I became omniscient about what world I am in, one might think, I might remain ignorant of which of these two people I am (or if my counterpart is actually me, having forgotten the Monday event on Tuesday, I might remain ignorant of what time it is *now*). One *could* say this, but one should not for several reasons. First, one does not need the science fiction story to make the point that some information is essentially indexical. The original, quite mundane story accomplishes this. (If the phenomenon of self-locating belief did depend on such science fiction scenarios, we could safely ignore it.) In the simple story, my belief is essentially indexical in the following sense: I cannot infer from a purely objective description of the world that I am at the east end. My objective description might tell me that there is a Prius at the east end, and no Prius at the west end, but I can use this information to orient myself only by putting it together with the information that there is a Prius *here*. More directly, of course, my objective description may tell me that Bob Stalnaker is at the east end, and not the west end, on Monday afternoon, but it is only because I know that I am Bob Stalnaker, and that it is Monday afternoon, that I can use this information. In normal cases, the indexical information we need to locate ourselves in the world is obvious enough to go unnoticed, but it is always essential. Stories about amnesiacs are not essential to the point; their job is just to make more prominent the role of the kind of information that usually gets taken for granted. Second point: even in the science fiction stories with two *actual* scenarios that are indiscernible, one can still assume that different epistemic alternatives are scenarios in different possible worlds. Even if, in *this* world, another event indiscernible from this one will take place tomorrow, or did take place yesterday (I don't know which) *that* event is not *this* one. Since I don't know whether it is now Monday or Tuesday, I don't know whether *this* token thought is taking place on Monday or on Tuesday, but I do know that whichever it is, the (token) thought that I am having on the other day (yesterday or tomorrow) is a different one. So one *can* assume that distinct epistemically possible scenarios are always different possible worlds without excluding the fanciful cases. But the third point is that one *must* take doxastic and epistemic alternatives to be different possible worlds, even in the fanciful cases, if one is to give a proper account of the role of belief and knowledge in action. Suppose I know that I will be in a similar situation—perhaps an absolutely indiscernible situation—on both Monday and Tuesday without knowing, on either day, which day it is. (I will be given an amnesia-inducing drug that ensures that, on Tuesday, I have no memory of the Monday situation.)[4] On each day, I must make a decision, perhaps to go left or right to find my car, or to accept or reject a bet about the result of a coin flip. In deciding what to do, I am making it true that this is what I do in all of the possible

---

[4] I am alluding here to the notorious Sleeping Beauty problem that Adam Elga introduced to the philosophical community in Elga 2000, and that has been extensively discussed in the literature since then. I discuss this problem, applying the modified centered-worlds framework to it, in Stalnaker 2008a, Chapter 3.

situations that are epistemically possible for me. Deciding is (at least normally) a way of coming to know. But it would distort the deliberative situation to think that, on Tuesday (or Monday) I was deciding what to do on the other day. I might be giving myself *evidence* about what I will or did do on the other day (if I have reason to think that my situation will be similar enough), but that is different from making a choice that decides it.

So we follow Lewis in using sets of centered possible worlds to represent states of belief, and we can use a doxastic accessibility relation on centered worlds to represent the beliefs of various believers, at various times, in a range of different possible worlds. If $\langle c,x \rangle$ and $\langle c',y \rangle$ are centered worlds, then $\langle c,x \rangle R \langle c',y \rangle$ holds just in case it is compatible with the beliefs of the individual at the center c at the time of that center in world x that she is the person at the center c', that the world is world y, and that the time is the time of c'. The assumption that I have been trying to motivate—that different doxastic or epistemic alternatives (for a given believer at a given time) have different centers only if the possible world component is also different, is formally expressed as follows:

$$\text{if } \langle c, x \rangle R \langle c', y \rangle \text{ and } \langle c, x \rangle R \langle c'', y \rangle, \text{ then } c' = c''$$

What this assumption does is to allow us to take the contents of belief to be sets of ordinary, centerless possible worlds, which makes it possible to compare the beliefs of different subjects (to say what they agree and disagree about) and to represent what one subject believes about what another believes. Essentially self-locating beliefs will have, as their contents, ordinary impersonal propositions; their distinctive self-locating character will be a feature of the subject's relation to that content, and not a feature of the content itself. The belief that Daniels expresses when, after discovering who Lingens is, he tells Lingens, "You are Rudolf Lingens" is not a self-locating belief (for Daniels), but on the account I am proposing it has exactly the same content as the newly acquired belief that O'Leary expresses when he echoes Daniels, "So, at last I know: I am Rudolf Lingens." But for Lingens, the belief with that content is a self-locating belief.

As we have seen, in the classical Hintikka models of knowledge and belief, the epistemic and doxastic accessibility relations are indexed to the subject. In the centered-worlds generalization that I am sketching, we need just one unrelativized epistemic or doxastic accessibility relation:

the subjects (and times) are determined by the relata, rather than the relation. Instead of saying that y is compatible with what A knows in x if and only if xR_Ay, we say that y is compatible with A's knowledge if and only if for some C, $\langle A,x \rangle R \langle C,y \rangle$.[5] Two subjects A and B have conflicting beliefs if the set of worlds compatible with A's beliefs is disjoint from the set compatible with B's. Agreement and disagreement is straightforward (whether the beliefs are self-locating or not), and the theory also provides the resources to represent iterated knowledge and belief, but here things are not quite so straightforward. Let me sketch another simple example to bring out two complications.

I am talking with John Perry at an APA meeting, but he is not wearing his nametag, and I am not sure who he is. I know Perry's work, but (let's suppose) I have never before met him. I am pretty sure the guy I am talking with is either John Perry or Fred Dretske, but I am not sure which. He is telling me what a fantastic book *Knowledge and the Flow of Information* is, and I am wondering whether he is bragging or praising the work of a colleague. I believe that the person with whom I am talking thinks that *Knowledge and the Flow of Information* is an excellent book, and I also of course believe that he believes that he is telling this to me (though he may not know who I am, since I am not wearing my nametag either). To represent these iterated beliefs (my beliefs about what John (or Fred) believes), we need to locate both the primary believer (me, in this case) and the person whose beliefs I have beliefs about (the person I am talking with) in the possible worlds that are compatible, according to what I believe, with what he believes.

The first and more obvious point here is that knowledge and belief are intensional: my knowledge and belief about what the person I am talking with believes are not the same as my knowledge and belief about what John believes, even though John is the person I am talking with. The classical Hintikka models, with their indexed accessibility relations ignore this complication. But the centered-world models, with the identity of the believer in the relata, can make the required distinctions. Suppose "f" is an individual concept, picking out a person as a function of a possible world. Then the pair $\langle f(x), x \rangle$ is a centered world, the one with the value of f for world x at the center. If f is a function whose value

---

[5] To simplify and avoid clutter, I am going to ignore, from now on, the time at the center, assuming a fixed time, and taking centers to be just individual subjects.

is the person I am talking with in each of the possible worlds compatible with my beliefs, then one can generalize about my beliefs about the beliefs of the person I am talking with (in one sense), and distinguish them from my beliefs about the beliefs of John, who is that person.

The second point is that to calibrate the beliefs of different subjects we need to locate them, not only in worlds compatible with their own beliefs, but also in worlds compatible with the beliefs of those whose beliefs they have beliefs about. To represent John's beliefs about what I believe about *him*, he needs to locate himself, not only in the worlds that are the way he takes things to be, but also in the worlds that are the way he thinks that I take them to be. Suppose John comes to realize that I am not sure whether he is Perry or Dretske. Then his "I" will pick out Dretske in some of the worlds that he takes to be compatible with my beliefs. ("This guy thinks I might be Fred Dretske," he thinks to himself. In this case, his "I" tracks my concept "the person I am talking with".) The "I" in this belief attribution has no special status for the proposition it is used to pick out, nor does it have a special status for the subject of the belief being attributed (there is nothing self-locating about my beliefs about John). But the iterated belief is self-locating for the person (John) who is attributing the belief to me. So there will be two different individuals that have a special status with respect to a possible world that is used to represent what one person believes about the beliefs of another person.

Say that an individual concept, f, is an *I-concept*, with respect to a possible world x if and only if for all worlds y and subjects B, if $\langle f(x), x \rangle R \langle B, y \rangle$, then $B = f(y)$. An I-concept f is an individual concept that picks out the individual that $f(x)$ takes himself to be in each of the possible worlds that are compatible with what he believes in world x. Any two I-concepts (relative to world x) that pick out the same individual in world x will agree with respect to all worlds that are compatible with what that individual believes in world x, but they may differ with respect to possible worlds that are not compatible with that individual's belief state in x. Consider, for example, Quine's story of Ralph and Ortcutt. Ralph knows Ortcutt in two guises—as a man he sees on the beach (who he thinks is a pillar of the community) and as a man he sees in a brown hat in a bar (who he thinks is a spy). Ortcutt, we may assume, knows perfectly well who he himself is, so any I-concept for Ortcutt will pick out Ortcutt himself in each of the possible worlds compatible with Ortcutt's beliefs. But suppose that he knows about Ralph's doxastic situation. Then to represent Ortcutt's beliefs about Ralph's beliefs about him, we need to distinguish two distinct individual concepts, both of which pick out Ortcutt himself in each world compatible with *Ortcutt's* beliefs, but one of which picks out the man on the beach in worlds compatible with Ortcutt's beliefs about Ralph's beliefs, while the other picks out the man in the brown hat. Each will be relevant in different contexts. If Ralph is across the room in the bar, looking suspiciously at Ortcutt, who is wearing his brown hat, Ortcutt might say to his companion, gesturing toward Ralph, "That guy thinks I am a spy."

So I-concepts represent possible extensions of a subject's self-location to epistemically inaccessible possible worlds: where an individual locates herself in worlds that, from her perspective, are counterfactual (including those she takes to be compatible with the beliefs of other subjects). Normally, when we can assume that everyone knows who everyone else is, we take the relevant I-concepts to be the one that always picks out the individual herself. But when a person is attributing beliefs to someone who is confused about or ignorant of that person's identity, more than one I-concept may be used, even within the same context. After our conversation, John might say to someone else, "I was talking with Bob Stalnaker, but he didn't realize that it was me that he was talking with. He thought I might be Fred Dretske." There is a shift here: consider the world that John correctly takes to be compatible with my beliefs in which the person I was talking with is Fred Dretske. The "me" in John's remark picks out Perry in that world, while the "I" picks out Dretske.

Finally, let's look back, from the perspective of this theory, at the idea of common ground: the infinitely iterated attitude with the structure of common knowledge that is our representation of a context in which a discourse takes place. We have seen, first, that iterated attitudes must be defined in terms of a way of identifying the individual whose attitudes one has attitudes about. (And while this is something that a consideration of self-location forces us to recognize, it is a general feature of iterated attitudes that we need to recognize in any case.) So to define something like the common knowledge of a group of subjects, we need to specify, not just the subjects, but also the ways they identify each other. In the context of a face-to-face conversation, this will be straightforward. Even if the conversation we are concerned with consists of a group of amnesiacs discussing together who each of them might be, they will still have a shared way of identifying each other—a basis for fixing the referents of the "I"s and "you"s in their conversation. As we have seen, in the iterated case, we get, in a sense, multiple centering: in worlds compatible with A's beliefs about what B believes, we need to locate both A and B (one center to represent who A takes herself to be in the world as she thinks B takes it to be, and another to represent who she thinks B takes himself to be in that same world). So in a representation of the common ground—the information shared in common between a group of n individuals—there will be n individuals at the center: the individuals that they all presuppose themselves to be.[6]

Here is a quick sketch of the formal definition of a notion of common knowledge in this framework:[7] for any individual concept f, we can define a relativized epistemic accessibility relation between (uncentered) possible worlds in terms of the epistemic accessibility relation between centered worlds as follows:

For any worlds x and y, $xR_f y$ iff $\langle f(x), x \rangle R \langle f(y), y \rangle$.

Provided that f is an I-concept, relative to world x, the set $\{y: xR_f y\}$ will be the set of (uncentered) possible worlds compatible with what the individual who is the value of f for world x knows in world x.

Now for any two individual concepts, f and g, we can define a binary relation R_{fg} as the transitive closure of R_f and R_g, and this relation will determine a common knowledge set, relative to a world x, provided that both f and g are I-concepts, relative to all possible worlds that are R_{fg} related to x.

That is, the set $\{y: xR_{fg}y\}$ will be the set of worlds compatible with the common knowledge, in world x, of the two individuals who are the values of f and g for world x (relative to those ways of identifying each other) if and only if for all worlds y in this set, and for all worlds z and individuals B, if $\langle f(y), y \rangle R \langle B, z \rangle$, then $B = f(z)$ and if $\langle g(y), y \rangle R \langle B, z \rangle$, then $B = g(z)$.

The formal definition is complex, but the intuitive idea is that two subjects have common knowledge only relative to a certain pair of ways

---

[6] See Ninan 2012 for a theory that makes use of multiply-centered possible worlds, though his use of them is different from the use to which I am putting them.

[7] I will characterize common knowledge for the two-person case, but it generalizes to n persons in the obvious way.

they have of identifying each other. The same two subjects might have different ways of identifying each other that give rise to different states of common knowledge.

I have sketched the definition of common knowledge, but if our basic attitude was acceptance for the purposes of the conversation, the result would be a representation of the common ground. Two observations about the consequences of this modification of the classical account: first, since the common ground is now represented by a set of multiply centered worlds, each with a center for each participant in the conversation, the context set look more like a set of K-contexts, and so helps to clarify the relation between the two notions of context that we have distinguished. The centers emerge naturally from the cognitive situations of the relevant individuals; assumptions about indexical pronouns played no role in the construction, but given the centers it will be a simple matter to apply the Kaplan semantics for personal pronouns to the members of the context set. The "I"s and the "you"s are interpreted in the obvious way by who is speaking in the relevant K-context. Second, as with common knowledge, the relativization of the common ground to the ways the individuals have of identifying each other means that it is possible for there to be two distinct contexts involving the same individuals, differing only in their ways individuating each other. This possibility is illustrated in the most Byzantine of the many Frege cases that have been discussed in the literature, a case that involves multiple identity confusion, indexicality, and contextual variation: Mark Richard's example of the phone booth.

5.3 Mark Richard's phone booth story

A woman in a phone booth is talking to a man.[8] She is also watching the man, who is waving at her, but she does not realize that it is the same man. The man also does not realize that the woman he is talking to is the same woman as the one he is waving at. The woman tells the man about the man waving at her. Then she says, "The man waving at me thinks I am in danger. But you don't think I am in danger, do you?" The man replies, "No, I don't think you are in danger."

---

[8] The story was first presented in Richard 1983.

Both the man and the woman are sincere, and it seems that what each says is true. That is, the woman's statements

"The man waving at me thinks I am in danger"

and

"You don't think I am in danger"

are both true.

But the singular terms, "the man waving at me" and "you", both refer to the same person, *and the terms occur outside the scope of the attitude verb.* So how can both statements be true?

We can model the essentials of the situation with three possible worlds: World α is the actual world in which there are two subjects A (the woman) and B (the man). They are talking to each other on the phone, and B is waving at A from across the street. A is in danger. World β is the world as the woman A takes it to be. There is, in β, a woman, A, who is not in danger, and two different men, B1 and B2. She is talking to B1, and B2 is waving at her. A (in α) centers herself at A (in β, the world as she takes it to be). That is, $\langle A,\alpha \rangle R \langle A,\beta \rangle$. World γ is the world as B takes it to be. There are two relevant women in this world, A1 and A2, and two men, B1 and B2. B (in world α) centers himself (in γ) at B1. (That is, $\langle B,\alpha \rangle R \langle B1,\gamma \rangle$.) B1 is talking to A1 in world γ, and is waving at A2. A1 is not in danger, but A2 *is* in danger.

Now the woman is aware (in the actual world α) of what the man she is talking to believes, and so she takes world γ to be compatible with what the man she is talking to believes. That is, $\langle B1,\beta \rangle R \langle B1,\gamma \rangle$. She is also aware of what the man who is waving at her believes: that he is waving at a woman who is in danger. The man (B1) is waving at a woman in danger in world γ, and so that world is compatible with what she believes the man waving at her believes.

We might distinguish two different I-concepts for A (relative to world α): both take world β to A (that is what makes them I-concepts for A in *x*), but one takes world γ to A1 and the other takes world γ to A2. The first I-concept is relevant to the context of the phone conversation with the man, where her "you" picks out B1 (in β), while the second is relevant to her attribution of belief to the man who is waving at her, who is B2, in world β, since in the context of this attribution, she identifies herself, in γ, with the woman who is in danger. Relative to the first I-concept, the clause "that I am in danger" refers to a proposition that is true in γ, while relative to the second I-concept, it refers to a proposition that is false in world γ. The man believes the first proposition, but not the second, and that is why "The man waving at me believes I am in danger" and "You don't believe I am in danger" said by the woman, are both true.[9]

It has been clear all along that the compatibility of the woman's two statements needs to be explained in terms of some kind of context shift. That was Richard's point. The framework I have sketched gives a precise account of the way that the referent of "I" in the scope of a second- or third-person belief attribution will vary with context, and so provides one way of pinning down just what kind of context shift is involved.

---

[9] Richard's story is of course fanciful and wildly unrealistic, but distinct parallel contexts involving the same individuals may occur in more mundane situations. Recall the story of my encounter at the APA meeting with John Perry. It could have been, that at that time I was also engaged in an email exchange with Perry. In the context of that exchange, we each knew who the other was.

6
May, Might, If

In the last chapter, we considered a way that our representation of the common ground needs to be refined in order to account for information about where the speakers and interpreters locate themselves in the world as they mutually take it to be. This self-locating information includes information about what the parties to a conversation agree and disagree about, and this is information that that they need to keep track of if the conversation is to run smoothly. Our main concern in this chapter and the next will be with the way information of this kind is expressed in speech and reflected in the common ground, the way it changes as the discourse proceeds, and the way expressions of this kind of information change the context. Both the facts about what is accepted and rejected and the knowledge of these facts are constantly changing, both by accommodation (by the mutual recognition of manifest events that take place) and as a result of conventional speech acts that reveal what a speaker accepts, and that aim to change what is mutually accepted. The common ground may change both by adding and by subtracting information. That is, the set of live possibilities that represents the common ground can expand as well as contract. Most of the discussion of context change, both as a conventional consequence of what is said, and by accommodation, has focused on the addition of new information (and so the contraction of the space of possibilities). The one speech act we have discussed is assertion, which (in the simple model of an assertion game) is interpreted as a proposal to change the context by adding information to the prior common ground. Discussions of the process of accommodation also tend to focus exclusively on the adding of new information: the speaker manifestly presupposes something, and "straightway" (to quote David Lewis on presupposition accommodation) it is then added to what is mutually presupposed. But we need also to consider speech acts that aim to open possibilities, rather than to eliminate them, and to keep in mind that one may accommodate by *adding* possibilities to the common ground in response to an interlocutor's manifest indication that she is *not* presupposing something that one previously assumed she was presupposing.

Modal words such as "might" and "must" are among the devices that help to express information about what is accepted or not accepted in a context, and to perform speech acts that open up possibilities. These words behave in puzzling ways that have stimulated a lot of interest in the recent literature, both in semantics/pragmatics and the philosophy of language, and I think the pragmatic framework we are developing may help to clarify some of their functions. The discussion of these functions will involve further consideration of the interaction of compositional structure with discourse dynamics, and further refinement of the points of the evolving space that represents the information that is mutually accepted.

Here is the plan for this chapter. I will approach the problem of epistemic modals indirectly by first giving an exposition of what David Lewis described as "a little language game" that he used to raise a problem about a *deontic* modality—permission. Lewis's game was not presented as an analysis of any natural language expression, but was the construction of an artificial game designed to throw light on the relation between the semantic and the pragmatic dimensions of the problem of understanding the role of certain modal expressions. The simplicity of the language and the game helps to make the relation between the content and force of the utterances that are moves in his game crystal clear, and I will argue that the pattern of dynamic interaction in the artificial game has enough in common with more realistic uses of modal expressions to make it an illuminating analogy and to provide some resources to explain some of the puzzling facts about the behavior of epistemic modals and conditionals. After describing this game and summarizing some features of its structure, I will look at Seth Yalcin's analysis of epistemic "might" and "must". Yalcin, like Lewis, is concerned with the relation between the compositional semantics for the modal expressions and their pragmatic function. I will point to some analogies between epistemic modals and the deontic operators in Lewis's game of commands and permissions.[1] Third, I will consider the semantics and

---

[1] Yablo 2011 also considers Lewis's permission game and the comparison of deontic and epistemic modals. I am indebted to his insightful discussion.

pragmatics of conditionals. So-called indicative conditionals are a kind of epistemic modal, and conditionals in general interact with other epistemic modals. An old controversy about whether conditionals express propositions connects with the more recent debates about epistemic modals, and I will argue that some features of Lewis's game of commands and permissions are also relevant to the issues about conditionals. With both epistemic "might" and "must" and with conditionals, I will aim to reconcile a truth-conditional compositional semantics with an expressivist thesis about the role of these expressions. One advantage of giving a truth-conditional form to the analysis is to facilitate the explanation of the interaction of conditionals with other expressions, and this chapter will conclude by arguing that the kind of semantic/pragmatic account I propose for indicative conditionals gives a good account of quantified indicative conditionals.

6.1 Commands and permissions

I start with what David Lewis called "a little language game" that he used to raise a problem about permission. Lewis's game was not presented as an analysis of any natural language expressions, but was the construction of an artificial game, played with an artificial language that is different in a number of ways from any natural language. The language is like a natural language in that it has modal sentences that have a declarative form, but that may be used to do something other than to make assertions about how things are. The language and the game aim to throw light on the relation between the content of modal sentences and the force with which they are expressed.

Traditionally, there are two ways to think about the role of modal notions, including the deontic modality involved in commands and permissions. On the one hand, one may think of a modal operator as determining a distinctive kind of proposition as a function of the proposition on which it operates (which, following the linguists, who are following medieval theorists, we will call the *prejacent*). But there is also a tradition of thinking of modality as determining the *mode* with which a proposition is expressed, and not being a part of, or a determinant of, the proposition itself. Lewis's game defines both a distinctive kind of deontic content, and a distinctive kind of imperative force, or mode, with which that content is expressed. First, the compositional semantics for the deontic sentences of the language that Lewis specifies determines propositions that state what one is obliged and permitted to do. Second, pragmatic rules are given for the use of the sentences in the playing of the language game. The pragmatic rules say how the things that the players might say will affect the state of play.

Specifically,[2] the language is a standard deontic propositional modal language, with sentence letters and two interdefinable modal operators, "!" and "¡" (which Lewis called "fiat" and "taif") for saying, respectively, what is required and what is permitted. In the standard Kripke-style semantics for such a language, a model consists of a set of possible worlds and a binary accessibility relation. The relation holds between worlds x and y if and only if world y is compatible with what is permissible in world x. Lewis's semantics is close to this familiar modal semantics, with world-time pairs playing the role of the possible worlds. Sentences of the form !ϕ and ¡ϕ, when used in possible world w at time t, say what is required or permitted at that time in that world. !ϕ is true, at $\langle x,t \rangle$ if and only if ϕ is true at $\langle x',t' \rangle$ for all x' and t' such that $\langle x,t \rangle R \langle x',t' \rangle$, and ϕ is true at $\langle x,t \rangle$ if and only if ϕ is true at $\langle x,t \rangle$ for *some* $\langle x',t' \rangle$ such that $\langle x,t \rangle R \langle x',t' \rangle$. Lewis calls the set of permissible world-time pairs, $\{\langle x',t' \rangle: \langle x,t \rangle R \langle x',t' \rangle\}$ the *sphere of permissibility* for $\langle t,x \rangle$.

There is little novelty in the language or in the truth-conditional semantics for it. The distinctive feature of the game is in the pragmatic rules, which are as follows. There are three players with distinctive roles: the master, the slave, and the kibitzer. The master controls the sphere of permissibility. When she issues a statement of the form !ϕ (at time t in world x), the sphere of permissibility adjusts to make the statement true at that time. More specifically, the master's command (at $\langle t,x \rangle$) makes it the case that the sphere of permissibility for time t in world x is the intersection of the sphere as it was before t with the proposition expressed by ϕ. The slave's job is to act in a way that ensures that the actual world remains within the sphere of permissibility. The kibitzer has no special powers or responsibilities, but can comment on the situation, perhaps reminding the slave what he must do, or the master what she has commanded or permitted. The point of having a kibitzer in the game is to bring out the fact that the same sentence, with the same content, can

---

[2] I will sketch just enough of Lewis's game to bring out the lessons I want to draw from it. See Lewis 1975b for the details.

be, in the mouth of one player, a command, and in the mouth of another an assertion. Both speech acts will have deontic content, but only one will have imperative force.[3]

The master can issue permissions as well as commands, and just as a command by the master makes it true that something is required, so a permission statement is supposed to make it true that something is permitted. In the case of a command, there is a straightforward answer to the question, what is the minimal adjustment to the prior sphere of permissibility necessary to make the content of the command true? So it is clear what the rule specifying the force of a command should be. But with a permission statement, there is no such answer. There is no unique way of "subtracting" a requirement in order to make a permission statement true. The task of finding a rule that says how the issuing of a permission statement by the master changes the context is the problem about permission that Lewis is referring to in the title of his paper. The paper does not offer a solution to the problem. It is argued that each of the proposed solutions that are considered either fails to be adequate, or is just a way of restating the problem.

I am not sure what Lewis would have counted as a solution to his problem (as contrasted with a restatement of it), since it is clear that any solution will require that new resources be added to the model, and any postulation of new resources sufficient to provide a determinate rule by which the spheres of permissibility evolve might be charged with being just a way of posing the problem. But a reformulation of the problem may still be helpful in sharpening it. Whether or not it counts as a solution, one can say something about the abstract structure of the resources that need to be added, and perhaps about the way the added resources might have application to other problems. Lewis's own work on the logic and semantics of counterfactual conditionals points the way, since there are parallels between the problem about permission and the problem of counterfactuals. The problem about permission might be put this way: suppose something impermissible was made permissible. What else would then be permissible? This looks a lot like the question: suppose a certain proposition that is in fact false were true. What else

---

[3] Lewis does not include any formal account of assertion in his game, but one could easily add a notion of common ground, represented by a set of world-time pairs, and the standard assertion rule.

would then be true? The rough idea of Lewis's analysis of counterfactuals is that a counterfactual, (φ □→ ψ), is true in possible world x if and only if ψ is true in all of the possible worlds in which φ is true *and which are otherwise minimally different from x*. A model for interpreting counterfactuals specifies a comparative "closeness" relation that determines what "minimal difference" comes to. One could add an analogous relation to the models for the commands and permissions game. There are alternative ways of making the structure precise, but one might suppose that the spheres of permissibility are nested in a succession of wider backup spheres, with some impermissible worlds "closer" to permissibility than others. When the master says "!φ" at a given world-time, the prior sphere of permissibility expands to include those points at which φ is true, and which are in the "closest" sphere that includes some points at which φ is true. Nothing substantive could be said about the relevant notion of closeness at this level of abstraction, but it seems reasonable to think that a permission game of the kind Lewis defined will require a relation with this structure, and if our models contained such a relation, it would yield a determinate rule for the evolution of the spheres of permissibility in response to permission statements by the master.[4]

It is this problem about permission that gets most of Lewis's attention, but there is also a small problem about commands (and permissions) that he does not consider, but that will be important for the analogy with

---

[4] Lewis has a detailed discussion of the parallels between his semantics for counterfactuals and a semantics for conditional obligation in Lewis 1973, section 5.1, and in a formal paper on dyadic deontic logic (Lewis 1974), but he does not mention, in the permission paper, the obvious connection between the structures proposed in those theories and the problem about permission. This is puzzling, but it may be because he was thinking of the command/permission game as a game where the spheres of permissibility do not represent some independently given value structure, but arise wholly from the speech acts of the master. It is specified, in defining the master/slave game, that in any model, before the master speaks, all is permitted. But even on this understanding of the project, the problem about permission shows that some further general conventions are needed to define a rule for permission, and it seems reasonable to think that the structures of the semantics for dyadic deontic logic would be relevant to stating such conventions.

One might hope that the structure that determines the permission rule would be the same as the structure that explains contrary-to-duty conditional requirements, one of the problems dyadic deontic logic is designed to address. But there will be some differences. Suppose the slave is commanded to carry rocks on Friday, and also (this is the contrary-to-duty command) to do penance on Sunday if he shirks his duty by not carrying rocks on Friday. That is the prior situation, but then the master gives the slave permission to take Friday off. It shouldn't follow that he still has to do penance on Sunday.

epistemic modals that I will develop. The problem is this: the force rule for the master's imperative utterances is clear enough for simple commands—simple sentences of the form !ϕ. But Lewis's game gives a complete compositional semantics for sentences of the deontic language, including truth-functions of sentences that mix deontic and descriptive content. We need to consider what should happen when the master utters a sentence with mixed deontic and factual content. Suppose the master (Scrooge, in this example) says to the slave (Bob Cratchit), after having reluctantly given him permission to take Christmas off: "If you do take Christmas off, you must work an extra hour the next day." Or perhaps Scrooge uses a disjunctive sentence to perform his speech act: "Either you work on Christmas, or you must work an extra hour the day after." (If "C" is "Cratchit works on Christmas", and "W" is "Cratchit works an extra hour the next day" then Scrooge's sentence, in Lewis's language, is (C∨!W)). What is the effect of the utterance of this disjunction? The general rule for the master's speech acts was supposed to be this: the sphere of permissibility adjusts in the minimal way required to make the master's sentence true, but it is not clear how to apply this rule to a disjunctive sentence with one imperative disjunct. If the sphere contracts to require that Cratchit is (categorically) required to work the extra hour, this will ensure that Scrooge's utterance is true, but this is too strong, since the statement might be true without this change. On the other hand, if the sphere contracts only enough to require that Cratchit is obliged to make the disjunction (C ∨ W) is true, this will not suffice to ensure that Scrooge's sentence, interpreted in a straightforward way, is true. Suppose Cratchit fulfills his obligation by taking Christmas off, and then working the extra hour the next day. Scrooge's statement will then be false since the first disjunct will be false, and because there is no categorical requirement, the second will be false as well.

The literal-minded Cratchit might be tempted to reason this way: "Either the command disjunct is true, in which case I have to work the extra hour whether or not I take Christmas off, or it is false, in which case I have no extra obligations, no matter what I do. In the former case, I prefer to take Christmas off rather than work Christmas, and also the extra hour the next day. In the latter case, I also prefer to take Christmas off (since in this case, I still won't have to work any extra hours). So in either case, that is what I should do. Of course I recognize that since I plan to take Christmas off, it must be that *if* the Master's command is true, it is the second disjunct that is true, but perhaps the master's statement is false, since it is at least *partly* a prediction, and therefore not automatically true. Furthermore, since I know that the master has not issued any new categorical command, I have reason to think that the second disjunct is false, whatever I do, and so (given that I am planning to falsify the first disjunct) it seems that the master's statement is just mistaken." Has the clever Cratchit found a loophole that will allow him to have his Christmas off, with no extra hours the next day? Scrooge might protest,

"What I *meant* to say was that you must either work Christmas, or work an extra hour the next day."

"But," Cratchit replies, "that is not what you said."[5]

Of course if Scrooge had said, "Either you work on Christmas, or you must work an extra hour the next day" in English, then it would seem reasonable to judge that Scrooge *did* say what he meant to say, and our semantics for disjunction and the deontic "must" should explain this. But we are assuming that he was speaking Lewis's little language, and what he said was "(C∨!W)". It is not clear what the stipulated rules of the game say about the case where the master says this. Lewis's game is just a made-up exercise, and we can adjust either the compositional semantics or the force rules in any way we like. One might simply stipulate that an utterance from the master counts as a command (or a permission) only if it is an unembedded deontic sentence. On this proposal, a sentence with an embedded deontic clause will always be treated as an assertion, even in the mouth of the master. On this stipulation, the reasoning that we put into the mouth of Cratchit is perfectly correct. To avoid this consequence, one might stay with this semantics, and this policy, for the official language, but allow commands to be made with *surface* sentences with imperative parts so long as they can be reinterpreted and formalized as categorical imperatives (for example taking the real form of "either C or ought-W" to be "!(C ∨ W)"). But these moves would rob the game of much of its interest, which is the promise that it can combine the advantages of a compositional semantics with a general account of speech acts that are used to do something different from what straightforward assertions do, which is to state what the world is like. The hope is

---

[5] I have to acknowledge that my Cratchit's personality is quite different from the original, and also that he is here asking for trouble.

that a game with this feature will throw some light on the way deontic and other modal expressions work in natural language. For this reason, the way we adjust the rules of the artificial game to solve the problem should be guided by the related phenomena in natural language, and it seems intuitively clear that complex sentences with embedded deontic clauses can be used (by a speaker with the right status) to change what is required. The problem for the game, and the adjustment to solve it, should help to explain why the natural language constructions that are the analogues of the operators in our simple game have some of the features they have.

The solution I will suggest modifies, not the force rule, but the compositional semantics, and it will make use of the notion of a subordinate context that was discussed in detail in Chapter 4. I emphasized in that discussion that subordinate contexts are wholly defined in terms of basic contexts, so in a sense they are features of the basic context—the common ground. Subordinate contexts, as discussed so far, have played no explicit role in the compositional semantics. Their role was to help to explain the dynamic process of accommodation, and to bring into focus the information provided by the basic context that is available for determining the propositions expressed or denoted by embedded clauses. But there is no reason why a language could not have modifiers or operators that are interpreted by semantic rules that appeal to relevant subordinate contexts, when the operators or modifiers occur in embedded clauses. If we interpret the deontic operators in Lewis's language this way, we can explain why some complex sentences with imperative parts can have the structure that they appear to have (a disjunction with one imperative disjunct, or a conditional with an imperative consequent), and also be governed by the general force rule when they are used by the master. This is the rule that says that the sphere of permissibility adjusts in the minimal way required to ensure that the sentence as a whole is true. So suppose we add to the semantics for Lewis's game an extra parameter of the interpretation, a *context*, represented by a set of world-time pairs. The semantic rule for the imperative, in the unmodified theory, was this:

$$[!\phi]\langle t,x\rangle = 1 \text{ iff } [\phi]\langle y,t\rangle = 1 \text{ for all } y \in S_{\langle t,x\rangle}$$

(where $S_{\langle t,x\rangle}$ is the sphere of permissibility at $\langle t,x\rangle$)

The modified rule will be this:

$$[!\phi]\langle t,x,C\rangle = 1 \text{ iff } [\phi]\langle y,t,C\rangle = 1 \text{ for all } y \in S_{\langle t,x\rangle} \cap C$$

(where C is the new parameter, a set of time-world pairs)

The default or initial context (for the interpretation of unembedded sentences) will be the set of all the relevant time-world pairs, "all of those such that t is a time during the game, and w is accessible (at the actual world) at the time at which the game begins."[6] So the modified rule will yield the same result as the original rule for unembedded commands. But the context parameter may be shifted by a compositional rule for another operator. With this modification to the semantics, the force rule can be general: the master's utterance of the sentence with the embedded deontic clause will adjust the sphere of permissibility to ensure the truth of the complete sentence.

It is not that every sentence with an embedded deontic clause will be suitable for making commands. There is no way, for example, that a belief attribution to someone other than the master could be used, by the master, to change the sphere of permissibility. If the master said to the slave, "The kibitzer believes that you must work an extra hour on the day after Christmas", this will be interpreted as an ordinary assertion, since no change in sphere of permissibility would suffice to make it true.

Though the suggested modification of the semantics is motivated by the role that we want imperative and permission statements to have in the overall game, the semantics remains independent of the force rule, and the modified semantics is still static in the sense that the semantic value of any sentence in a given context, and at a given time, is a function of the semantic values of the parts at that same context and time.

We haven't said exactly how the parameter shifts in a disjunctive or conditional context—that will depend on the semantics and pragmatics of disjunction and the conditional. Conditionals we will discuss later in this chapter. Disjunction is complicated, as we have seen, with the order of the disjuncts sometimes mattering, and sometimes not. (It seems to matter in this case.) The parameter shift might in some cases be optional, allowing for scope distinctions, though some possible interpretations that make sense for the kibitzer's assertions might not make sense for

---

[6] Lewis 1975b, 21.

the master's commands. If the shift is optional, then even with the modified rule, the disjunctive sentence, in the Scrooge example, might have the interpretation that Cratchit took it to have. The kibitzer, for example, might recall that either the master commanded the slave to work an extra hour, or else the slave decided to take Christmas off, but can't remember which. But the master could not use the sentence, interpreted this way, to issue a command.

One could say more about refinements and extensions of Lewis's game, but this is enough for our purposes. To conclude this section I will point to some features of the game that are relevant to our general concern with the relation between the content and the force of sentences containing modal expressions.

To the question, "Should the distinctive character of a command or the issuing of permission be represented with a modal operator, affecting the content, or by a force operator, determining the way that a given content affects the context?" Lewis's answer was "both". Deontic content is explained independently of force, so we can account for propositions about requirements and permissions that are embedded in complex statements, and explain how propositions about requirements and permissions can be the content of speech acts of different kinds. But the theory also gives a precise account of a distinctive kind of imperative force, and an explanation of the relation between the distinctive kind of content and the distinctive kind of force. The semantic account of the content is *static* in the following sense: the compositional rule for a deontic sentence, !ϕ or ¡ϕ, specifies the proposition expressed at a given point (world-time pair) as a function of the proposition expressed by the prejacent ϕ at that same point.

The pragmatic force rule is like the rule for assertion in that it explains force in terms of the way that the speech act changes the context, as a function of the content of the speech act. But commands and permissions issued by the master contrast with assertions (including assertions of deontic propositions) in this way: the sentence uttered changes the context by changing a parameter of interpretation (the sphere of permissibility) so as to ensure that the sentence expresses a proposition that is true relative to the changed context. The result is that in these cases the determination of the content of the speech act is *prospective* in the following sense: the content of the deontic sentence is interpreted relative to the *posterior* context—the context as it is after the force rule is applied.

Because of this feature of imperative force, it contrasts with assertive force, where the content of the assertion is determined relative to the *prior* context. The prior context (as the extensive discussion of presupposition accommodation in Chapter 2 brought out) is not the context as it was before the speech act took place, but the context as it is after the manifest fact that the speech event has occurred is recognized. But the context change, in the case of the imperative speech acts of Lewis's game, is not a case of presupposition accommodation. In these cases, it is the application of the force rule itself that brings about the change in the parameter of the context relative to which the content of the speech act is determined.

The form of this dynamic rule (context is changed as a function of a proposition that is determined as a function of the context that results from the change) introduces an obvious threat of circularity. The strategy for avoiding circularity is to specify that the context is to be changed in the minimal way required to make the sentence express a true proposition. In the case of commands, it is clear what the unique minimal change is, but in the case of permission, additional structure must be added to the models in order to get a determinate force rule that avoids circularity.

So let me sum up the lessons of Lewis's little language game, lessons that will carry over to the other modal expressions I will consider. First, the semantics is static, and is explained independently of force. Second, the way imperative speech acts change the context is *prospective*. Third, the prospective character of the force rule requires (in the case of permission) that structure beyond that required for the static semantics be introduced in order to give a determinate account of the dynamics of the game.

6.2 Epistemic modals

The traditional view about epistemic "might" and "must" is that they quantify over the possibilities that are compatible with the knowledge or potential knowledge of some contextually specified individual or group. When Alice says to Bert that it might rain, she says that she doesn't know that it won't rain, or perhaps that neither she nor Bert knows it, or that she is, or they are, not in a position to know it or to come to know it. The puzzle is that no way of pinning the relevant knowledge state down seems to be able to explain both why we are in a position to make the epistemic "might" claims we seem to be in a position to make, and also why it is often reasonable to disagree with "might" claims made by others. If Alice's statement were about just her own state of knowledge, then how could Bert disagree with her (as it seems he could)? On the other hand, if Alice's claim is about what information is available or potentially available to some larger group, then Alice will not be in a position to know what might be true in cases where it seems, intuitively that she is. Different versions of the traditional view—what von Fintel and Gillies have called "the canon"[7]—try to find a way to pin down the constraints on the relevant informational state that can explain the data.

Seth Yalcin's account of epistemic modals[8] began with a striking observation that raised a new puzzle. First, he observed that, as one would expect on the canonical view of epistemic modals, there are versions of Moore's paradox for epistemic modals that parallel Moore's paradoxes for explicit knowledge claims. Just as one cannot coherently say, "It will rain, but I don't know that it will," so one cannot coherently say, "It will rain, but it might not." In the case of explicit knowledge claims, the paradoxical conjunctions are shown not to be *semantic* contradictions by the fact that they can be coherently *supposed* even if they cannot be asserted. There is no paradox or incoherence is saying, "Suppose it will rain, but that I don't know that it will," or "If it will rain and I don't know it, then I will get wet." But with epistemic modals, the incoherence persists in the supposition context: "Suppose that it is raining, but that it might not be raining" is just as bad as the simple conjunctive assertion. So the conflict between "is" and "might not" is deeper than in the familiar cases of Moore's paradox.[9] The new puzzle shows that "φ, but it might be that not-φ" cannot simply mean, "φ, but not-φ is compatible with X's knowledge", for any choice of X, since whatever the choice of X, it should be perfectly coherent to suppose that φ is true, but that X does not know it. But despite this fact, "φ, but it might be that not-φ" still cannot be a

---

[7] von Fintel and Gillies 2011. [8] Yalcin 2007.
[9] Wittgenstein, in his discussion of Moore's paradox in the *Philosophical Investigations* mentions an example with an epistemic modal ("Es dürft regnen, aber es regnet nicht"), but he does not note the contrast, in the case of supposition, with the version of the paradox that is explicitly about knowledge or belief. (Wittgenstein 1953, 192).

straightforward contradiction, since that would imply that the claim that it might rain entails that it will rain, which is obviously wrong.

Yalcin offers a detailed semantic and pragmatic account of epistemic modals that is designed to solve both the traditional problem about bare epistemic modals, and his new problem about epistemic modals embedded in contexts of supposition, and in propositional attitude ascriptions. I will exploit some of the insights of his account, but will spell out my take on the problem in my own way, which will emphasize the analogy with Lewis's game of commands and permissions. I follow both Yalcin and Lewis in separating the task of giving a compositional semantics for the relevant modal expressions from the task of explaining the pragmatic role of the resulting semantic value. And I will follow them in doing the semantics in the familiar truth-conditional framework. Despite the truth-conditional form of the semantics, Yalcin describes his account of epistemic modals as *expressivist*, and the basis for that description is that the speech act that epistemic modal sentences are used to perform (according to the account) contrasts with the speech act of assertion, which aims to describe the world as being a certain way. Lewis's account of the speech acts of the master in his language game might be called expressivist for the same reason.

As we saw, what is distinctive about the force of the master's speech acts in Lewis's game is that the content of the command or permission sentence is determined by the *posterior* context, rather than the *prior* context, as is the case with assertions. My proposal is to make the same move in explaining the distinctive force of a statement made with an epistemic modal. In the master/slave game, the relevant feature of the context is the sphere of permissibility. In the case of epistemic modals, the changing contextual feature will be the context set itself.

As with Lewis's master/slave game, we start with the static compositional semantics, and as with the semantics for Lewis's game, the semantics will be close to an orthodox Kripke semantics (at least if we ignore certain complications that we will consider later). Our framework already provides us with a binary relation that is determined by a common-ground context. The context, in this sense, is a set whose elements are possible worlds centered on a time and a sequence of individuals, the participants in the conversation. (Call these multiply centered worlds "*s-worlds*".) The conversation is taking place in each of the possible worlds in the context set, at the time, and involving the parties that define the center. So for any s-world x in the domain of the common ground, there is a set of s-worlds that are compatible with what is common ground in x. So this gives us a binary accessibility relation on s-worlds, R, defined as follows: xRy if and only if y is compatible with what is common ground in x. If we restrict our domain, for the moment, to possible worlds compatible with the common ground of a given conversation, and assume that our context is presupposed to be non-defective, then the accessibility relation will be an equivalence relation, and so the logics of the "might"s and "must"s interpreted by it will have a simple S5 structure. (We will come back later to the question what happens when we interpret an epistemic "might" or a "must" in a possible world outside of the context set.) That is the compositional semantics for the "might" and "must"; as with Lewis's game, the innovation comes when we specify the force rule, and we will start, as Lewis's game does, just for unembedded modal claims. The proposal is to make the rule *prospective* in exactly the sense in which the commands and permissions issued by the master in Lewis's game are prospective. In saying might-ϕ, one is not *asserting* that ϕ is possible, relative to the *prior* context. Rather, one is proposing to adjust the context (if required) to bring it about that what the sentence says, relative to the *posterior* context—the context as adjusted—is true.

In Lewis's game, one player—the master—had complete authority over the relevant parameter—the sphere of permissibility—and so that parameter automatically adjusts in response to her speech acts. But in the assertion game, no one player controls the context set; it is subject to negotiation, and this will lead to complications not found in Lewis's simple game. While the slave cannot reject the master's commands or permissions, epistemic "might" statements, like ordinary assertions, can be rejected. Just as an ordinary assertion may be rejected, so any party to a conversation may decline to accept an epistemic modal claim. Since the context set models what is commonly accepted, if one party refuses to rule out a possibility, that possibility must remain in the context set. But parties to a conversation can still disagree about whether they are in a position to rule out a possibility. I will look at disagreement in more detail in the next chapter, but let's start with a standard and unremarkable case where an epistemic modal speech act changes the context, but does not result in disagreement. Alice says, "Noam might be in his office," and Bert responds, "No, I just saw him leaving for lunch." Alice's statement (on the semantics sketched above) was true, relative to the *prior* context, but we are taking it to be a proposal about the posterior context, a proposal that possibilities compatible with Noam being in his office remain in the context set so as to ensure that the sentence remains true. Bert rejects the proposal, since he has information sufficient to rule these possibilities out.

If it was already compatible with the prior context that Noam be in his office, why did Alice need to say what she said? In the assertion game, we assume that it is inappropriate to assert what is already accepted, since the assertion would have no effect on the context. This question points to two related ways in which we need to refine the simple picture of the common ground, ways that are independently motivated, and that we have noted before. First, as Kripke's discussion of presupposition brings out, there is a difference between information that is general background knowledge and information that is presupposed in an active context. Assertions may be appropriate as reminders, even if they are not really news.[10] Such assertions serve to bring an item of background knowledge into the active context—to make it salient. Second, both philosophers and linguists have recently emphasized the importance of recognizing the questions that are at issue in a given context.[11] Formally, a representation of context needs, not just a space of those possibilities that are compatible with what is presupposed, but also a partition of the possibility space, with the questions at issue being those that distinguish between the cells of the partition. If we add this kind of structure to our representation of the common ground, then there will be the following two ways in which a "might" statement can change the context: (1) In some cases, the speech act will expand the space of relevant possibilities in the minimal way required to make the "might" statement true, relative to that revised context (this kind of change is just like the change induced by a permission statement by the master in Lewis's game); (2) in other cases, the job of the "might" statement will be to refine the "modal resolution" (to use Yalcin's term)—to add a new distinction between the possibilities. The following example is a clear case of the first kind of change: Bert says, "The butler didn't do it, so it

---

[10] There is some discussion of reminders in Abbott 2008, and in my response to this, Stalnaker 2008b.
[11] See Roberts et al. 2009, Yalcin 2011, and Schaffer 2007.

must have been the gardener," presupposing that the guilty party was one of the two. Alice replies, "Wait, it might have been the chauffeur—we forgot about him." To illustrate the second kind of context change, Yalcin uses this example: the speaker says, "It might be raining in Topeka." It was not previously presupposed that it was *not* raining in Topeka—the issue was not on the table. The statement neither made nor retracted a claim, but served only to make the question salient.

Because of the prospective character of the force rule, the interpretation of those "might" statements that are not compatible with the prior context faces a problem that parallels Lewis's problem about permission. Without additional structure beyond that required by the static semantics, we don't have a determinate context change rule for the epistemic "might". The kind of structure we need is the same as that required for Lewis's game: nested spheres of possibility around the basic context set. This is exactly the kind of modal structure that semanticists such as Kratzer and Fintel have used in their accounts of modality and conditionals.

The problem about embedded commands and permissions that I raised for Lewis's game also has a parallel in the epistemic case, and the solution is the same. If Alice were to say, "If it rained, the game must have been called off," or "Even if the Yankees lost, they might still win the division," how is she proposing to adjust the context? Unless we modify the semantics, no adjustment to the basic context will be both minimal and sufficient to make the statement true. But if we interpret the "must" and "might" relative to a derived context, the complex sentence can be a proposal of the right kind: one put forward as true relative to the posterior (basic) context.

This modification gives us a solution to Yalcin's puzzle about "might" in the scope of a supposition, a solution that is close to (and modeled on) the one that he proposed. Yalcin's theory, formulated in Lewis's CI framework, proposed that an information state (represented by a set of possible worlds) be added to the index, and this coordinate will be "shifted" for the interpretation of embedded clauses. If we formulate my suggestion in the CI framework, it would add a set of s-worlds to the index. I don't agree with Yalcin's original proposal about the way this coordinate of the index shifts in the scope of propositional attitude ascriptions, for reasons that his later work has brought to light, but

I agree with the basic idea, and I think the prospective form of the force rule helps to motivate it.[12]

The move that Lewis made in defining his little language game (with the adjustments I proposed) allowed for the combination of a smooth compositional semantics with a force rule that made sense of speech acts that do something different from conveying information. On this kind of account, nonassertive speech acts and assertions have in common that a proposition determined by the semantics is put forward as true. In both cases, the end result of a successful and uncontested speech act is a context in which the content of the speech act is accepted—true in all possible worlds in the context set. The contrast between assertions and the other speech acts is in the means by which this is accomplished.

Neither Lewis nor Yalcin discuss the case of deontic or epistemic modals in the scope of quantifiers, but one advantage of a theory that uses a truth-conditional semantics, even for determining the contents of nonassertive speech acts is that it can give a smooth semantics for such cases. There could be a version of Lewis's game with many slaves, and in such a game the master could issue general commands and permissions such as this: "Each of you may take a day off on your birthday." With epistemic modals, we have examples such as this: "Any one of the candidates might be selected." (Though with both the Lewis game, and the parallel proposal about epistemic modals, not every quantifier would be suitable for issuing permissions, or for altering the common ground.

---

[12] Yalcin's proposal, in Yalcin 2007, was that in the scope of propositional attitude ascriptions to a subject J, the information-state coordinate of the index shifts to the set of possible worlds that is compatible with J's attitude. So if Alice says, "Jones believes that it might rain," the statement will be true if and only if its raining is compatible with Jones's beliefs. One problem with this hypothesis is that, because of the context shift, the proposition about what Jones believes will be different from what Alice would say, or propose, if she said (or denied) that it might rain. Suppose Alice said, "Jones believes that it might rain, but I disagree—I think we can count on fine weather all day." To account for the disagreement, I think we should interpret the "might" in the belief attribution in terms of the same contextual parameter, or an extension of it. Whether this is right or not, it is clear (as Yalcin himself brings out in later work) that his proposal does not generalize to the case of knowledge. Suppose Jones mistakenly takes himself to know that it won't rain, while in fact it will rain. Then it is clearly false that he knows that it might rain, but it is compatible with his knowledge that it will rain. I will leave questions about epistemic modals in the context of attitude ascriptions for another time, but my tentative conjecture is that they should be interpreted relative to an extension of the information-state parameter determined by the basic context to possible worlds outside the context set (those compatible with the subject's attitudes), and not to an index shift.

If the master were to say, "Some of you may take a day off on your birthday," this would have to be interpreted as an assertion. If Alice were to say, "Several of the candidates might be selected," this will require (or at least favor) a wide scope reading for the "might" (it might be that several of the candidates are selected), or else a nonepistemic interpretation of the "might".)

In giving the semantics for the epistemic "might" and "must", we restricted the specification of the accessibility relation to s-worlds that are compatible with the given context. But what about possible worlds outside of the context set? For example, Alice says that it might rain tomorrow in a context in which it is presupposed that the weather forecaster predicted rain. Now consider a possible world w in which the weather forecaster did not predict rain (perhaps no prediction was made) and in which it in fact did not rain on the relevant day. Is Alice's "might" statement true or false in that possible world? Since presupposition and common ground are not factive notions, it could be that Alice's presuppositions in world w are the same as they are in the actual world. In fact, w might be the actual world. So we know what the context set is, in world w, but what is the set that is R related to world w, where R is the relation that is relevant to determining the truth-value of the epistemic modal sentences in that world? One might be tempted to say that the relevant R is just the relation that holds between an s-world w and the s-worlds that are compatible with what is presupposed in w, and this would be the right thing to say if the modal statement were simply the proposition that something is compatible with what is being presupposed. But there is a subtle difference between a proposition that states something *about* the context and a proposition that expresses something that is context-dependent. φ is compatible with the common ground if and only if we are presupposing that it might be true, and that is enough to tell us whether the "might" statement is true or false in the worlds compatible with the context, but it leaves open the question whether the proposition expressed in that context is true or false (or neither) in possible worlds outside the context. So our theory, thus far, remains silent on the question whether the "might"s and "must"s are true or false (or neither) in worlds outside of the context set. Should this gap be closed, and if so how?

To get a more concrete sense for this kind of question, let's look at some examples. In many cases, there will be a clear and unproblematic fact of the matter about whether some statement is true or false, even if the statement is made in a context in which a relevant presupposition is in fact false. Suppose I try to call Sam Smith, but dial the wrong number and am in fact talking to someone else. "Is this Sam?" I ask, and because my interlocutor happens by coincidence to have the same first name, he answers "yes". Presupposing that I am talking to Sam Smith, I say, "The department voted to offer you the job." It is clear enough what I have said: I referred, with my use of "you" to my actual interlocutor, and inadvertently said something false about him. But in other cases, the semantics may not provide an answer, or it may be controversial what the answer should be. Suppose my interlocutor and I are presupposing of Jones that he is the unique man drinking a martini and I say, "The man drinking a martini is a philosopher."[13] Jones is in fact a philosopher, but our presupposition that he is drinking a martini is false—it is Perrier in his martini glass. Russell, Strawson, and Donnellan will all agree about the way the assertion affects the context, since they all agree about the truth-value of the statement with the definite description in possible worlds compatible with what is being presupposed in the context. But their analyses of definite descriptions will disagree about the truth-value of the statement in the *actual* world, which is outside of the context set: assuming that no unique man in the room is actually drinking a martini, Russell will say the statement is false, Strawson will say that it is neither true nor false, and Donnellan (assuming the description is being used referentially) will say that it is true.

On the dynamic *pragmatic* story, it is a minimal requirement on appropriate speech that one use a sentence that has a truth-value *at least* for all the possible worlds compatible with the CG-context. That is, it is required that the function from possible worlds to truth-values determined by the semantics be a total function, relative to that domain. On the dynamic *semantic* story, where the semantic values are context-change potentials, truth-values are determined *only* for possible worlds in the context set. On the pragmatic theory that separates the determination of content from the force of the speech act, the proposition expressed *may* extend beyond the possibilities compatible with what is being presupposed. On this kind of account, some speech acts are more

[13] This classic example comes from Donnellan 1966.

robust: what is asserted may be detached and added to one's stock of beliefs. In other cases, what is said may be more fragile, succeeding in distinguishing between the possibilities compatible with a local context, but not extending much or at all beyond it. The silence of the account we are considering about the relevant information state for interpreting epistemic modals in possible worlds outside the context set, implies that sentences with bare epistemic modals will, or at least may, be cases for which the proposition expressed is partial, and so the statement gets no truth-value in the actual world. But in some cases, there may be a natural extension of the relevant parameter to worlds outside the context set. Consider this extended example. It is the last day of the baseball season, and the Yankees are one game ahead of the Red Sox. Each team has one game to play, though not with each other. If the Yankees win, or if the Red Sox lose, the Yankees win the division. But if the Yankees lose *and* the Red Sox win, they will then be tied, so there will be a playoff game to determine the division champion. All of this is common ground in the context. Alice says: "The Yankees lost, so the Red Sox still might win the division." This is true in all of the possible worlds compatible with the (posterior) context. But, let us suppose, Alice was wrong about the Yankees—they in fact won. Alice's "might" statement was appropriate, and succeeded in changing the context in a determinate way, but was it true *in the actual world*? We know that the Red Sox won't be the division winner, but we have information not available either to Alice or to her interlocutors. It could have been that one of the interlocutors knew that Alice's assertion about the Yankees was mistaken, in which case he would reject both that assertion, and her proposal that the possibilities in which the Red Sox win the division remain in the context set. But no one in the conversation had this information, and so the possibility that the Red Sox win does, in fact, remain in the context. The "might" statement was accepted, but was it *true*? In this case, was Alice in fact wrong not just about the Yankees game, but about her epistemic "might" statement about the Red Sox? Now consider the reverse situation: suppose Alice said, "The Yankees won, so the Red Sox must be out of the running for the division title." Alice got it wrong in this version of the example too: the Yankees in fact lost. But alas, the Red Sox also lost (though none of the relevant parties know this), so the Red Sox *are* in fact out of the running, but is Alice's statement that they *must* be out of the running true in the actual world? Her reasoning was based on a false premise, but is this enough to make it false? I don't think these questions have obvious answers. There is some inclination to fill the vacuum left by our theory's silence by shifting to *our* context—the context of the theorist giving the example, bringing in the stipulated facts about the story that are used to raise the problem. There is also some inclination to shift to a nonepistemic modality to give an answer. (If the Yankees lost, and the Red Sox game is still undecided, then even if we stipulate that they *will* lose, we can say that, as of now, they still *might* win. But if we say this, we are using the "might" in a nonepistemic sense.) Further elaboration of the example, or of the theory, might give reason to assign a truth-value, outside of the context set in such cases, but for some cases, the semantics might resolutely retain its silence.[14]

The semantics will give a definite answer, even outside the context set, in the case where the prejacent of the "might" statement is true in a given world, or when the prejacent of a "must" statement is false. Whatever anyone believes, knows or is presupposing, if the Red Sox actually did win the division in the end, then the statement that they might win was actually true, relative to any context in which that statement was made, or denied. That follows from the reflexivity condition on the relevant accessibility relation, which it seems intuitively clear should hold. And this condition will hold for deontic "must" and "may" as well as for the epistemic modals. Lewis's little language game used an artificial language, with "!" and "¡" for the command and permission operators, but if Lewis's commands and permissions were made with "must" and "may", with their normal senses, then a disobedient slave will be a problem, not just for the master, but for the semantics. The master can make it the case, just by her speech act, that the slave is obliged to stay out of her wine cellar, but she cannot make it the case, by her speech act, that the slave does what he is obliged to do. If either the master or the kibitzer says to the slave, "You must stay out of the wine cellar," she or he must presuppose that the slave will do what he must do. If one wants to allow for the possibility of the disobedient slave, one must put the command or

---

[14] There has been much discussion in the literature on epistemic modals about so-called eavesdropper cases: situations where speakers in one context comment on epistemic modal claims made in a different context, and intuitions about these cases are mixed or uncertain. (See Yalcin and Knobe (unpublished) for experimental evidence about this.) Eavesdropper cases are one example of the problem of assessing the truth of an epistemic modal claim relative to possible worlds outside of the context in which that statement is made.

statement differently—for example, with "should" or "ought" rather than "must".[15]

6.3 Indicative conditionals

Debates about whether indicative conditional statements express propositions predate the recent flurry of discussion about epistemic modals, but the parallels are clear. I will argue that we can reconcile the propositional and non-propositional approaches, and my attempt to do this will replay the same themes seen in our discussion of deontic and epistemic modals. On the one side of the old debate about conditionals is the hypothesis that a conditional statement, whether indicative or subjunctive, expresses a proposition that is a function of the propositions expressed by its constituents, the antecedent and the consequent. The function is usually assumed to be context-dependent. On the other side is the hypothesis that the indicative conditional is used to make a distinctive kind of speech act involving just two propositions—those expressed by antecedent and consequent. A conditional assertion is not the unqualified assertion of a conditional proposition, but a qualified assertion of the consequent, with the antecedent expressing the qualification. On this hypothesis, the conditional sentence does not purport to state a fact, but expresses an epistemic attitude, or makes a qualified commitment. Dorothy Edgington has been the most prominent proponent of the conditional assertion account.[16] Building on earlier work by Ernest Adams, she has given both challenging arguments against the proposition analysis, and a constructive development of the view. Allan Gibbard has also argued for what Jonathan Bennett labeled the NTV (no truth-value) analysis of indicative conditionals, which Bennett also endorses.[17] Gibbard and Bennett accept a propositional analysis of *subjunctive* conditionals, arguing that the two kinds of conditionals should receive separate analyses, while Edgington opts for a unified account according to which even counterfactuals should be understood as sentences that express certain probabilistic relations but do not express propositions. On the propositionalist side, some philosophers

---

[15] cf. Dilip Ninan 2005, where it is observed that one cannot say things like "He must go to confession, but he won't."
[16] See Edgington 1986 and 1995.   [17] Bennett 2003.

and linguists have defended the material conditional analysis for indicative conditionals, attempting to explain away apparent counterexamples as cases that are true, but conversationally inappropriate. Grice adopted this strategy in his William James lectures. David Lewis, Frank Jackson, and Barbara Abbott have also argued for this analysis. Others have argued for a unified truth-conditional analysis for both kinds of conditionals. I have been on both sides of the debate between the propositionalists and the proponents of a conditional assertion account, first arguing, in a paper published in 1975,[18] that the same abstract possible-worlds semantics developed for the interpretation of counterfactuals should also be used for the interpretation of indicative conditionals, with the semantic differences between the two kinds of conditionals explained by different constraints on the contextually determined parameter of the interpretation. I still think this is the right approach, though I later acknowledged, in response to arguments by Allan Gibbard, that if indicative conditionals are to play the roles that they seem to play, they "must be too closely tied to the epistemic states of the agents who utter them to express propositions which could be separated from the contexts in which they are accepted."[19] In a recent paper,[20] I argued that one could reconcile the conditional assertion analyses with a propositional account, seeing the former as equivalent to a special case of the latter. The general strategy parallels the one we have seen in the language game of commands and permissions, and in the semantic/pragmatic account of epistemic modals. In all of these cases, the aim is to combine the advantages of the compositional semantics that comes with a propositional approach with an acknowledgement that the expression in question is being used to do something other than to communicate an item of information.

To spell out how this idea applies to indicative conditionals, I will first review the semantic/pragmatic analysis of indicative conditionals that I have defended, and then spell out the sense in which one version of this account coincides with a conditional assertion analysis. The proposal will be that indicative conditional statements are *prospective* in exactly the way that permissions, commands, and epistemic "might" and "must" are prospective. After sketching the idea as it applies to simple conditional statements, I will look at indicative conditionals within the scope of

---

[18] Stalnaker 1975.   [19] Stalnaker 1984, 111.   [20] Stalnaker 2011b.

quantifiers. As with the other modal expressions, quantified cases illustrate the advantages of the propositional form of analysis, but they also bring out problems raised by the interaction of the semantics with the pragmatic constraints. The discussion of conditionals will continue in the next chapter, where I will consider the relation between the fact-stating role of conditionals and their role in expressing epistemic attitudes.

On the propositional account of conditionals that I have defended,[21] the semantics interprets the conditional in terms of a context-dependent selection function taking a possible world w and a proposition ϕ to a possible world, $f(w, \phi)$—intuitively, a world in which ϕ is true, but which otherwise differs minimally from w. Nothing substantive is said in the abstract theory about the criteria for minimal difference, but formal constraints are put on the selection function to ensure that it orders the possible worlds, with the base world, w first in the order (since any world is minimally different from itself). The semantic rule is a follows:

$(\phi > \psi)$ is true in possible world w if and only if ψ is true in $f(\phi,w)$.

This semantic rule gives the truth-conditions for any conditional in a given possible world, and it also determines the *subordinate context* for the conditional supposition. If C is the context set (the set of possibilities compatible with the common ground), then the subordinate context for the supposition ϕ is $\{f(w,\phi): w \in C\}$.

For indicative conditionals, the pragmatics adds a contextual constraint on the selection function. Where C is the context set, say that a selection function is *admissible* if it meets the following condition:

If $w \in C$, then $f(w, \phi) \in C$.[22]

The effect of the constraint is to ensure that all of the presuppositions of the basic context are preserved in the subordinate context.

That is the truth-conditional semantics. We can also formulate, very simply, a conditional assertion analysis in our pragmatic framework, as follows: there is a speech act of *supposition*, which like the speech act of

---

[21] See Stalnaker 1968 and Stalnaker 1984, Chapter 6.
[22] Since by definition, $f(w,\phi) \in \phi$, this constraint presupposes that $\phi \cap C$ is nonempty. It is required that the antecedent of an indicative conditional be compatible with the prior context.

assertion, adds the content of the speech act to the common ground, but in this case it is added temporarily, and with no commitment to the truth of the supposition. The consequent of the conditional is then asserted in this temporary subordinate context. At the end, the possibilities that were temporarily removed are added back.[23]

Though one of these stories is propositional and the other is not, they have much in common. Each can explain why an indicative conditional assertion is very similar, in its effect, to the assertion of a *material* conditional, but each can also avoid some of the problems with a simple material conditional analysis. For example, each can explain why the rejection or denial of a conditional is very different from the rejection or denial of a material conditional. The similarity between the two analyses can be made precise by defining a version of the propositional analysis that is essentially a terminological variant of the conditional assertion view.[24] First, we note that any contextual parameter relative to which truth-conditions are specified (a modal base, a domain of discourse, a selection function, the referent of a demonstrative) may be underdetermined by the actual context. In such cases, a proposition may be partial—a truth-value determined for some, but not all possible worlds. Suppose we adopt a version of our propositional semantics for indicative conditionals that is maximally cautious, determining a truth-value for a conditional only when the rules we have specified suffice to determine one, as a function of the antecedent, the consequent, and the common ground. This is accomplished by saying that all *admissible* selection functions are on a par. A conditional is true (relative to a given CG-context) if true for all admissible selection functions, false if false for all, and neither true nor false otherwise.[25] The upshot will be that a conditional sentence will be false in possible worlds compatible with the context if and only if that possibility would be excluded by the conditional assertion, according to the conditional assertion analysis. So one can see this version of the propositional theory as an implementation of the conditional assertion account. But this will work only if we assume that the

---

[23] The scope of the supposition may, in some cases, continue beyond a conditional sentence.
[24] This was suggested in Stalnaker 2011b, but I did not discuss there the prospective character of conditional assertions.
[25] The supervaluation account of truth-value gaps was first proposed in van Fraassen 1966, and has been widely applied since.

interpretation of the conditional sentence is *prospective*. Here is the argument that this assumption is necessary: suppose I *believe* that learning ϕ would be sufficient reason (given my other beliefs) for accepting ψ, but that this is not common ground, since (ϕ&~ψ) is compatible with the prior context. A conditional assertion would clearly be appropriate in this situation, since in a context in which ϕ is supposed, I am in a position to assert ψ. But on the maximally cautious version of our truth-conditional semantics, if we interpret the conditional (if ϕ, then ψ), relative to the *prior* context, the conditional will be neither true nor false in the possible worlds in which ϕ is false. Since I am not in a position to rule out these possibilities, the conditional, interpreted this way, would not be assertible. But if we interpret the conditional relative to the *posterior* context, where that context is the result of the minimal adjustment necessary to make the conditional true, relative to the adjusted context, then the conditional statement will be appropriate, and we get the equivalence between our two accounts. Just as with the epistemic "may" and "must" statements, the effect is to adjust at once a parameter of the interpretation and the set of possibilities compatible with the common ground. In the epistemic modal case, the changing common ground *is* the parameter of the interpretation; in the case of conditionals, the parameter is closely constrained by the changing common ground. The general account explains both how the expressive speech acts are like assertions, and how they are different. In all cases, the end result of a successful speech act will be a context in which the proposition expressed is true in all of the possible worlds compatible with what is then the common ground. In the non-assertion cases, this success is achieved, in part, by changing the determinants of the truth-conditions for the proposition.

If the upshot is the equivalence of the conditional assertion analysis and (one version of) the propositional account, why is it important to go with the truth-conditional semantics? Part of the answer is the familiar one—that it provides a semantics for sentences in which conditionals are embedded in other constructions—but of course this is an advantage only if the compositional semantics gets the right result. Lewis appealed to compositionality in defending the presumption that indicative conditionals express propositions: "We think we know how the truth conditions for compound sentences of various kinds are determined by the truth conditions of constituent subsentences, but this knowledge would be useless if any of those subsentences lacked truth conditions."[26] But the particular analysis of indicative conditionals that Lewis defended was the material conditional analysis, and it is precisely with the embedded conditionals that this analysis gets things wrong. As we have seen, simple assertions of indicative conditionals have essentially the same effect as the assertion of the corresponding material conditional, on both the conditional assertion analysis, and on our minimal truth-conditional hypothesis, but the most dramatic divergence between ordinary indicative conditionals and material conditionals occur with denials, rather than assertions, or with conditionals embedded under negation. The truth-conditional account I am defending does better with embedding under negation, and I will argue that it also does better with conditionals in quantified sentences.

A second advantage of a truth-conditional semantics for indicative conditionals is that it allows for continuity between cases where conditionals seem to express an epistemic attitude and cases where their aim seems to be to communicate information about the world, information that is independent of the epistemic situation of the participants in a conversation in which the information is exchanged. It may be a matter of debate and negotiation, not only what the facts are, but what there is a fact of the matter about, and it is good to have a framework that does not require that such questions be settled in advance. I will have more about this issue in the next two chapters, but let's look first at the compositional considerations—particularly at the interaction of indicative conditionals with quantifiers.

6.4 Quantified indicative conditionals

Jim Higginbotham argued that quantified conditionals present a prima facie case of non-compositionality.[27] He begins by comparing two examples, with different quantifers, each with a conditional open clause in the scope of the quantifier:

(1) Everyone will succeed if he works hard.
(2) No one will succeed if he goofs off.

He claims that the first can be interpreted as a conditional in the scope of a quantifier, but that the second cannot. Higginbotham is not explicit

[26] Lewis 1976, 305.   [27] Higginbotham 2003.

about how he is interpreting the conditional at this point in the discussion, but what he says about (2) suggests that his noncompositionality claim is based on a strict conditional interpretation. Suppose we interpret (2) as saying that for no x (in the relevant domain) is it true that if x goofs off, x succeeds. His claim is that it would then say that goofing off is in no case a sufficient condition for success, while the actual meaning is that in no case is goofing off compatible with success. The point is all the more obvious if we interpret the conditional as a material conditional, for then (2) would assert that everyone will goof off, and that no one will succeed, which is obviously not what it says. Higginbotham then suggests that compositionality can be restored if we give the semantic analysis that I proposed, and that I have sketched here, though he does not consider the pragmatic constraint. On this analysis, one could paraphrase (2) this way:

(2')   The following is true of no x (in the relevant domain): in the world minimally different from ours (in relevant respects) in which x goofs off, x succeeds.

This seems to get things right.

Higginbotham considers an alternative analysis that takes "if" clauses to be restrictors on the quantifier, rather than sentential connectives. On this analysis, (1) and (2) could be paraphrased this way:

(1r)   Everyone who works hard will succeed.
(2r)   No one who goofs off will succeed.

This also seems to get things right for these cases, but Higginbotham argues that the analysis does not generalize. The clearest counterexamples are with the quantifiers "most" and "few", though there are also problem cases with all, some and none. Compare

(3)   Most (of these) students will get As if they work hard.
(3r)   Most (of these) students who work hard will get As.

(3r) will be true if a majority of the hard-working students will get As, while (3) will be true if a majority of *all* the students meet the condition that they will get an A if they work hard. Neither statement entails the other. It might be that only a few students will work hard, and most of them will get As, but that the majority of students would get B or lower, however hard they worked. On the other hand, it could be that hard work would be sufficient for an A for most of the students, but unfortunately, only a minority of those who will actually work hard are among those capable of achieving an A.

Higginbotham argues that even with universal quantifiers, there is a difference between the quantifier restrictor analysis and the quantified conditional analysis, though in this case the latter entails the former. He uses the following minimal pair to illustrate the difference:

(4) Every professor will retire early if offered a generous pension.
(4r) Every professor offered a generous pension will retire early.

"There might be," Higginbotham says, "many professors (but even one will do) who we can be sure will not retire early, quite independently of any pension they may be offered." In this case, (4) will be false, while (4r) will be true, if all the professors who are *actually* offered a generous pension choose to retire early.

We get the same contrast in the negative universal case, again using Higginbotham's examples:

(5) No professor will retire early if not offered a generous pension.
(5r) No professor not offered a generous pension will retire early.

"If Professor X is going to retire early, period, then he is a counterexample to [(5)], but if he is amongst those offered a generous pension, then he is no counterexample to [(5r)]." As Higginbotham notes, to get the right result for (5), by straightforward application of compositional rules, we need to assume the principle of conditional excluded middle (CEM), which is validated by the semantics sketched above.[28] Assuming that "no x" means "for all x, not", (5) has the structure: for all x, it is not the case that [if x is not offered a generous pension, x will retire early]. CEM gets us from this to: for all x, [if x is not offered a generous pension, then x will not retire early], which seems to be the right result.

Higginbotham's discussion ignores the distinctive features of *indicative* conditionals: both the contextual constraint on the selection function used to interpret conditionals, and the prospective character of the interpretation. As he notes, his treatment of the examples "very much depends on the sensitivity of the conditional to counterfactual situations," but one

---

[28] CEM is the thesis that the following schema is valid: $(\phi > \psi) \vee (\phi > \sim\psi)$

cannot assume, in general, that the correctness or adequacy of an indicative conditional claim (if Professor X is offered a generous pension, he will retire early) will correspond to the truth or acceptability of the corresponding counterfactual (if Professor X, who will not in fact be offered a generous pension, *were* offered a generous pension, he would retire early). Suppose we know that our administration will offer pensions only to those they predict will accept, and while we have no idea who will be offered a pension in exchange for early retirement, or who is disposed to accept the offer, we believe the crafty administrators are very good at such predictions. Then we might believe, of each professor, that he or she will retire early if offered a pension, while not being prepared to accept that every professor *would* accept the deal, if offered. But this hypothesis is contrived. Higginbotham's examples still work if we assume, as is plausible for this example in the normal case, that there is no epistemic or causal correlation between those who will be offered pensions in exchange for early retirement and those who are disposed to accept them. For some other examples, however, including one discussed by Higginbotham, the distinctive features of indicative conditionals matter, and ignoring them raises new problems.

Suppose (to use another of Higginbotham's examples) I have been told by someone I trust, and who shares my standards for boringness, that

(6*)   every book on that shelf with a red cover is boring.

At least if we assume that we don't know anything in advance about what books are on the shelf, this seems to be enough to justify my statement:

(6)   Every book on the shelf is boring if it has a red cover.

But, Higginbotham observes:

We know in advance that giving a book a red cover does not alter its contents, so does not affect whether it is boring. Let *b* be a book on that shelf with a blue cover. In the closest possible world, whatever it is, in which *b* has a red cover, it is boring or not, just as it is boring or not as things are. But then it seems that [(6)] should be false if there are non-boring books on the shelf whose covers are not red, although they might have been!

This is, as Higginbotham observes, the wrong result. I don't understand his response to the problem, but it seems to be an ad hoc fix. Instead, I think we should recognize what we have independent reason to recognize: that the contextual and epistemic relations that are relevant to the interpretation of indicative conditionals can come apart from the causal relations that are relevant to counterfactual conditionals.

Suppose I learn that one of the books on the shelf is *Infinite Jest* by David Foster Wallace. I know nothing about the book, let us suppose. I plan to check the cover before deciding whether to read it, since I believe (based on the information from my trustworthy informant) that if it has a red cover, it will be a boring read. The same could be said for any of the books on the shelf, assuming that I don't have an independent opinion about any of them. On the other hand, suppose I do know about *Infinite Jest*—I've read it, and it is definitely not boring. I conclude (again, based on the information from my informant) that it must not have a red cover. I don't, however, have any independent reason to have an opinion about the color of this book's cover, so if I were to learn that it has a red cover, I would conclude that the informant was mistaken. In this case (after I have learned that *Infinite Jest* is on the shelf, but before learning what color its cover is), I still believe that every book on the shelf with a red cover is boring, but I am not any longer prepared to say, of every book on the shelf, that it is boring if it has a red cover.

For simple indicative conditionals, on our account, it is a constraint that the antecedent must be compatible with the CG-context. I can say "if φ" (indicative) only in a context that allows that it might be that φ. When the constraint is not met by what the addressee takes the common ground to be, he must accommodate.[29] The same constraint should be met with quantified conditionals: if I say that all or most or some of the Fs are H if they are G, then it should be true of each of the Fs that it might be G. But it is not always straightforward how to apply this constraint, since even when it seems, in a sense, true of each of the Fs that it might be G, there may be ways of describing one of the Fs such that it is *not* compatible with the common ground that an F fitting that description be a G. Suppose

---

[29] "Presupposition accommodation" usually refers to a situation where a proposition is *added* to the common ground when appropriate speech requires it. But as noted above, sometimes appropriate speech requires that a proposition *not* be implied by the common ground, and in this case accommodation requires changing the common ground so that the proposition is no longer presupposed.

we know that not all of the books on the shelf have red covers. It is common ground that there are some blue ones. It is compatible with this assumption that each of the books on the shelf (the first one, the second one, etc.) might have a red cover. But it is of course not true that the first *blue* one might have a red cover. It may be unclear, in some cases, whether it is right to say that each of the Fs might be a G, but these will be just the cases where it is unclear whether the quantified conditional is acceptable. Higginbotham mentions this example:

??(7)   Every coin is silver if it is in my pocket

which is distinctly odd, in contrast with

(7*)   Every coin in my pocket is silver

which is fine. It would be equally odd to say that every coin is such that it might be in my pocket.

My original discussion of the account of indicative conditionals that I am defending here began with what I called the direct argument:

> Either the butler or the gardener did it, so if the butler didn't, the gardener did.

The puzzle was that if this argument, which seems compelling, is *semantically valid*, then the material conditional analysis of the indicative conditional must be right. But it seems that we have other reasons to reject that analysis.[30] The solution to the puzzle was to use the dynamic interaction of the semantic analysis with the pragmatic constraint to explain how the argument could be a compelling inference, even though not semantically valid. The acceptance of the premise changed the context in a way that ensured that the proposition expressed by the conclusion, relative to that revised context, would be true. So the semantic/pragmatic analysis accepts, and explains, the data that motivate the material conditional analysis without being saddled with the

---

[30] Dorothy Edgington, in Edgington 1986, also appealed to the fact that acceptance of the material conditional seems to be sufficient reason to accept the indicative conditional, at least in cases where it is an open question whether the antecedent of the conditional is true. This implies, she argued, that the indicative conditional does not express a proposition stronger than the material conditional. This, together with arguments against the material conditional analysis, sufficed for the conclusion that indicative conditionals do not express propositions at all.

problems faced by that analysis. The possible-worlds semantics for the conditional is a part of the theory that accommodates and explains these data, but the contextual constraint, distinctive to the indicative, is also an essential part of the explanation. Barbara Abbott, in her Gricean defense of the material conditional analysis, presents counterexamples to the possible-worlds semantic analysis, but she ignores the pragmatic side of the analysis, which shows why the examples she gives are not counterexamples. Nevertheless, her main example is interesting, involving quantifiers, so let's look at it, and see how our semantic/pragmatic account explains her, and our, judgments about it.

Here is Abbott's Snodgrass example:

We have received a number of letters about the water shortage. Almost all of them were 5 pages or less, and all of those received an answer. One letter (from Byram Snodgrass) was 5 pages plus a few words, and the last letter was 8 pages. We did not reply to the last two letters. The 8-page one was just too long to consider, and Byram Snodgrass is a crank who has been writing incoherent letters to us about everything under the sun ever since we took on the post of Water Commissioner. We never answer his letters.[31]

Byram called our office to find out whether his letter had been sent a reply. Based on the truth in (12),

(12) Every letter no longer than 5 pages was answered.

we said (13):

(13) If your letter was no longer than 5 pages, it was answered.

Our reply was truthful.

There is a sharp contrast between the true indicative conditional in (13) and the corresponding subjunctive conditional in (14), which is not true:

(14) If your letter had been no longer than 5 pages, it would have been answered.

As noted, we never answer letters from Byram Snodgrass.

All of this seems right, and it is exactly as predicted by our analysis of the indicative conditional. The reply to Byram's inquiry was *misleading*, as I am sure Abbott would agree, since it implicated that the speaker was not in a position to give a complete answer to his question ("Was my letter answered?"). But our account agrees that it is truthful, since even though both the speaker and the addressee know that the letter was longer than five pages, and so that the antecedent of the conditional is false, this is not common ground (the indicative antecedent indicates

---

[31] Abbott 2010.

that it is not). On our analysis, the conditional is true in all possible worlds compatible with the prospective common ground, and we may presume that this includes the actual world, since none of the relevant presuppositions are false. The indicative conditional claim (on our modal analysis) does exactly what the assertion of the material conditional does: it excludes possible worlds in which the antecedent is true and the consequent false.

The Water Commissioner's office might have replied to Snodgrass's inquiry (equally truthfully, and equally misleadingly) with a universal generalization:

(15)   Every letter was answered if it was no more than 5 pages long.

Both our analysis and the material conditional analysis predict that this is true. Or, the office might have replied (again, misleadingly but truthfully) with a negative universal generalization:

(16)   No letter was answered if it was more than 5 pages long.

In this case, the reply will inform Byram (assuming he remembers how long his letter was) that his letter was not answered, but will be misleading because it implicates that the answer explains why it was not answered, and this is false. But in this case, the material conditional analysis gets the truth-conditions dramatically wrong, since the negative universal material conditional falsely implies that every letter was longer than five pages, and that none of them was answered. We can save the material conditional analysis, in the negative universal case, only by giving up compositionality. But our truth-conditional version of the conditional assertion account gives a compositional analysis that I think gets the facts right.[32]

---

[32] I am grateful to Seth Yalcin for extensive comments on an earlier draft of this chapter, and email correspondence that helped me to better understand both his view and my own.

7
Disagreement and Projection

On the pure expressivist account of epistemic "might" sketched in the last chapter, statements such as "Noam might be in his office" are not used to say what the world is like—to convey a piece of information. They do not aim to eliminate possibilities, as assertions do, but to expand the set of possibilities that are live options in the context, or sometimes just to add new distinctions between the possibilities that are already there. But, following Lewis and Yalcin, we gave the expressivist analysis a truth-conditional formulation. As we saw, this kind of formulation allows for an orthodox compositional semantic explanation for expressions in which the modal clauses are embedded in complex constructions involving propositional attitude verbs and quantifiers, or conjoined with fact-stating sentences.

On the pure conditional assertion account of indicative conditionals, statements such as "If Noam is not in his office, he is out of town" are not used to convey, categorically, a piece of information, at least not a piece of information that goes beyond what is expressed by the material conditional. But the conditional assertion account can be given a truth-conditional formulation (a formulation that was different from the material conditional analysis) and I argued that this kind of formulation has the same benefit as the truth-conditional analysis of "might" and "must", providing an explanation for embedded conditionals (an explanation that also explained why embedded conditionals do not behave as embedded material conditionals would behave).

The compositional benefit of a truth-conditional analysis is the one that is usually emphasized, but I want to suggest that this kind of analysis has the following additional advantage: it helps us to see both the pure expressivist account of epistemic "might", and the pure conditional assertion account of indicative conditionals, as special cases at one end of a spectrum that also includes more full-blooded truth-conditional modal and conditional claims. It seems that modal and conditional statements sometimes express propositions that get truth-values in possible worlds beyond those in the local context in which they are made, and that they sometimes make claims about what the world is like that are detachable from the contexts in which those claims are made. It is useful to have a representation of the modal and conditional constructions that helps to explain the transition between the expressive and the fact-stating uses of these constructions, and that allows for uncertainty and for disagreement, not only about what the facts are, but also about epistemic priorities, and about what there is a fact of the matter about.

7.1 Partial information and contested common ground

To see how this transition might go, I will start with two examples that illustrate the dynamics of discussion involving modals and conditionals in contrasting kinds of situations. The first example is a familiar one. With apologies to those who have heard the story too many times, let's look at Allan Gibbard's notorious Mississippi riverboat case:

Sly Pete and Mr. Stone are playing poker on a Mississippi riverboat. It is now up to Pete to call or fold. My henchman Zack sees Stone's hand, which is quite good, and signals its contents to Pete. My henchman Jack sees both hands and sees that Pete's hand is rather low, so that Stone's is the winning hand. At this point the room is cleared. A few minutes later Zack slips me a note which says 'if Pete called, he won,' and Jack slips me a note which says 'if Pete called, he lost.' I know that these notes both come from my trusted henchmen, but do not know which of them sent which note. I conclude that Pete folded.[1]

The two pieces of information are conveyed to the narrator (call him "Allan") independently, in separate contexts. The story was designed to ensure that the context sets of the two *prior* contexts (between Allan and Jack, and between Allan and Zack) are the same in all relevant respects (since it is stipulated that Allan does not know which note came from which informant). On the truth-conditional analysis sketched in the last chapter, if the conditionals were interpreted relative to the prior contexts, they would be inconsistent with each other, so the story confirms the idea

---

[1] Gibbard 1980, 231.

that the conditional statement is to be interpreted relative to the proposed *posterior* context. Trusting his henchmen, Allan accepted each proposal, leading to two different posterior contexts, one including just the call-and-lose and the don't-call possibilities, the other including just the call-and-win and the don't-call possibilities. He concluded that Pete folded by pooling the information from the two contexts.

The information might instead have been conveyed in sequence in a three-way conversation between Allan and his informants. First Jack says, "If Pete called, he lost." Supposing that Zack accepts what Jack says (this is not a case of disagreement, but a case of two people with different partial information about the situation), he might then say something like this: "In that case, he must have folded. Or if he did call, he must have missed my signal." On the analysis I am defending, the informants (in both the original story and in this variation) express propositions, with truth-conditions, but the truth-conditions are fragile, subject to change with a small change in the story, a change that alters the speakers' evolving epistemic situations.

Contrast this with another example that I have discussed (inconclusively) in a recent paper[2]—an example that does involve disagreement. I will repeat the example—call it the whodunit case—and then say what I think it shows about the process of negotiating over the common ground.

There are just three possible suspects for the murder—the butler, the gardener, and the chauffeur—and it is common knowledge that whoever did it acted alone. Alice was with the gardener at the time of the murder (although she is reluctant to reveal this fact), so she is absolutely certain that he is innocent. Bert has conclusive evidence that rules out the chauffeur, which he has shared with Alice, so it is common knowledge between Alice and Bert that either the butler or the gardener did it. Alice concludes that since it wasn't the gardener, it must have been the butler. But Bert has what is in fact misleading evidence that he takes to exonerate the butler, so he infers that it must have been the gardener. Alice and Bert each tell the other who he or she believes was the guilty party, but neither is convinced by the other. Alice, in particular, is far more certain of the innocence of the gardener than she is of the guilt of the

---

[2] Stalnaker 2011b.

butler. Were she to learn, to her surprise, that the butler was innocent, she would conclude that the chauffeur's alibi must not be as good as it looks, and that he must be the guilty party. But that won't happen, since in fact, the butler did it.

Bert says, "We disagree about who did it, but we agree – it is common knowledge between us – that either the butler or the gardener did it, and each possibility is compatible with our common knowledge. So even though you are convinced that the butler is the guilty party, you should agree that if the butler didn't do it, the gardener did." Bert is just giving what I called the direct argument, which all of the accounts on the table have assumed to be compelling.

Alice agrees that it is common knowledge that either the butler or the gardener did it, and that each of these two possibilities is compatible with their common knowledge. But she will be reluctant to accept the conditional, which conflicts with her conditional belief—perhaps with her conditional knowledge—that even if the butler didn't do it, the guilty party is still not the gardener.

If, in this case, we assume that common knowledge (what Alice and Bert both know, know that they know, know that they know that they know, etc.) coincides with the common ground (the context set), then if Alice reasonably refuses to accept Bert's conditional conclusion ("If the butler didn't do it, the gardener did"), we have a counterexample to the pragmatic constraint imposed by our account of indicative conditionals. The example also seems to conflict with a simple conditional assertion account, which implies that one should accept B, conditional on A, if A, added to the common ground, entails B. But on the other hand, if Alice accepts the conditional that Bert invites her to accept, she will be apparently violating a conditional knowledge norm, and (from the point of view of the Bayesian account of assertability) asserting something unassertable.[3] What we seem to have is a case where the requirement to select a possible world from the context set conflicts with

---

[3] I assume that in an appropriate Bayesian account, conditional probabilities may be defined even when the probability of the condition is 0. Such conditional probabilities represent conditional degrees of belief, on conditions that are entertainable, even though they are taken to be certainly false. Alice is disposed, should she be surprised by the information that the butler was certainly innocent, to revise her beliefs so that she would still assign very low credence, relative to that condition, to the proposition that the gardener did it.

the requirement to select a possible world from the set of possibilities compatible with the individual's conditional knowledge.

The source of the problem, in my view, is that in this example, the common ground is contested: Alice thinks that that she and her interlocutor are in a position to accept that the butler did it, since she takes herself to know that he did, and she asserts it. Bert, however, rejects her assertion, and in cases of disagreement, the "might"s are supposed to trump the "must"s, since a proposition can be common ground only if all agree that it should be accepted. But "might" statements can also be contested. It is agreed by all sides in the debates about epistemic modals that parties to a conversation can disagree about what might be true, and when a statement of any kind is contested, it cannot be common ground that it is true. In this case, Alice rejects not only the claim that the gardener did it, but also the claim that he might have done it. The upshot is that (1) it must be compatible with the common ground that the gardener did it, since one of the parties to the conversation (Bert) accepts that he did, but (2) it is not common ground that the gardener might have done it, since one of the parties to the conversation (Alice) rejects the claim that he might have done it. It follows that in this case (and more generally in any case in which there is disagreement about what might be true) we cannot identify what might be true with what is compatible with the common ground. The claim that the gardener might have done it will be true in some possible worlds compatible with the (posterior) context, and false in others. On the simple expressivist account sketched in the last chapter, the domain of possibilities relative to which the "might"s and "must"s were interpreted was (for each possible world in the context set) the whole context set. But in cases of disagreement, the relevant domain will be a proper subset of the context set, and will vary from world to world.

So what determines the relevant information state, or the accessibility relation that specifies the relevant information state, for a given possible world? That is, what determines the modal bases relative to which the epistemic "might"s are interpreted in disagreement cases? The rough idea is that for each party to the disagreement, there must be possibilities in the context set where the modal base reflects what that party manifestly accepts—what that party is *proposing* that the context set should be. There is inevitably a tension in any situation in which there is a divergence of opinion about what the common ground should be.

This calls for negotiation, but one can negotiate only in a context guided by agreed upon presuppositions. Since the context set plays a role in determining the content of what is said, some at least temporary resolution will be required if conversation is to continue. The parties may decide just "to agree to disagree" about some matter. In this case, since it would beg the question to presuppose a proposition that is contested, possibilities compatible with both sides must remain in the context. That is, in the context for resolving the dispute in the whodunit case, the possibility that the gardener did it must remain open. But one party to the dispute thinks that they are in a position to rule out that possibility, and this must be reflected in the common ground as well. In this kind of case, the possibilities compatible with the common ground will differ, not only about what the facts are, but also about what *might* be true.

Kai von Fintel and Thony Gillies, in their discussion of epistemic modals, say, "There is no such thing as 'the context', only the contexts admissible or compatible with the facts as they are. The context[4] of the conversation really does not provide a determinate resolution and we propose to model this by saying that there is a cloud of contexts at the given point of the conversation."[5] This seems right, particularly in situations of disagreement. In cases where there is a dispute about what the context set should be, the different candidate context sets may be what defines the cloud. It may be enough for conversation to continue that the context sets in the cloud are similar enough so that, with care, one can avoid equivocation and misunderstanding.

The relevant domains of possibilities in contested cases can also be understood as derived contexts of a kind that was discussed in Chapter 4. At any point in a conversation between Alice and Bert, there is the set of possibilities compatible with what it is presupposed that Alice accepts. In asserting that the gardener didn't do it, Alice makes manifest that she accepts that he didn't, and if she does not retreat when Bert rejects her assertion, it remains common ground that she accepts that the gardener is innocent. In a stable context—one that is in an uncontested

---

[4] This use of "context" seems to refer to the informal notion of context, the concrete situation in which discourse takes place (the first of the three notions of context distinguished in Chapter 1). This obviously contrasts with the context sets—contexts in one of the technical senses—which are the members of the cloud.

[5] Von Fintel and Gillies 2011, 118–19.

equilibrium—the common ground will coincide with what it is presupposed that each of the parties accepts. That is, the set of possibilities compatible with what it is presupposed that Alice accepts will be the same as the set of possibilities compatible with what it is presupposed that Bert accepts, and with the possibilities compatible with the common ground itself.[6] In such a context, there will be agreement about what might be true, so the simple expressivist account of "might" works in this kind of case. But when the derived contexts that reflect what is accepted by the different individuals come apart from what is common ground, the "might"s will be interpreted relative to the information states that defined the derived contexts. What this requires is that the relevant epistemic state is projected onto the world, leading, in some cases, to a finer grained partition of the space of possibilities. To see this, consider the following development of our whodunit example: suppose Bert becomes a bit more concessive: "Okay, *perhaps* the butler did it. I agree that his alibi is not quite so airtight as the chauffeur's. But I continue to think that the gardener might be guilty." Since Bert grants the possibility that the butler is guilty, there must be a possibility compatible with what Bert accepts (and so compatible with the common ground) in which the butler did it. But since this is a possibility compatible with everything that Bert accepts, it will also be true in this possible situation that the gardener *might* have done it. That is, there will be a possible situation compatible with the common ground in which the butler did it, but the gardener might have done it. This possibility is therefore *not* compatible with what Alice accepts, since she rejects the claim that the gardener might have done it. So in the context in which the dispute is discussed, we need to distinguish two possibilities: one in which the butler did it, but the gardener might have done it, and one in which the butler did it, but it is false that the gardener might have done it.[7]

---

[6] That a context is stable in this sense does not imply that there is nothing to talk about—no information to be exchanged. It might be common ground, in such a stable context, that Alice, but not Bert, knows *whether* φ, even if it is not yet common ground that Alice knows that φ, or that not-φ.

[7] The argument is that there must be a possibility in which the butler did it, while the gardener might have done it, but it is hard to describe that possibility without seeming to contradict oneself. As Yalcin's examples and arguments brought out, if we *suppose* that φ, and then consider whether ψ might be true, we are shifting to a subordinate context in which φ is (temporarily) accepted. So it will be true in that subordinate context that it might be that ψ only if ψ is compatible with φ. So if I say, "Consider a possibility in which the

It is important to distinguish the account of the epistemic modals I am proposing (for the disagreement cases) from a *contextualist* account of the difference between Alice's and Bert's statements. On a contextualist analysis, the "might" (in the mouth of Alice) is interpreted relative to the derived context that is defined by the set of possibilities compatible with what it is common ground that *Alice* accepts, while the "might" (in the mouth of Bert) is interpreted relative to the different derived context defined by the set of possibilities compatible with what it is common ground that *Bert* accepts. On this account, Alice and Bert are not disagreeing in what they say, but are using contradictory *sentences* in different contexts to say things that are compatible with each other (as when Alice says, "I was born in New Jersey" and Bert says, "I was not born in New Jersey"). On the contextualist analysis, Alice would agree that what Bert said was true, and Bert would agree that what Alice said was true. In contrast, the account I am proposing says that the epistemic disagreement (about how the context should change) is projected onto the worlds, so that the butler-did-it possibility is divided in two, one in which it is true that the gardener might have done it, and the other in which it is false that the gardener might have done it. On this account, Alice and Bert agree in their interpretation of what is said with the "might". They disagree about whether the possibilities in which the "might" statement is true should be admitted to the context that they are negotiating about.

We have been discussing the source of the puzzle that arises in our whodunit case, but we have talked just about epistemic "might", and still have not said how the problem about indicative conditionals should be resolved. Bert has argued that Alice should accept that if the butler didn't do it, the gardener did, since it is common knowledge that one of the two is guilty, and the guilt of each is compatible with what is agreed to be common ground. The puzzle was that if Alice reasonably rejects Bert's conclusion, which she should, then we seem to have a counterexample to the pragmatic constraint on indicative conditionals—that the conditional possibilities relative to which the consequent is evaluated should

---

butler did it," I am supposing that the butler did it, and given that supposition, it will be false that the gardener might have done it. It is difficult for the theorist to avoid injecting herself into the context that she is attempting to describe, but with effort, we can make sense of what is true relative to a context different from the one we are in when we talk about it.

be compatible with the common ground. The solution that I tentatively proposed, and want here to endorse, is that in the contested context in which the discussion takes place, Alice should refuse to allow the disjunctive claim (either the butler or the gardener did it) to be included in the common ground. It would be natural, in this situation, for Alice to say something like this: "If it might have been the gardener who did it, then it also might have been the chauffeur." She can reasonably insist that the chauffeur can be excluded as a suspect only if we also exclude the gardener. The upshot will be that all three possibilities remain open, and Alice will be in a position to assert what she believes: that if it wasn't the butler, it must have been the chauffeur.

It is surprising that one might reasonably reject a disjunctive assertion while being prepared to accept an assertion that entails it, but our account of conditionals and epistemic modals helps to explain how this can happen, and to provide a framework for modeling it. The context set represents not just the possibilities that one or another of the conversational parties is not now prepared to exclude, but also the priorities that will determine the way the common ground will evolve in the subsequent discourse. The negotiation about it may be more complex that it initially seemed to be.

Lewis's problem about permission showed that the dynamics of permission given in his language game required additional deontic structure beyond what was required for the static semantics. Specifically, we needed nested spheres of permissibility to provide for the expansion of the basic sphere. We noted that exactly the same kind of additional structure is required for the interpretation of epistemic modals: we need backup spheres of possibility to provide for expansion of the "modal horizon" (to use Angelika Kratzer's term) when the acceptance of a "might" statement raises new possibilities. We also need this kind of structure (the same kind of structure used in belief revision theory) for the derived contexts in the contested cases. So Alice's preferred context comes with a backup plan for a retreat, and so does Bert's. These will play a role in determining the common ground in which the discussion takes place. To allow for the possibility that it might be the gardener, Alice must expand the modal horizon enough to bring in some worlds in which the gardener did it, but to do so she must include the "closer" worlds (given her epistemic priorities) in which the chauffeur did it. (It is not that Alice *accepts* that the gardener might have done it—it's just that, in order not to beg a question in dispute, she allows for the possibility that the gardener did it, and so also for the possibility that the chauffeur might have done it.)

Paralleling the retreat from the pure expressivist account of "might" in the disagreement case, we also get a retreat from the pure conditional assertion account of indicative conditionals. Even after the rejection, by Bert, of her proposal to change the contexts so that "If the gardener didn't do it, the chauffeur did" becomes true, Alice continues to accept that conditional, and it will be common ground that she does. The contrary conditionals, "If the butler didn't do it, the chauffeur did" and "If the butler didn't do it, the gardener did" will each be true in (different) possible worlds compatible with the context of the dispute. But in this case, the disputes, both about the "might" statement, and about the conditionals, remain disputes that are grounded in epistemic priorities, and do not, in the end, reflect a disagreement about matters of fact. To see this, consider what would happen if we ask in retrospect, after it becomes clear to all that the butler did it, which of our two disputants was right, Alice or Bert? Is the actual world one in which Alice's conditional claim was true, or one in which Bert's was true? It wasn't the gardener who did it, so Bert was wrong about that, but was he wrong when he said that the gardener *might* have done it? The questions are not about counterfactual or causal possibilities. Bert and Alice will probably agree, in retrospect, that if the butler hadn't done it, no one would have. And when Alice insisted that even if the butler was innocent, it wasn't the gardener who did it, she was making no claim about what would have happened if the butler hadn't done it. So the projection of the epistemic disagreement onto the worlds is (in this case) ephemeral. In our model of the contested context, we split the butler-did-it possibility in two in order to represent the disagreement. But the two possibilities merge again when the epistemic situations of the disputants change. The actual world, or any of the worlds compatible with Alice and Bert's retrospective context, does not distinguish between the possibilities that divided Alice and Bert in the earlier context. We will look more closely, in the next and last chapter, at cases like this of what has been called "faultless disagreement".

While in this particular case the dispute between Alice and Bert is about epistemic priorities, and not about the facts, in other cases a dispute about "might"s and "if"s may reflect an underlying factual dispute—one that will emerge when the disputants discuss the issue, giving their reasons for their epistemic priorities. Consider this different, and less problematic, version of our whodunit case: Alice and Bert agree that the butler is probably the culprit, since they know that he was planning to do it. They also agree that the butler had an accomplice who was prepared to do the deed if the butler was unable to. But they disagree about who that accomplice was—Bert thinks it was the gardener, while Alice is convinced it was the chauffeur. So as in the original example, Alice says that if it wasn't the butler who did it, it was the chauffeur, while Bert disagrees, insisting that if it wasn't the butler, it was the gardener. In this version of the case, unlike the original, it seems that the facts about which was the accomplice will determine which of the two indicative conditionals was right, even if the butler was in fact the one who did it.

In cases where it is agreed that there is a factual question underlying the epistemic modal question, one may not need disagreement to get a divergence between the domain of possibilities that determines the common ground and the domain that determines what might be true. Here is an example of a kind much discussed in the literature on epistemic modals: there is a medical test for a certain cancer where a negative result is highly reliable, but where there are many false positives. The doctor knows the result of the test, but we do not, so we don't know whether the patient might have cancer. Here it is not disagreement that prevents the context from being in a stable equilibrium, but the recognition of a salient and potentially available but presently unknown fact on which the question whether something might be true depends. Sometimes what might epistemically be true seems to be a fact that an expert may be in a position to tell us.[8]

Cases where a piece of unknown or disputed factual information underlies the epistemic disagreement are cases where the "might" is less fragile, and where assessment of the epistemic modal statements is more easily extended to possible worlds outside of the common ground. This may include retrospective contexts in which we consider who was right in an earlier dispute, eavesdropper cases, where we assess the truth of a modal claim made in one context from the perspective of the

---

[8] Yalcin gave an example, based on the title of an article published in *Nature*: "Late Antarctic spring might be caused by ozone depletion." (Yalcin 2007, 1012)

different context of an observer, and contexts in which knowledge or belief about a modal claim is ascribed to agents who are not participants in the context in which the attitude is ascribed.

Consider this example of a retrospective assessment of an indicative conditional, given by Dorothy Edgington:[9]

You cancel your booking on flight 007, and it crashes, killing all on board. The crash was a horrible fluke. No one was in a position in advance to say, reasonably, "if you take that plane, you will be killed," though after the fact it does seem correct to say "if you had taken that plane, you would have been killed." But now suppose a fortune teller had said, before the fact, "if you take that plane, you will be killed." You, quite reasonably, didn't give this any credence—you canceled for quite independent reasons. But when you learn of the crash, you say, "My god, she was right." You don't conclude that she *knew* that what she said was true, or that she was justified in believing what she said—just that she was right, by complete coincidence.

Since Edgington defends the "no truth-value" thesis about indicative (as well as subjunctive) conditionals, she does not identify "being right" with saying something true. But if the example works at all, it shows that there is a sense in which one can be right in saying or believing an indicative conditional, even if it was, at the time, an unreasonable thing to say or to believe. The judgment that the fortune teller was right is not any kind of assessment of the epistemic attitude that she was expressing; it seems that in this case the conditional assertion has a content that can be detached from the context in which it was made, and judged, in retrospect, to have been correct.

In both the modified whodunit case and Edgington's plane crash example, it is clear what the factual information is on which the questions turn—one can state, in unproblematic terms, the facts in virtue of which what was said with the indicative conditional was correct, or not. In more complex cases, it may be less clear how to state, except with the conditional itself, or with terms that are explained in terms of conditionals, what the facts are in virtue of which a conditional assertion is true. You think that the vase will probably break if we drop it, while I think it won't. I am right, as it turns out, since the vase is not at all fragile, which means (to oversimplify) that it lacks the property of being

---

[9] Edgington 2004. See also Bennett 2003, 367–9 for discussion of her example. I discuss this example in more detail in Stalnaker (forthcoming).

disposed to break if dropped. Of course there will be some underlying explanation for the fact that fragile things are fragile, and that nonfragile things are not fragile—but the explanation may vary from case to case, and the underlying explanation may involve dispositional properties, explained with the help of conditionals, all the way down.

I think Thorpe will win the election if Wilson doesn't, while you think Heath will win, in that case.[10] The winner, it turns out, was Wilson. Maybe the facts (about what would have happened if certain things had gone slightly differently) will make it clear that one of us was right—perhaps Thorpe couldn't have won, but Heath might have. On the other hand, maybe the disagreement reflects just a difference in our epistemic priorities, or in the different partial information we have. Perhaps I know certain facts in virtue of which Heath could not have won, while you know some different facts in virtue of which Thorpe could not have won. In this case, the example will be more like the Sly Pete case. In retrospect, we say that the question which of us was right does not arise.

At the end of inquiry (a time that will never come, even in the long run, when we are all dead), we will be able to distinguish, in all cases, the disagreements that turn just on the different epistemic perspectives of the disputants from those that turn on the facts. Usually we don't have to wait that long: we can see, with further discussion, or in a retrospective context after a bit more information comes in, whether it is reasonable to say that one of us was right, and the other wrong. But at the time, it may remain open where this line should be drawn. It is useful to have a way of representing the structure of discourse that allows for both possibilities, and for continuity between them.

7.2 The so-called subjunctive

In the cases of disagreement about an indicative conditional statement where one judges, in a retrospective context, that one or the other of the disputants was right, one shifts to what has come to be labeled a "subjunctive" conditional to say what turned out to be right. In Edgington's example, the fortune teller said, "If you take that plane you will be killed," and when you learn of the crash, you say, "My god, she was

---

[10] This is an old example, based on an example from Grice's William James lectures (Grice 1989, 64), that I discussed in Stalnaker 1984, 113.

right—if I had taken that plane, I would have been killed." This very natural way of putting the claim that she was right supports the idea that (at least sometimes) the subjunctive conditional sentence is a way of stating the same proposition that, in a different context, was stated with an indicative conditional. In the literature about the relation between so-called indicative and subjunctive conditionals, the emphasis has been on the contrasting cases (pairs such as the notorious "If Oswald didn't kill Kennedy, someone else did" and "If Oswald hadn't killed Kennedy someone else would have")—cases where it seems clear that the contrasting conditionals make very different claims. But one should also attend to the cases like Edgington's plane crash example, where the two kinds of sentences seem to be used to say the same thing in different contexts. In the remainder of this chapter I will consider the distinctive kind of conditionals that are labeled "subjunctive", and their relation to the indicative conditionals that we have mostly been considering thus far.

Let me start with a brief remark about grammar.[11] It is a familiar fact that the label "subjunctive" is not wholly accurate as a word for the distinctive kind of conditional that contrasts with the ones we have been calling "indicative". Jonathan Bennett quotes an English grammar text from 1860 saying: "The subjunctive is evidently passing out of use, and there is good reason to suppose that it will soon become obsolete altogether."[12] Some subjunctive forms in English have passed out of use, but despite what Bennett says, I think it is clear that many of the conditionals we label "subjunctive" are literally subjunctive. For example, the singular "were" in, "If the Democratic party were now in control of the House of Representatives, Nancy Pelosi would be the speaker" is an unambiguous sign of the subjunctive. But it is tense, rather than mood, that is doing the work in marking this as a *so-called* subjunctive conditional. If we transpose this example into the (archaic) present tense subjunctive, the antecedent would be "If the Democratic Party be now

---

[11] See Iatridou 2000 for discussion of the grammatical devices in various languages.
[12] Bennett 2003, 11. Robert Fogelin once started a paper on conditionals this way: "Linguists have remarked that subjunctive constructions are in the process of dying out of our language, and if this be true, it lends urgency to the enterprise of giving a proper account of them." A copy editor changed this to "if this *is* true," confirming not only what linguists have remarked, but also the suspicion, common among authors, that copy editors sometimes miss the point. (Fogelin 1967, 15.)

in control of the House of Representatives," and the sentence that results from this substitution means (or meant) what we mean by the present tense *indicative* conditional.

So it is tense that is doing most of the work, but what exactly is tense? Of course the paradigm function of tense is to mark temporal distinctions, but it is not clear that this is its only job. The example above of a past tense subjunctive conditional is statement about the present (as indicated by the "now"). It has been held that the so-called past tense sometimes represents a nontemporal distance from the actual present. There is in any case a tension between a notion of tense that is grammatical or morphological and a notion that is definitionally tied to the function of representing temporal information. On the one hand, it is sometimes said that there is no future tense in English: we use the modal "will", and sometimes the verb "to go" to represent futurity. Other times it is said that the future tense in English is expressed with the modal "will". In French, the form used to express the conditionals that we call "subjunctive" (the "conditionelle") is called a tense, even though its primary semantic function is not to express temporal information.[13]

There are interesting issues here concerning the syntax–semantics interface in English and other languages, but I am going to pass them by, sticking with my strategy of trying, as best I can, to keep the focus on structures that are relevant to the dynamic of discourse, while remaining neutral on questions about the linguistic mechanisms that are used to convey information about those structures.[14]

I am going to assume that we can identify at least paradigm cases of the contrasting categories of conditionals independently of any contentious theoretical assumptions about the grammatical marks by which we

---

[13] See Howell (forthcoming) for an interesting discussion of the role of the conditional tense in French.

[14] I say "try as best I can" because I recognize that is not easy to separate questions about functions from questions about the linguistic devices used to fulfill those functions. The data by which we judge hypotheses about discourse structures inevitably come to us as facts about the use of expressions of particular languages, and one cannot use that data without making some assumptions about the semantics of those expressions. But the problems of understanding how our languages work are daunting ones, and I think it is worth the effort to try to disentangle different parts of the problem, and to divide the labor. This methodological problem has been an underlying theme throughout this book; my adoption and development of the Gricean program is in part motivated by it.

are identifying them, and then ask what work are those grammatical marks, whatever they are, doing? That is, what is the functional difference between a so-called subjunctive and a so-called indicative conditional?

In the conditional assertion account sketched in the last chapter, the antecedent is used to make a supposition which determines a subordinate or derived context, a context that is the same as the one that would result from an assertion of the antecedent, except that the context is temporary, with no commitment made to the truth of the proposition expressed by the antecedent. The consequent is then asserted in that derived context, after which the possibilities from the original context that were temporarily removed by the supposition are restored. Our truth-conditional implementation of this account was an attempt to reconcile it with the kind of selection function analysis that was originally designed primarily with counterfactual conditionals in mind. On this analysis (at least on my version of it) a conditional is true in a given possible world (the base world) if and only if the consequent is true in a possible world that is selected, relative to the antecedent and the base world. The selected world is one in which the antecedent is true, but that is otherwise minimally different, in relevant respects, from the base world. For the (so-called) indicative conditionals, a selection function was *admissible* only if the antecedent was compatible with the context set—the set of possible worlds compatible with the common ground. In application, the selection function may not be fully determinate, and in the limiting case—the most cautious version of the application of this account to indicative conditionals—we assumed, first, that all admissible selection functions were on a par, and second, that the interpretation was prospective in the sense that the semantics is applied to the proposed posterior context. This account, I argued, was essentially equivalent to the expressivist conditional assertion analysis. In this chapter, we have considered reasons for moving away from the limiting case, reasons involving disagreement, deference to experts, and retrospective assessment of claims made in a previous context. But while we allow for further constraints, beyond admissibility, on the selection function, we retain the admissibility constraint (for the indicative conditional). What this means is that all of the presuppositions that are in force in the basic context are retained in the derived context defined by the selection function.[15] But the admissibility constraint obviously fails to hold for the so-called subjunctive conditionals. My hypothesis is that the function of the grammatical/morphological marks of the so-called subjunctive is to indicate that in the derived context created by the supposition, some presuppositions are being suspended, which is to say that when the conditional has these distinctive grammatical marks, the admissibility constraint on the selection function relative to which the conditional is interpreted is waived. Since it is a default assumption, in general, that propositions expressed (as assertions or as assumptions) are compatible with what is taken for granted as common ground, one needs a conventional indication when this is not the case.

The admissibility requirement applies to the context relative to which indicative conditionals are interpreted on our prospective account, and so may be incompatible with the context as it was before the conditional statement was made. As we emphasized in Chapter 2, even with ordinary assertions we must allow for accommodation. For example, suppose I not only believe, but also took it to be uncontested common knowledge that Barack Obama was born in the United States, but you say that he was not, or perhaps only that he might not have been. I may contest your statement, but I must change my assumptions about what we both are taking for granted. The same is true if you *suppose*, in the indicative, that Barack Obama was not born in the United States. You are opening up the possibility (even if only for the purposes of the discussion) that he actually was born elsewhere. But the kind of presupposition suspension induced by the distinctive grammatical form of the so-called subjunctive is different from this. One is not changing the basic context, as in cases of accommodation, but instead creating a parallel, subordinate context, one that does not by itself change what is presumed to be the actual common ground.

This kind of presupposition suspension means that the subordinate context is of a quite different kind from the basic context. To use the terminology introduced in Chapter 5, it is a parallel rather than a simple

[15] Formally, the picture is this: selection functions map worlds onto worlds, relative to a given antecedent, and this determines a function from sets of worlds to sets of worlds—the "images" of the worlds in the given set. When the selection function is only partially defined, the images are blurred, and in the maximally indeterminate case, (with just the admissibility constraint) we have a holistic function that takes a set (the context set) to that subset of it in which the antecedent is true.

subordinate context. The crucial contrast is between subordinate contexts that share the iterative structure of the basic context and those that do not. When we are engaged in conversation, it is common ground that we are engaged in that particular conversation. This is crucial for the role of common ground in constraining the means used to communicate, and is built into the iterative structure of common ground. (The iterative structure implies that information presupposed includes information about what is being presupposed in the conversation in question.) The common ground context will have this feature even if it is a context involving pretense—even if we are presupposing things that diverge from what we believe, and mutually recognize that we believe.[16] This essential feature of the basic context carries over to the kind of derived context determined by an *indicative* supposition. Although the set of possibilities is temporarily shrunk, it retains its iterative structure, and its centering, since it is a subset of the basic context. So in each of the possible worlds compatible with the indicative subordinate context, the conversation in question is taking place. The same is true for another kind of subordinate context we have considered, first in discussion of presupposition projection, and again in this chapter: the context of what it is presupposed to be presently accepted by one of the participants in the conversation. But this feature of basic contexts and of the simple subordinate contexts does not hold for the subordinate contexts created by a subjunctive supposition. The set of possibilities compatible with what is being supposed (the images of the possible worlds in the basic context that are determined by the selection function) need not be worlds in which the conversation is taking place—need not be possible situations in which the participants even exist. Although these subordinate context sets are defined in terms of sets of possibilities with centers and an iterative structure, they do not themselves have this kind of structure. This kind of subordinate context is, in a sense, an information state, but it is not an information state with a subject, or a set of subjects, whose knowledge (or presumed common knowledge) it represents. It could be an information state that tells a story in which there is no one there to tell the tale.

---

[16] There are cases of pretense that stretch this assumption: after revealing some top-secret information, I say, "We never had this conversation." Despite the content of this remark, the demonstrative reference presupposes that we did have the conversation. (Just to play along, and show me that you got the point, you might reply, "What conversation?")

Parallel derived contexts do not have the iterative structure of a basic context, but the "subjunctive" subordinate contexts can be centered on times and persons. If x is a multiply centered world of the basic context, then its image in a subordinate context determined by a conditional supposition will normally be centered on the same time and individuals on which x is centered. So if I say, "If the coin had landed heads I would have won the bet," the "I" will refer, in the counterfactual world, to the speaker in the actual world. If the statement is made by the amnesiac, Lingens, in a context where it is an open question whether he is Lingens or Lauben, then the counterfactual world selected relative to the Lingens world in the basic context will refer to Lingens, and in the counterfactual world selected relative to the Lauben world of the basic context will refer to Lauben. The contrast between the way the centering works in indicative and subjunctive cases can be seen most clearly in complex conditionals with a subjunctive conditional embedded in an indicative. Consider the notorious case of Sleeping Beauty, who woke up not knowing whether it was Monday or Tuesday. The procedure was this: she was put to sleep on Sunday night, woken up on Monday, and then again on Tuesday if, but only if, a fair coin landed tails. Before being waked up on Tuesday (in the case where the coin landed tails) she would be administered an amnesia-inducing drug, and so would have no memory of the Monday waking. When she wakes up, Sleeping Beauty might reason this way: "If it is now Tuesday, then the coin must have landed tails."

"Why?" asks her companion, the slow-witted Sleeping Ugly.

"Because," she answers, "if today is Tuesday, then if the coin had landed heads, I would not now be awake." The indexical "now" is variable in the basic context, picking out Monday in some possible worlds and Tuesday in others. But the counterfactual image of the Tuesday world (in which the coin landed heads, rather than tails) is centered on Tuesday.[17]

Despite the contrasts between the two kinds of contexts, the information implicit in a parallel derived context will play the same role that information plays in a basic context. If presuppositions are required by

---

[17] See Santorio 2012 for related examples of the contrasting behavior of indexicals in indicative and subjunctive contexts. Santorio's examples and arguments are discussed in section 2 of the Appendix.

the use of some expression, then what is required is that the relevant proposition be entailed by the derived context, and if information is required for the interpretation of a pronoun, then it suffices if the information is implicit in the derived context. Since the derived context does not supplant, but is parallel to, the basic context, there will be two different information states that may be exploited in interpreting what is said in the consequent of a subjunctive conditional. A pronoun, for example, might pick up its referent from the basic context, or from the derived context. (Compare "if a woman had written plays like Shakespeare's, *they* would probably have been ignored" with "if Shakespeare had not written the plays he wrote, *they* would never have been written.")

We are giving a selection function semantics for both indicative and subjunctive conditionals, but is this plausible for the conditionals in natural language? Angelika Kratzer and other semanticists following her have argued that it is a mistake to interpret the word "if" as a binary connective. It is instead an operator that (together with its complement clause, the antecedent) determines a restrictor that restricts an implicit or explicit modal. But there is no conflict between the Kratzer-style analyses and the kind of formal semantic analysis that I and David Lewis proposed for conditionals. Those analyses are not guilty of a "syntactic mistake"[18] since they make no claim about the syntax of any natural language. Let me digress to develop the point.

7.3 Methodological digression

Both David Lewis's and my semantic analyses of the conditional were given for an artificial language of the kind used to study truth-functional and modal propositional logic, and first-order predicate logic. The method of clarifying concepts and logical structure by the construction of formal languages was a familiar one from the beginning of analytic philosophy, and was a dominant method of philosophizing in the logical empiricist

---

[18] Kratzer's famous soundbite is this: "The history of the conditional is the story of a syntactic mistake. There is no two-place *if...then* connective in the logical forms for natural languages. *If-clauses* are devices for restricting the domains of various operators." (Kratzer 1986) I don't want to suggest that Kratzer would disagree with the distinction I am making here, or that she intended a serious criticism of the kind of semantic account that Lewis and I gave. The sound bite was just a dramatic way of emphasizing the contrast between the different syntactic structures.

tradition. The focus, in the early years, was on the syntactic properties of the constructed languages, and on proof theory for the logics, since semantics for such languages was initially unsystematic and informal, but with the advent of Tarskian semantics for extensional quantification theory, and with the development of richer model theoretic structures for the interpretation of more expressive languages ("possible worlds" semantics, as developed by Kripke, Montague, Hintikka, and others), it became possible to study the structures used to interpret the formal languages, independently of the languages they were used to interpret.

Different philosophers who used the formal-language method had different ideas about the relation between constructed and natural language. Artificial languages were often viewed, in the early days, as recommended replacements for what was regarded as vague, unsystematic and equivocal natural languages that were poor vehicles for the perspicuous representation of what there was to be said about what the world is like, and for the clarification of concepts and logical relations. But the method itself does not require the benighted view that natural language is an unsystematic mess, best replaced for the purposes of serious cognitive enterprises. I think it is better to think of the construction of formal languages, with clear and straightforward semantics, as part of a device for the division of labor. One sets aside, or abstracts away from the means that natural language uses to accomplish certain tasks in order to focus on the tasks themselves. The Quinean notion of regimentation can be understood in this light. The poster child for the success of the formal language method of conceptual clarification, and the one that Quine emphasized, is the semantics for quantifiers. I think I can safely say that no one knows, in full generality, how quantifiers work in natural language, but one thing is clear: they do not work the way that the quantifiers in a first-order quantificational language work, with scope determined exclusively by word order, and with an infinite sequence of variables serving to link quantifiers to the places that they bind. These formal languages, with their semantics, should not be seen as approximations to a natural language, but as representations of what can be said in a natural language, and of how what can be said by complex expressions depends on the semantic values of certain component parts of those expressions. The formal language, and its semantics, helps us to be clear and precise about the scope distinctions that quantification makes possible, and when extended to modal languages, with the ways that the scopes of quantifiers may interact with other kinds of expressions. One ignores questions of how scope is marked by word order, lexical differences, intonation patterns, and contextual presuppositions, focusing instead on the semantic significance of scope, however it is indicated. Or consider a tense logic, with its semantics. As is often noted, tenses in natural language are not sentential operators. But tenses, along with other devices, do mark the kinds of temporal differences that are perspicuously represented in a formal language with tense operators. Tense and modality interact in subtle ways, and the issues about how they interact involve a mix of substantive and linguistic questions. A formal semantics for an artificial language that contains both tense operators and time-dependent modal operators has the resources to clarify some of the issues without commitment about the precise means used in natural languages to represent the structures that the formal semantic models are modeling. Giving a precise and detailed account of the structures that play a role in what is represented helps to sharpen the questions about how the linguistic devices that do the representing work.

Formal languages, and the semantic structures constructed to interpret them, allow for two kinds of conceptual separation: first, we can separate what language is used to do from the particular syntactic, morphological and lexical means for doing it; second, we can separate questions about the language used to talk about some aspect of the world from philosophical questions about the subject matter itself. There is no simple and uncontentious way to separate the different kinds of questions, but one move toward disentangling the issues is to construct formal languages with a clear semantics. The disentangling is not easy, since as Quine emphasized in his general characterization of the method of regimentation, we have to explain our semantic structures with the languages we have, and so we cannot avoid some implicit commitments concerning the interpretation of natural language, but as the example of the success of the standard formal semantics for quantifiers illustrates, we can often rely on an unsystematic and informal understanding of unproblematic parts of our language in order to explain the concepts that are needed to interpret the constructed languages. Regimentation may not solve or eliminate problems, either about the interpretation of natural language, or about the subject matter of that language, but it often helps us to bring them into focus.

So long as the general semantic job of a sentence of a natural language was assumed to be to express a proposition, the regimentation project was reasonably clear: say what kind of thing the semantic values of sentences and other simpler expressions are, and what the different ways are that those expressions can interact. The division of labor is not very difficult. But the separation of function from means of accomplishing it becomes more complicated in the context of a broader conception of the general function of language, and with the recognition of the interaction of semantic and pragmatic considerations. The task of natural language semantics (or semantics/pragmatics) is not just to explain what propositions are expressed by the sentences, but also to tell a larger story about the way the use of language determines the way in which a communicative situation evolves. But it is still possible and fruitful (and I would argue all the more urgently required) to separate questions of function from questions of the means used to serve the functions. The construction of "little language games" such as Lewis's master/slave game, with a formal language embedded in a dynamic setting, and of artificial quantificational languages with a dynamic semantics are ways of doing this.

The semantic analysis of a conditional, expressed in an artificial language that extends the language of modal propositional calculus, should be understood in this light. As I wrote when I first proposed a theory of conditionals, I regarded the semantic analysis as "an *explanation* for a commonly used concept.... This does not imply, however, that the theory is meant as a description of linguistic usage. What is being explained is not the rules governing the use of an English word, but the structure of a concept."[19] The conditional was represented as a binary connective, not because the word "if" is a conjunction with a syntax just like "and" and "or", but because what a conditional is used to say is a function of what is expressed by two sentential clauses. The selection function in the semantics aims to represent a structure (an ordering of possible worlds based on something like similarity in some respects to the actual world) on which the truth-conditions for the conditional depend. This is exactly the structure given by an "ordering source" on a modal base that is used in Kratzer's semantics. Kai von Fintel has given

---

[19] Stalnaker 1968, 108.

an analysis of counterfactuals in the Kratzer framework that, as he makes clear, assigns exactly the same truth-conditions as those given in my original analysis.[20] The implementation is different, with the differences motivated both by consideration of the syntax–semantics interface, and by the role of conditionals in a wider pragmatic setting. The details of the implementation do matter, but agreement about the basic structure represented by a selection function or an ordering helps to sharpen the issues that depend on the differences.[21]

7.4 The role of presupposition suspension

This ends the methodological digression. Let's now go back to the hypothesis that the role of the distinctive grammatical form we label "subjunctive" is to indicate that we are moving to a parallel subordinate context in which some of the presuppositions of the basic context are suspended. There are at least four different kinds of cases in which presuppositions are suspended in this way. The most familiar is the case of a counterfactual, where the supposition itself is presupposed (in the basic context) to be false, and so it is obvious that a consistent derived context will be determined only if presuppositions are suspended. There has been some unclarity in the literature on conditionals about exactly what is meant by the term "counterfactual", but I use this term to refer to a conditional statement made in a context in which the antecedent is presupposed to be false. By this definition there are conditionals that are not counterfactual, but still require, for their interpretation, the suspension of presuppositions.

A second kind of case is what has been called an Anderson case after an example that Alan Anderson used to show that there were subjunctive conditionals that are not counterfactual.[22] His example was something like this: "If she had taken arsenic, she would show exactly the symptoms that she is in fact showing." This statement is made as part of an inductive argument for the conclusion that she probably took arsenic. So the conditional is obviously not counterfactual, since the truth of the antecedent remains a live option. But the indicative version of this

---

[20] von Fintel 2001. See also Kratzer's papers on conditionals collected in Kratzer 2012.
[21] For discussion of some of these issues, see Moss 2012.
[22] Anderson 1951.

conditional would be anomalous, since it would be trivially true: "If she took arsenic, then she is showing just the symptoms that she is in fact showing." It goes without saying that, whatever she took, she is showing the symptoms that she is showing. In this case, it is clear that the presupposition that is being suspended in the derived context is the presupposition that she is showing these particular symptoms—the ones she is in fact showing. The point of the claim is to say something like this: were we in a situation in which we did not know her symptoms, and then supposed that she took arsenic, we would be in a position to predict that she would show these symptoms.

A third kind of case is a conditional in a modus tollens argument. An example: "There were no muddy footprints in the parlor, but if the gardener had done it, there would have been muddy footprints in the parlor, so the gardener must not have done it." Here, the subjunctive conditional cannot be counterfactual, in the sense defined, since one is arguing that the gardener did not do it, and one cannot presuppose something one is arguing for. That is, the argument is appropriate only in a context in which it is initially an open question whether the gardener did it. In this case, the presupposition that is suspended is the proposition, made explicit in the first premise of the argument, that there are no muddy footprints in the parlor. The idea behind the conditional claim is something like this: suppose we didn't know that there were muddy footprints in the parlor, and in that context supposed that the gardener did it. That would give us reason to predict muddy footprints, and so to conclude that if we don't find them, he didn't do it.

The fourth and most puzzling cases are subjunctive conditionals about the future.[23] Here the distinction between subjunctive and indicative is more subtle and controversial, but I think the presupposition suspension hypothesis helps to clarify them. I will start with an example of an alleged puzzle about counterfactuals that Jonathan Bennett has discussed, and then modify it to give us a case about the future.[24] Here is Bennett's exposition of the example:

---

[23] See Iatridou 2000 for a discussion of cases of this kind.
[24] I say an *alleged* puzzle because I don't think Bennett's example, in the past tense where both interpretations are counterfactual, quite works. The second of Bennett's two contrary counterfactuals, stated as it is, seems false. As interpreted, it is what has been called a backtracking case, which would normally be put differently—something like "if he had

Mr. D'Arcy and Elizabeth quarreled yesterday, and she remained angry with him this morning. So *if he had asked her for a favor this morning, she would have refused.* On the other hand, he is a proud man (and a percipient one, who knows anger when he confronts it); he would never risk being turned down; so if he had asked her for a favor this morning, they wouldn't have quarreled yesterday, in which case Elizabeth would have been her usual accommodating self, and would have granted the favor. So *if he had asked her for a favor this morning, she would have granted it.*

Now convert this example into a situation about the future, where we are pretty sure that there was a quarrel, but are not certain. Assume that the background facts of the story, as Bennett told it, are *presupposed*: he wouldn't ask if he didn't expect to be accepted, and he knows anger when he confronts it. So the indicative, *if he asks, she will accept*, seems good, since if we add the supposition that he asks to all that we are presupposing, it will follow that there was no quarrel, and so she will accept. But what about *if he were to ask, she would accept*? The distinction is much more subtle here, but it seems reasonable to say that probably, if he were to ask, she would not accept (since probably they quarreled) so for that reason, he probably won't ask. The case is difficult since tense, concerning time, interacts with tense used to indicate presupposition suspension.

Subjunctive conditionals are the clearest cases of this kind of presupposition suspension, but the phenomenon is more general. As we have seen, "might" statements can be used to express what the speaker thinks we are not in a position to rule out (in the basic context), but they are also sometimes used to make a possibility claim that requires a derived context that suspends presuppositions. One could, for example, say to a child,

(1) You shouldn't have been playing with matches; you might have started a fire

in a context in which it is presupposed that the child did not in fact start a fire. The linguistic signs of presupposition suspension are less clear in the modal case, at least in English. Tense differences play a role. One couldn't use "may" rather than "might" to say what is said in (1). Consider

---

asked her for a favor this morning, that would have been because they hadn't quarreled, in which case,..."

(2) You shouldn't have been playing with matches. You may have started a fire.

An appropriate use of this sentence requires a context in which it remains an open question whether a fire was started. Lexical differences also play a role: "could" instead of "might" tips the balance in the direction of the interpretation that involves presupposition suspension, but in some cases, both interpretations are possible with either of these modal words. Further idiosyncrasies in the English modals emerge when one looks at the strong modal "must", which can have either an epistemic or a deontic interpretation. But unlike its duals "may" and "might", it has no tense, and it cannot be used in a derived context in which presuppositions are suspended. So compare (3) and (4) with counterfactual counterparts of each:

(3) If the Yankees lost the game, the Red Sox might still win the title.
(4) If the Yankees won the game, the Red Sox must have lost the title.
(3') If the Yankees had lost, the Red Sox might still have won the title.
*(4') If the Yankees had won, the Red Sox must have lost the title.

It seems that with "must", the relevant modal base must be one that is compatible with the basic context.

As we have seen, the lexical and grammatical devices for marking the distinctions between different kinds of conditionals and different modal bases vary across and within languages, but the notion of presupposition suspension helps to locate the different function that the different devices serve. Locating the function also helps to bring out a more general question: what is the point of suspending presuppositions, and making a claim in a subordinate context that is explicitly marked to indicate that the speaker is not committed, even conditionally, to the actual truth of the claim? In the cases of ordinary indicative conditional assertions, one is making an implicit claim of epistemic relevance: roughly, one is expressing the idea that if one learned that the antecedent was true, one would have reason to conclude that the consequent was true. Debates about epistemic modal claims are negotiations about what the basic context should be—about what the discourse participants are in a position to accept. The relevance of claims of these kinds to inquiry and to contingency planning is clear. But what is the point of a discussion of what to accept in a context that allows possibilities that are acknowledged *not* to be compatible with what the parties to the conversation take to be open? And what are the priorities that determine the modal bases and orderings that are relevant to such a discussion? The answer, I think, is that the epistemic connections that are relevant to discussions involving epistemic modals and indicative conditionals are holistic, and in the general case may be highly unstable, depending on what we happen to know, and be ignorant of. The conclusions we reach about what indicative conditionals and epistemic modals to accept do not necessarily provide us with pieces of information we can detach from our local epistemic situation. Cases like Allan Gibbard's Sly Pete story indicate that contrary epistemic conditionals may be justified with contrasting configurations of knowledge and ignorance, each compatible with the actual facts. But we have an interest in finding stable and robust epistemic connections—facts that would tend to provide evidence for a certain conclusion in a wide range of circumstances. Reasoning in subordinate contexts, in which presuppositions are suspended, is a way of articulating hypotheses about this kind of fact.

8
Contextualism and the New Relativism

In the discussion of disagreement in the last chapter I argued that the possibilities that are the points in the space that defines the common ground are sometimes to be individuated in a way that reflects contrasting epistemic priorities, and not just contrasting beliefs about matters of fact. The thesis that there may be disagreements that are not, in the end, resolved by the facts can be described as a kind of relativism, and in this final chapter, my plan is to look at a family of approaches to semantics, or to the semantic analysis of particular concepts, that has been given this label. Semantic relativism is sometimes contrasted with contextualism (for example, about knowledge, or epistemic modals), but context-dependence and relativism are interconnected. Relativism (or a relativist analysis of a particular concept) is also sometimes contrasted with expressivism (or with an expressivist analysis of a particular concept), but one may also think of relativism as a way of implementing a kind of expressivism. There are different versions of relativism, and my discussion in this chapter will be critical of some of the relativist doctrines, but my hope is that the framework for representing context I have been using in this book can help us to get clearer about the phenomena that motivate relativism, and about the relativist response to those phenomena.

Here is my plan for this chapter. In section 8.1, I will take a quick look at relativism as traditionally conceived, starting with the notorious Protagorian doctrine, and then relativism about morality, and about about spatial location and motion. In section 8.2, I will ask what it means to be a relativist about truth, as the contemporary versions of semantic relativism seem to be. To try to answer this question, I will look at three particular applications of the relativist strategy, first (in section 8.3) at a relativist doctrine about future contingents, second (in section 8.4) at a relativist account of predicates of personal taste, and third (in section 8.5) at gradable adjectives. These examples do, I will suggest, help to clarify what it means to be a relativist about truth, but I remain skeptical about the notion of "faultless disagreement", and about MacFarlane's notion of a variable context of assessment. In a concluding section 8.6, I will look back at some of the examples discussed in the last chapter from the perspective of semantic relativism.

8.1 Traditional kinds of relativism

Any discussion of relativism must begin with the notorious Protagorean doctrine. According to Protagoras (or at least according to Protagoras, according to Socrates, according to Plato), "man is the measure of all things: of the things which are, that they are, and of the things which are not, that they are not... As each thing appears to me, so it is for me, and as it appears to you, so it is for you."[1] This is the classic version of relativism about truth, and it is the kind of view that teachers of philosophy all hear, or at least used to, from their students in introductory classes. It is hard to make sense of the doctrine; the arguments for it seem to involve equivocation between truth and belief, and to reveal some ambivalence about what there is a fact of the matter about. The new relativism about truth (of the kind promoted by John MacFarlane, Mark Richard, Max Kölbel, and Andy Egan, among others)[2] is a more sophisticated and carefully formulated doctrine, and it is responding to real problems, but I am suspicious that it reveals some of the same ambivalence about what there is a fact of the matter about that is behind the Protagorean doctrine. On the other hand, I argued in the last chapter that the question what there is a fact of the matter about is a question that can be contentious, and that we can reasonably be uncertain about, so perhaps there is room for a theory that helps to blur this line.

One final remark about the Protagorean doctrine, before moving on from it: whatever the differences between recent versions of relativism and the old Protagorean doctrine, the new relativists—at least some of them—do see a connection, and are not afraid to use the appeal of the

---

[1] Plato 1990, 152a–b.
[2] MacFarlane 2003 and 2011, Richard 2004 and 2008, Kölbel 2002, and Egan 2007.

Protagorean doctrine to motivate their own brand of relativism. Perhaps Mark Richard is just trying to annoy the bourgeoisie when he says that there is "a deeply entrenched use of 'true' which is relative", and refers to the use that is in play when we hear, from our students, "It was true when the Greeks said it that the earth was flat."[3] As Richard goes on to say, "Philosophical resistance to this use is as deeply entrenched as the use itself", but I think this particular way of talking about different uses of the word "true" muddies the waters. It is just flat out false (in the absolute sense of false) that it was true when the Greeks said it that the earth was flat. If there are mistakes, either conceptual or empirical, that are made with some regularity, then there will be, in a sense, entrenched uses of words to say false things with them. However often some may say otherwise, being true according to the Greeks is not a way of being true, any more than being flat according to the Greeks is a way of being flat.

I am not going to dwell on the Protagorean straw man, but I do want to say something about more traditional kinds of relativism that have been seriously defended before looking at the issues that motivate the new relativism about truth. Then, after some general remarks, I will look at some of the specific applications of the new relativism: to future contingents, to predicates of personal taste, to moral expressivism, to gradable adjectives, and finally, to epistemic modals and conditionals.

The main idea behind relativism about some particular concept or family of concepts seems to be that what appears on the surface to be an absolute claim (the ascription of a monadic predicate) is really a relational claim. So, for example, according to a moral relativist, the claim that it is wrong to torture prisoners of war is really a claim that some contextually determined set of norms requires one not to torture prisoners of war. A relativist about space (of the Galilean or Leibnizian kind) holds that the claim that some body is in motion is really a claim that the body is in motion relative to certain other objects, or to a frame of reference determined by certain other objects. In both cases, the relativism is motivated by the thesis that there is no fact of the matter of the kind needed to make an absolute claim true. So, according to the moral relativist, there is no fact of the matter about which set of norms is the

---

[3] Richard 2004, 234.

right one, but there is a fact of the matter about what some given norms (perhaps those that are endorsed by the members of some community) require. According to the relativist about space, there is no fact of the matter about whether some object is in motion, but only facts about changes in the distances between objects.

These brands of relativism contrast with a contextualist thesis, according to which the relativity is in the determination of what is said, and not in the content of what is said. A claim might be an absolute one, even if one needs a reference to a feature of the context in order to determine what claim is being made. For example, an absolutist about space will still need a frame of reference—a coordinate system—in which to locate objects, and the coordinate system may be fixed by context. The conception of space will still be an absolute one if the referents of context-dependent expressions for locations are absolute locations. But context will also enter into the relativist's story, since the other terms of the relativist claim (the norms, in the case of moral relativism, or the frame of reference in the case of relativism about motion) are implicit, and so determined by context. Still, the contextualism is independent of the relativism, since a relativist might choose to speak a language in which the relational claims that she takes statements about morality or motion to be making are made explicit, in a context-independent way. ("Body x is in motion, relative to frame of reference y", or "Torturing prisoners of war is wrong, relative to system of norms N.") So relativism (of this kind) and context-sensitivity are in principle independent.

8.2 Semantic relativism

The familiar kinds of relativism I have been talking about are motivated by metaphysical or factual theses—theses about the kind of facts there are for our statements to make claims about. It is reasonably clear what is going on in such cases, but this is not relativism about truth. It is the idea that truth itself is a relational notion that is hard to make sense of.

Or, on some ways of clarifying the idea, it is too easy to make sense of. There are many abstract objects (for example the meaning of a sentence) that will determine a truth-value, but only relative to something else (for example, certain facts about a context). Functions from something or other to a truth-value are cheap, and such functions will determine truth-values only relatively. In the case of context-dependent sentences in particular, the claim that the sentence is true will state a relational fact—that it is true relative to such and such a context—and it may be true relative to some contexts, and false relative to others. But this is not the kind of relativism about truth that we are interested in. As we have noted, context-dependence is the relativity of *what is said* to something, but the thing that is said in context—the proposition expressed—might still have its truth-value absolutely. The idea of the new relativism (like the old Protagorean relativism) seems to be that the proposition itself—what is determined by meaning plus the context of utterance—is something that has a truth-value only relatively. But what is at stake in calling some abstract object that may be the semantic value, in some sense, of a sentence, and that determines a truth-value (either absolutely, or relative to something) a proposition?

Start with the simple notion of a proposition as a function from possible worlds to truth-values.[4] This conception of proposition is motivated by the idea that the content of a belief, or of an assertion, serves to distinguish certain ways the world might be from others, for the purpose (in the case of assertion at least) of locating the actual world on one side of the line. As John MacFarlane has noted, even this orthodox notion of proposition exhibits a certain kind of relativity. Consider a possible world that certain neo-conservative theorists and liberal hawks thought, before George W. Bush's Iraq war, might be actual (call it "Dick Cheney's dream world"): in this world, when the US invaded Iraq, the troops were met with flowers, as expected, and the mission was accomplished. Peace broke out, the Iraqi Jefferson or Nelson Mandela emerged and was acclaimed by all. The Arab Spring arrived early, and democracy flourished throughout the Middle East. George Bush said, "Our Iraqi policy has been a success." Is what he said true? The proposition that he expressed in that counterfactual world is true relative to that counterfactual world, but not true relative to ours. One might be tempted to distinguish the context of utterance, which includes the world in which the utterance event took place, from the context in which we assess the proposition, and judge it to be false. But this is not really relativism about

---

[4] In the framework we are using, this is what propositions are, but the questions we are asking about relativism about truth can be raised in a more neutral framework that assumes only that a proposition, though perhaps more fine-grained, at least determines such a function.

truth, since the claim that the proposition is true is not a relational claim. What is true in a counterfactual world is what would be true if things were different, and not what is true, in any sense. Truth is an absolute property of propositions, if propositions are understood as functions from possible worlds to truth-values, or as things that essentially determine such functions.[5]

The new relativism about truth claims that there is an additional source of relativity. Even when the context of utterance has done its work to determine a proposition, and even when the objective facts about what possible world is actual are determined, there are further parameters that need to be specified before a truth-value is determined; the same proposition might be true, relative to some specifications of these additional parameters, and false relative to others, even relative to the same possible world. MacFarlane provides a label for the additional parameter: a *context of assessment*. So on this view, a sentence plus a context of utterance determines a proposition, which is a kind of abstract object that takes a possible world, plus a context of assessment to a truth-value (or equivalently, if we call the relativist's propositions R-propositions and the orthodox propositions O-propositions, then R-propositions will be functions that take contexts of assessment to O-propositions).

Now this notion of a proposition—R-proposition—is formally exactly like Kaplan's notion of character. One might describe the abstract form of this kind of relativism this way: a context should be divided into two parts (called "context of utterance" and "context of assessment"), and the process by which "what is said" is determined should add an additional step: the first part of context determines an R-proposition, which is a function from the second part of context to an O-proposition, which given the facts, will determine a truth-value.

But it seems to be an important part of the new relativist doctrine that this new intermediate entity—the function from contexts of assessment to propositions in the old sense—is really a *proposition*, in some sense. To know what relativism about truth is saying, we need some account of what this sense is.

---

[5] In saying this, I am assuming an actualist conception of possible worlds: they are a certain kind of property that a world might have. On a modal realist metaphysics defended by David Lewis, one might more naturally think of truth as a relational property.

David Lewis's account of self-locating belief helps to motivate some brands of relativism, since it provides an abstract object (a property, or "centered-world proposition": a function from centered worlds to truth-values) that plays some of the roles of a proposition (it is, on his account, an object of the attitudes), but that takes a truth-value only relative to something in addition to a possible world. But Lewis's centered-worlds propositions are not what most relativists have in mind. (Andy Egan is an exception.[6]) For the relativist, part of the point of calling this intermediate entity a proposition seems to be that when two speakers affirm conflicting propositions (or when one affirms one, and the other denies it), they are (in some sense) *disagreeing,* even if they can both be right, relative to different contexts of assessment. When I say I was born in New Jersey, and you deny that you were born in New Jersey, what I affirm is the same centered-worlds proposition that you deny, but no one thinks that there is anything appropriately called disagreement here. The way that the truth of sentences with demonstratives and personal pronouns is relative to context is a paradigm of the kind of relativity that the relativists want to contrast with the kind they are interested in. But what is the basis for the line that they want to draw? To try to get a handle on this question, I will look at some particular applications of the doctrine of semantic relativism, starting with what I think is John MacFarlane's best case for relativism about truth, the best case for the applicability of his distinction between a context of utterance and a context of assessment, and the best case for a notion of proposition that determines a truth-value only relatively.

8.3 Future contingents

According to one metaphysical view about time, there is (now) no fact of the matter about which of a range of possible future courses of events will be realized.[7] Let me give my take on what is going on in this case. Assume, first that the future course of events is open but that the past is settled. There are alternative ways that things might go, but only one past that leads to each of these futures. We can model this assumption with a branching time structure, where the moments of time are nodes in

---

[6] Egan 2007. [7] MacFarlane 2003. See also Thomason 1970.

a tree, branching upward, and converging downward. Now even if one accepts this kind of model as a good model of the causal possibilities, one might insist that there is a fact of the matter about what will happen—a fact that that is grounded in the occurrence of a future event. But the temporalist metaphysics holds that all facts must be grounded in the present or the past, and so if there are alternative possible futures, there is no fact of the matter, at any moment of time, as to which of those alternatives will be realized. The open possibilities (at that moment) are all on a par; no one of them can be truly said to be the *actual* future. A semantics for a formal language based on our branching time model might define truth relative to two parameters: a moment of time, represented by a node of the tree, and a total history that includes that moment, represented by a complete path through the tree that passes through the node that represents that moment. So, for example, suppose someone makes a prediction at a certain moment, m_1: "There will be a suicide bombing in Damascus tomorrow", and suppose there is a suicide bombing in Damascus at moment m_2, one day after m_1 in history h_1, but not at m_3, one day after m_1 in a different history h_2. Then the prediction will be true at m_1 relative to h_1, but false at m_1 relative to h_2. We might say that the prediction is true (false) simpliciter (at a moment) if and only if it is true (false) at that moment, relative to all histories containing it. More generally, we might define a *proposition* as a set of histories, and say that a proposition is true, relative to a given history just in case it contains that history. A tensed sentence will determine a proposition, in this sense, only relative to the *time of utterance*, but even after specifying the time of utterance, which fixes the proposition, there remain two ways in which the truth of the utterance is relative to a further element: first, the proposition, and so the utterance, may be true relative to one history, but false relative to another. Second, the proposition may be neither true nor false simpliciter at one moment (the time of utterance), but determinately true relative to another (later) moment within the same history. The later moment (for example, m_2, in the history h_1) might be a *context of assessment* for the prediction made at m_1. At that later time, we correctly judge the prediction to be true, even though it was neither true nor false, relative to the time of utterance.

In this semantic/metaphysical model, the notion of a *possible world* comes apart into two different notions: first, one may think of a possible total state of the world as something that determines "all that is the case", or all that would be the case if that state were realized: all that there is or would be a fact of the matter about. Second, one might instead think of a possible total state of the world as something that determines all that we need to represent the distinctions between the possibilities that thinkers and speakers distinguish between. On the temporalist metaphysics that we are following MacFarlane in assuming, a moment of time determines all that there is a fact of the matter about. But we need finer distinctions to represent the content of a prediction, and to do the compositional semantics for the expressions used to make predictions, guesses, and suppositions about the future. The relativity that results from this distinction seems to be a genuine relativism about truth. The relativity is something like the relativity in the Cheney dream world example, since the different contexts of assessment are, in one sense, different "possible worlds". And this kind of relativity is not just contextualism, since the relativity remains after we fix the time of utterance, which serves to fix the proposition that is determined relative to the context-dependent word "tomorrow". We get both the relativity of the truth of something reasonably thought of as a proposition (since it is the content of, or the information conveyed in, a speech act), and a distinction between a context of utterance and a context of assessment. But in this application of the MacFarlane relativistic framework, the context of assessment will not be an independent parameter: the speech act, if not its content, determines a unique appropriate context of assessment. The prediction is appropriately assessed only tomorrow, since (assuming the temporalist metaphysics) a prediction does not make a claim that the content is true at the time it is made. And we don't get, from this particular kind of relativism, a feature that seems to be characteristic of some of the other applications: disagreement where neither party to the disagreement are making a mistake. If I predict (at m_1) the bombing the next day, and you predict (at that moment) that there will be no bombing the next day, then even though we both acknowledge that neither of our predictions are either true or false at the time made, we will also agree that both of our statements should be assessed only tomorrow, and that at that time, one of us will be shown to have made a mistake.

Does this picture of relativism generalize? If it does, I think it will exploit the idea, present in this case, of a split between the two conceptions of a possible world: (i) a possible world as *all that is the case* (all that there is a fact of the matter about); and (ii) a possible world as a point[8] in the logical space that we divide up in our debates, deliberations, and investigations. I think one can make sense of some of the relativist moves with the help of this distinction, but I also think that the relativist analysis is sometimes a way to equivocate about what one thinks there is an objective fact of the matter about, and what one thinks is at root just a fact about oneself, or about the participants in some discourse situation.

8.4 Predicates of personal taste (and value)

One kind of expression that has been a paradigm application of the relativist strategy is the category of predicates of personal taste: words such as "tasty", "fun", and "funny".[9] Let me begin with a somewhat crude and oversimplified contrast between a contextualist and a relativist account of such words. Both accounts will share the assumption that statements such as "Sea urchin is tasty" or "Riding roller coasters is fun" are assessed as true or false relative to a standard of taste, which might be determined by what one particular person enjoys eating or doing, or what the person *ought* to enjoy, or is *disposed* to enjoy, or by what the members of some group enjoy, or ought to enjoy, or are disposed to enjoy. The contextualist takes the relevant standard to be determined by the intentions of the speaker, or at least by the context of utterance. One who assesses the statement relative to a different standard is simply misunderstanding what was said. The relativist, in contrast, says that the *content* of the statement (determined by the context of utterance) leaves the standard variable; it is only when the statement is *assessed* that the standard comes into play. I might assert that sea urchin is tasty on the ground that I enjoy eating it, and you might then reject my statement (disagreeing with me) on the ground that you do not. Even though we

---

[8] Or better, given that we want our common-ground contexts to have a modal resolution, representing the distinctions between the answers to the questions at issue in the context, the second notion of a possible world might be identified with an equivalence class of the points in a possibility space (rather than a point in the space). The sensitivity to questions recognizes that our context may cut up logical space more coarsely than is allowed by the totality of facts (or what there is a fact of the matter about). The present point is that we might sometimes also have reason to cut the space up *more* finely than is determined by what there is a fact of the matter about.

[9] See Lasersohn 2005 and Stephenson 2008.

are disagreeing (assigning opposite truth-values to the same statement), we both may be right, relative to our different contexts of assessment, which are determined by our own tastes. But I think this crude version of a relativist analysis distorts the phenomena. If my aim, in asserting that sea urchin is tasty, was simply to express my liking of them, then it seems to me that you miss the point if you reject my statement because you do not share this taste. It must be granted that it is natural to describe the contrast as a difference of opinion, but I think to the extent that we take this difference to be a *disagreement*, we are adopting at least the pretense that there is a common standard that the speaker intended his judgment to be assessed against, and that the addressee who disagrees is disagreeing about the result of applying the standard intended by the speaker to the case at hand. And in many cases this will be more than a pretense. Two people with divergent tastes may share the presupposition that there is a standard that their tastes ought to meet, and that at most one of them succeeds in meeting.

Of course there is no simple way to distinguish a difference in standard from a disagreement about how to apply it to cases. Suppose A judges that sea urchin is delicious because he thinks that any discerning and properly educated eater with an appreciation of subtlety and an open mind will enjoy eating it, while B thinks that only pretentious phonies who are taken in by the latest fad will be able to stomach the stuff. Are they applying different standards, or disagreeing about how a common standard applies to this case? There are different levels of specificity on which one might characterize a standard, but I think the divergence will be properly described as a disagreement, rather than a misunderstanding, only if the context of utterance, or the intentions of the speaker, determine a standard, at some level of generality, that both parties can be said to be aiming to meet.

But this does not imply that, in a case of genuine disagreement, there must be a fact of the matter about who is right. I suggested above that what often lies behind the relativist intuition is a contrast between two ways of thinking about the possibilities in terms of which one might represent a discourse or an inquiry: first, one may take a possibility, or "possible world" as a representation of all that there is, or might be, a fact of the matter about; second, one may understand a possibility as a point in the logical space with which we model the discourse, deliberation or inquiry. On a simple picture, the two ways of understanding possibilities go together. The participants in a discourse distinguish between the points in a space of possibilities, claiming that the world is this way, rather than that, or perhaps requesting that an addressee act so as to make the world this way, rather than that, or asking whether the world is this way, rather than that. The truth of the statement, the conformity to the request, or the correct answer to the question is determined by which of the points in the logical space is or represents the actual world. But in some cases, a discourse may be carving up logical space too finely for the facts to determine which of a range of possibilities being distinguished is the actual one. This may happen because the participants in the discourse are falsely presupposing that there is a fact of the matter when there is not, but for the relativist, who does not usually take his account to be a kind of error theory, we should expect this divergence between the distinctions made in a discourse and the facts that decide who is right to be recognized and acknowledged by the participants. It is clear enough what is going on, in the simple picture in which the participants in a discourse distinguish between the possibilities: they are aiming to describe, or find out about, or change, the actual world. But in a situation in which the participants take themselves to be disagreeing, while acknowledging that there are no facts to decide who is right, we need an account of what the aim or point of the discourse is. That is the recognized challenge to the relativist, and in some cases I (as suggested in our discussions of conditionals and epistemic modals in the last chapter) think the challenge can be met.

Suppose you and I are resolute moral expressivists. I hold that it is wrong to torture prisoners of war, while you think it is just fine to do so. We sort out the underlying values, and reach the conclusion that our difference is rooted, not in a factual disagreement, but in commitment to different norms. Do we disagree? We may have a *practical* disagreement (about what to do). And we will have contrasting attitudes toward each other. Perhaps we each like to be respected, and recognize that we both lack respect for people with values that differ in certain ways from our own. I may want you to have my values, and you do not want that. In such a case, we share the view that the situation is unsatisfactory when the norms we each accept diverge, and the attempt, through discussion, to reduce or eliminate the divergence may have the same structure as a discourse whose goal is to arrive at the truth.

In the framework that Allan Gibbard developed[10] to reconcile an expressivist account of normative judgments with a truth-conditional account of the contents expressed in such judgments, the points of the logical space that we are distinguishing between in our discourse consist of pairs, one term of which is a system of norms, and the other a possible world in the strict sense. One can model Gibbard's analysis with a two-dimensional space, the horizontal lines representing alternative factual possibilities, the vertical lines representing alternative complete systems of norms, and the points representing the pairs. The content of a speech act will be a set of points. We disagree if the content of what you assert or accept is disjoint from the content that I accept. But the disagreement may be nonfactual if we don't disagree about the factual component of our content.

Max Kölbel, in his exposition and defense of relativism,[11] takes expressivism and relativism as contrasting and incompatible theses, and argues that Gibbard's theory is best understood as a version of relativism, rather than of expressivism. But I see the two doctrines (relativism and expressivism) as parts of a single approach to normative discourse. It is because the expressivist believes that there are no facts to determine the correctness or incorrectness of normative judgments that he must say that such judgments are true or false only relative to something like a set of norms. And there is room for a relativist account of content only when there is reason to for speakers or thinkers to make finer distinctions between possibilities than are made by the facts. One might think of the relation between moral relativism and moral expressivism this way: In my discussion of moral relativism in the introductory section of this chapter, the idea was that there are moral facts, but they are relational facts—facts about the relation between a set of norms and a moral judgment. For example, it will be fact that some action is wrong, relative to some given set of norms (and it might be a contingent fact, since the norms might characterize wrongness as a function of the facts). There is nothing expressivist about this theory: the expressivism comes in with the *acceptance* of a set of norms, relative to which certain moral

---

[10] Gibbard 1990, especially Chapter 5. The basic ideas developed in this early book have undergone a number of refinements since, but for our purposes, the refinements introduced later won't matter.

[11] Kölbel 2002.

judgments are correct. To be committed to a moral judgment, on the expressivist theory, is to *accept* a set of norms relative to which the moral judgment is true. The expressivist, unlike the plain moral relativist, has the burden of explaining what it is to accept a set of norms.[12]

8.5 Gradable adjectives

In Gibbard's formal model, the factual dimension and the non-objective dimension to which truth is supposed to be relative are sharply separated, and it is reasonably clear what the non-objective dimension represents: practical norms or values, plans or "hyperplans". In other applications of the relativist strategy, the non-objective dimension may be semantic, conceptual, or epistemic, and the line between the factual and the non-factual may be less sharp. I will look in a little more detail at an example that Mark Richard discusses in his defense of relativism. Richard's real concern is with knowledge attributions, but he begins with a philosophically uncontentious example of a gradable adjective, the word "rich". Here is Richard's basic example:

Suppose...that Mary wins a million dollar lottery. Didi is impressed, and remarks to a friend "Mary is rich." Naomi, for whom a million dollars is not all that much, remarks in a conversation disjoint from Didi's, "Mary is not rich at all."[13]

We are to assume that there is no difference between the two conversations in the relevant comparison class, or in the point of assessing people as rich or not. We may also assume that there is no simple factual disagreement about Mary's income, property or savings, or about the distribution of income or wealth in the relevant comparison class. Nevertheless, Richard claims, one who hears both conversations might *report* the two as disagreeing about whether Mary is rich. And even though the remarks were made in different contexts the two might later *argue* about who was right (presupposing that their statements were in conflict). Richard asks, "What disagreement is reported in The Report?"

---

[12] See Field 2009 for an incisive discussion of the relation between relativism and expressivism.
[13] Richard 2004, 218.

and "What disagreement are Didi and Naomi having in The Argument?"[14]

On a simple contextualist story (rejected by Richard) the apparent disagreement (the disagreement that is the subject of The Argument as well as the disagreement reported in The Report) is simply a misunderstanding. The contextual standard that determines the content of Didi's statement is different from the standard that determines the content of Naomi's statement, and despite appearances, the two propositions are compatible. But if the difference between Naomi and Didi is really a disagreement in *belief*, then it seems reasonable to take it as a disagreement about where the actual world is located. To get clearer about this, we should try to get clearer about how Naomi's and Didi's belief worlds differ. Whether they are right or not, it seems that the two take themselves to be disagreeing about whether the property of being rich (as determined in a certain common context) applies to Mary or not. But they agree about how much money and income Mary has, about the general distribution of wealth, and about the relevant comparison class. What are they disagreeing about? It seems reasonable to say that this property, being rich, gets its identity from a cluster of generalizations and associated conditions, some more general, some more local and specific to the context of their discussion, or of their separate discussions, some more plausibly thought of as contextual factors that fix the criteria (in this context) for being rich, and some more naturally thought of as generalizations of fact about the differences between the rich and the non-rich. Perhaps Didi or Naomi think, at least tacitly, of the rich as a social/economic class, and that there is a substantive theoretical issue about exactly how the line between it and contrasting classes is to be drawn. Richard suggests that the issue is about how it is best to conceptualize things. A "statement, that Mary is rich, is as much an invitation to look at things in a certain way as it is a representation of how things are."[15] But Quine taught us that the line between decisions about how to use words and judgments, using those words, about the facts are often arbitrary. The question whether there is a fact of the matter about who is right in a dispute in which factual and semantic questions are intertwined may itself be partly a factual question. In "The Argument" (if it is

---

[14] Richard 2004, 219. [15] Richard 2004, 226.

a reasonable argument), Didi and Naomi are doing two things at once: first, trying to understand each other, and second, trying to make a point about the facts. The differences between the world Naomi takes us to be in, and the world Didi takes us to be in may be, in part, a difference in the way that the word "rich" is and ought to be used. But even if, in the *actual* world, the difference is really mainly a semantic one, if the disagreement is not just silly, then Didi and Naomi will take it to be mainly a substantive one, and so the difference between their belief worlds will be substantive. If, in the end, there is no fact of the matter about who is right, then they will, in some sense, both be wrong, since they are presupposing that there is something that they are disagreeing about.

The key part of the story is "The Report": the third party attribution of a disagreement between people making contrasting statements in different contexts. But we need to keep in mind that the attribution is made in its own context: the reporter characterizes the contents of the statements he is ascribing by distinguishing between the possible situations in a derived context. In reporting a disagreement, the reporter takes Naomi's and Didi's statements to distinguish between the possible situations in the same way. The two statements may be contradictories, relative to the possible worlds compatible with the derived context even if the statements themselves were made in different contexts. So the reporter is presupposing, in The Report, that there is a substantive disagreement, and so that only one of them can be right, just as Didi and Naomi are presupposing this in The Argument. In both cases, this presupposition may be wrong. Even if the two statements are incompatible, relative to the set of possible situations compatible with the context of The Argument, or relative to the derived context of The Report, they may agree (or at least not disagree: perhaps the truth-values of both statements are undefined, relative to some possible worlds) outside that context.

Here is a simple and unproblematic case where there is disagreement, even though both parties are right in what they *say*, but in which both they and a reporter reporting what they say are wrong in what they *presuppose*. Examples to illustrate the point could involve gradable adjectives, but the example I will give involves the paradigm case of a *non*-gradable adjective, an adjective that might be described as the F such that it is said that one cannot be just a little bit F: Didi said, on Tuesday, "Mary is pregnant." Naomi said, on Thursday, "Mary is not pregnant." Sam reports, on Saturday, "Didi said that Mary is pregnant, but Naomi said that she is not." This is The Report. The tenses in the report (past of "say", but present in the clause) indicate that the reporter is presupposing that Mary's pregnancy status is the same at all the relevant times (Tuesday, Thursday and Saturday, the times of the statements and the report). Relative to possible worlds compatible with this presupposition, the two statements are contradictories. But, let us suppose, the presupposition is false: Mary was pregnant on Tuesday, but no longer so on Thursday. So both Didi and Naomi spoke the truth; the actual world is outside of the (derived) context set in which the report is made.

8.6 Facts and epistemic priorities

In deliberation, inquiry and conversation, we cut up spaces of possibility in various ways, both to get a handle on what the actual world is like, and to figure out how to change it. In doing so, we may sometimes cut the space up more finely than is justified by the facts that determine which possibility is the actual one. I think this is at least a part of what brings together the diverse phenomena that various versions of semantic relativism are trying to explain. Nevertheless, I think that at least some of the disagreements that are described as "faultless" or "blameless" disagreements do not really fit the intended description. The intended meaning is that a disagreement is faultless, not just if neither party is at fault (which can happen with ordinary factual disagreements), but also that despite the disagreement, neither is making a mistake.[16] When we disagree (dividing the space of possibilities in conflicting ways), we are usually *presupposing* that there is a fact about who is right. Where that presupposition is wrong, it might be better to say, not that both parties are right, but that neither of them is.

But perhaps there are some cases that really do fit the description. I suggested in the last chapter that it sometimes unclear or controversial, not only what the facts are, but what there is a fact of the matter about. For this reason, it is useful to have an account of how rational discussion can proceed even when such questions are open. Let's look back, from the perspective of Richard's discussion of his example, at some of the cases of conditionals and modals discussed in the last two chapters.

---

[16] Kölbel uses this terminology, with this sense. See Kölbel 2002, 29–30 and 92, among other places.

In particular, let's consider analogues of Richard's case of Didi and Naomi (apparently conflicting statements made in separate contexts, perhaps later leading to an *Argument*, and a third party *Report*).

The case of Sly Pete was a case that involved, not disagreement, but a difference in context. If it led to an analogue of The Argument, this would be an argument based on a mistake—a failure to recognize the difference in context. An analogue of The Report would be inappropriate, and perhaps incorrect, suggesting mistakenly that the two were disagreeing when they were not. For The Report to be accurate, it must be made with a common derived context relative to which what Jack said contradicted what Zack said.

In this case, let us suppose, each of Allan's henchmen had *knowledge* of all the facts on which they based their conditional claims, and they also knew what they did not know. So it would seem reasonable for Jack to assure Allan, in his note, that he *knew* that Pete lost if he called, and for Zack to say that he *knew* that Pete won if he called. But it would be paradoxical for Allan to report that Jack knew that Pete lost if he called and Zack knew that Pete won if he called. The conditionals are not both true in the same context, and in particular they are not both true relative to the context Allan is in after getting and accepting the two messages.

But now consider the apparently conflicting statements by Alice and Bert about whether the gardener might have done it and about who did it if it wasn't the butler. (Consider the version of the case where Bert grants that the gardener *might* be innocent, but disagrees with Alice about whether he *might* be guilty.) Here we do have an analogue of The Argument, and a genuine disagreement. On our account of the case, we have a common context in which the two parties to the dispute interpret "the gardener might be guilty" in the same way. That is, this sentence in the mouth of Bert divides the space of possibilities compatible with their context in the same way as the sentence in the mouth of Alice. What they disagree about is how the proposition expressed by this sentence should be used to determine the posterior context that represents the information they are in a position to accept. A report could correctly represent their difference as a case where the same proposition that is accepted by one is rejected by the other. But when one looks back at the case after all the facts are in, one may reasonably judge that there was no fact of the matter about who was right. Furthermore, the parties to the disagreement may anticipate that this will probably be their retrospective judgment, at least if it turns out that the butler did it, which they both acknowledge is possible. So while they are disagreeing, they are not presupposing that one or the other will, in the end, be proved right by the facts.

This account of the case gives relativists some of what they want, but it does not support the kind of assessment sensitivity that is the essential element of MacFarlane's version of relativism. There is not a proposition that is actually true, when assessed relative to the earlier context, but false when assessed in the retrospective context, after the facts are in. Neither Alice nor Bert need *retract*, in the later context, the statements that they made in the earlier context. In the retrospective context, they are not in a position to express the proposition that divided the possibilities in the earlier context. It was an essentially contextual proposition.

In one of the variants of the whodunit case that we considered, the retrospective judgment is different. This is the case where the butler had an accomplice who was prepared to do the deed if the butler was unable to do it, but where Alice and Bert disagreed about whether that accomplice was the gardener or the chauffeur. Because of this disagreement, they disagree about who did it if was not the butler. In this case, when they look back after the facts are in (both that the butler did it, and that the chauffeur was the accomplice), they will judge that Alice was right, and that Bert was wrong. Bert will retract his statement, but this is still not a case of assessment sensitivity. The facts show that Bert was wrong all along, and that is why he takes back what he said.

Some disagreements are practical, and not factual, but there is no easy way to draw the line between disputes that will be settled by the facts and those that never will be. Some disagreements (both practical and factual) are robust and, if not resolved, will lead to continuing disagreement. Others are ephemeral, and will in the end disappear, or be settled by arbitrary and inconsequential stipulation. But there is sometimes no way to tell in advance which way a given dispute will go. For these reasons, it is appropriate that we should be flexible about the relation between the way we cut up the space of possibilities in our thought and discourse and the way the world we talk and think about settles the questions we ask. I don't know whether granting this flexibility counts as a kind of relativism, but I do think it is a reasonable thing to grant.

Appendix

As I have emphasized throughout this book, my main concern is not with compositional semantics, but with the development of concepts for describing and theorizing about the dynamic structure of discourse. The aim is to do so in a way that makes minimal commitments about the details of semantic mechanisms, interesting as those questions are. But issues do not divide neatly, and one needs to make at least some tentative and speculative assumptions about semantics to get clear about pragmatic structures, and to engage with other work. I have made use of David Lewis's abstract Context/Index framework at various places, and this appendix is mainly a series of digressions about this framework, and about some related issues.

1 The nuts and bolts of the CI framework

Here is a concise summary of David Lewis's Context/Index (CI) semantic framework, with a few examples of the kind of semantic rule it licenses. A semantics of this kind for a language assigns to each sentence a function that takes a pair of abstract objects (each with its own complexity) to a truth-value. The first argument of the function is a *context* (what I have called a K-context), which is a centered possible world: a pair consisting of a possible world, and a center, where a center is itself a pair consisting of a person (the *agent* of the context) and a time. The K-context is intended to represent the context of utterance for an utterance in the world by the agent at the time. Since a K-context includes a whole possible world, it determines all the facts on which the content or the truth of an utterance might depend. The second argument of the function is an *index*, which will be an n-tuple consisting of a sequence of *coordinates*, each of which is a feature of a kind that is determined by a K-context. In a simple example for illustration, an index will be a triple consisting of a time, a location, and a possible world. The coordinates of the index are independent of the K-context that is associated with it; that is, in a given context-index pair, $\langle c,i \rangle$, the time, location, and possible world coordinates of i may be different from the time, location of the agent, and world of c. But for any K-context, there will be an initial index, the index *of* that context, for which the time coordinate is the time of the context, the world coordinate is the world of the context, and the place coordinate is the location of the agent of the context. Notation: "c" and "i" will refer, respectively, to an arbitrary context and index, $c = \langle a_c, t_c, w_c \rangle$ and $i = \langle p_i, t_i, w_i \rangle$. The index of the context, c, will be $\langle p_c, t_c, w_c \rangle$, where p_c is the location of a_c at t_c in w_c. I will use square brackets for the semantic value of a sentence. "$[\phi]\langle c,i \rangle = 1\ (0)$" says that sentence ϕ is true (false), relative to the context/index pair, $\langle c,i \rangle$.

The form of a semantic rule, for a temporal, locative or modal operator, "o", will be something like this:

$$[o\phi]\langle c,i \rangle = 1 \text{ if and only if } [\phi]\langle c,i^* \rangle = 1$$

for some or all i*, where i* is defined in some specific way in terms of c and i.

For example:

$[\text{somewhere } \phi]\langle c,i \rangle = 1 \text{ iff } [\phi]\langle c,i^* \rangle = 1$

for some i^* that differs from i at most in the location term.

$[\text{Once } \phi]\langle c,i \rangle = 1$ iff $[\phi]\langle c,i^* \rangle = 1$ for some i^* that is like i, except that $t_{i^*} < t_i$.
$[\text{Now } \phi]\langle c,i \rangle = 1$ iff $[\phi]\langle c,i^* \rangle = 1$ where i^* is like i, except that $t_{i^*} = t_c$.
$[\text{Actually } \phi]\langle c,i \rangle = 1$ iff $[\phi]\langle c,i^* \rangle = 1$ where i^* is like i, except that $w_{i^*} = w_c$.
$[\blacklozenge\phi]\langle c,i \rangle = 1$ iff $[\phi]\langle c,i^* \rangle = 1$ where i^* differs from I at most at the world component, which must meet the condition that $w_i R w_{i^*}$.
(R is a binary accessibility relation, determined by the context.)[1]

The rule for the first-person singular pronoun will, of course, be this:
$[\text{I}]_{\langle c,i \rangle} = a_c$

The truth-value of a simple sentence, such as one that means the same as "it is raining" will depend entirely on the index. So if it is raining on

---

[1] I use a solid diamond, rather than an open one in order to contrast a metaphysical or causal modality with the epistemic "might", represented "$\Diamond$", which will come in for some discussion later.

Tuesday in Pittsburgh in world *w*, then if the *index* time and place are Tuesday and Pittsburgh, and the *index* world is *w*, then "it is raining" will take the value 1 (true) even if the *context* time and place are Monday and Cambridge, where it is dry in the context world.

The semantics gives us a truth-value, relative to an arbitrary context-index pair, but how do we get from this to the truth-value of an actual token utterance? Specifically, how do we get the particular *c* and *i* that are relevant to determining the truth-value of the utterance? We need to connect the abstract object, the semantic value, to the concrete situation. The relevant *c* is the one determined by the circumstances of the utterance—the actual speaker and time of utterance, and the actual world. (Or if we are interpreting a counterfactual utterance event, an utterance that takes place at a certain time and place in another possible world, then that time, place and counterfactual world will be the relevant contextual parameters.) To get the relevant index for the interpretation of the token utterance, we note that any context determines a corresponding index, the index *of* the context. So the final step, to get an actual truth-value, will be to use the index of the context. The upshot is that an utterance of a sentence S by agent *a* at time *t* in world *w* will be true simpliciter if and only if S is true relative to the CI pair, $\langle\langle a,t,w\rangle, \langle p,t,w\rangle\rangle$, where *p* is the location of *a* at *t* in *w*. For example, if a particular token of "it is raining" is uttered by RS on July 23, 2012 in the actual world, @, and if RS is in Cambridge at that time, then the utterance will be true just in case the sentence takes the value 1 relative to the context-index pair, $\langle c,i\rangle$, where $c = \langle$RS, July 23, 2012, @$\rangle$, and $I = \langle$Cambridge, July 23, 2012, @$\rangle$.

2 Monsters

The compositional rules of Lewis's CI semantics all define the value, relative to $\langle c,i\rangle$ in terms of the value at $\langle c,i^*\rangle$, where i^* may differ from *i*, but the *c* always remains the same. Why, one may ask, is the indexical semantics constrained in this way? This is the question, why the semantics rules out what David Kaplan called "monsters". The answer I gave in Chapter 1 is that this restriction is no substantive constraint, since the general abstract theory puts no constraints on what can go in the index. The idea is that the index should include all of the "shiftable" elements. If one wanted to use a Lewisian CI semantics to account for a language that shifted something that looked a lot like the abstract object that we use to represent context, or something determined by it, then one can put an object of this kind into the index. For example, Philippe Schlenker, in his brief on behalf of monsters, reports that in Amharic, the first-person singular pronoun can shift, in the scope of a propositional attitude verb, to refer to the agent of the attitude, rather than to the speaker in the context of utterance. So the pronoun that means "I" in a simple sentence that translates "I am happy", may refer to John, and be translated "he" in a sentence that means that John$_1$ believes that he$_1$ is happy. This pronoun would not be a monster, in a CI semantics, since a semantics of this kind for this language will put an "agent" place into the index. The agent coordinate of the index *of* the context will be the speaker, but that coordinate will shift in the scope of the attitude verb.[2]

I think this is the right way to think about monsters in the Lewis CI framework, but that is not the end of the story, since the framework in which Kaplan made his notorious remark about monsters was not exactly Lewis's framework, and there are other interpretations of what a monster might be. In Kaplan's semantics for demonstratives, the semantic value of a sentence is a *character*, which is a function from context to content. Kaplan's prohibition of monsters was the claim that, while our compositional semantics should allow any operators or connectives that defines the *content* of the complex expression in terms of the *contents* of the parts, we do not allow operators that define the *character* of the complex expression in terms of the *character* of the parts. But in Lewis's framework, the notion of propositional *content* plays no role at all, either in the compositional semantics, or in his pragmatic story of the conventions and rules governing speech. As a result, Kaplan's notion of character also plays no role in the CI theory. I argued in Chapter 1 that it was a mistake to leave propositional content out of the pragmatic story, but it is a separate question whether a notion of content should play an essential role in the compositional semantics.

Despite the differences between Kaplan's and Lewis's frameworks, there is nevertheless a clear abstract analogy between Kaplan's requirement that the language contain no monsters and the requirement of the CI framework that indices, but not contexts, can be shifted by the compositional rules. The Kaplanian dogma that there are no monsters

---

[2] Schlenker 2003, 31.

is essentially the assumption that the compositional process has the following structure: *context* determines the values of indexicals, which fix the *contents* of all the sentential constituents. Context has then finished its job: the compositional rules take over, giving the contents of complex expressions as a function of the contents of their parts. On the CI picture, neither content nor anything analogous to content plays an *essential* role, since Lewis argued that in a CI semantics there is only a notational difference between a two-stage process (function from context to function from index to truth-value) and a one-stage process (function from a context-index pair to a truth-value). But the two-stage representation facilitates comparison with the Kaplan picture, and if we describe the CI semantic framework that way, the abstract structure is exactly the same as it is on the Kaplan picture: the context determines, prior to the compositional process, the values of some parameters, and these will then determine functions from indices to truth-values (the abstract analogues of content), in context, for each of the sentential clauses. The job of context is then finished; the compositional process operates on the index-to-truth-value functions. The question is, why does the structure of a semantic theory have to take this form?

If a "context" were really a *context*—the concrete situation in which an utterance event takes place—then it would be hard to make sense of a compositional rule that shifted the context. But if we think of a "context" as an abstract object—a centered possible world that does not necessarily represent the situation in which an utterance being interpreted takes place—then it is not clear what the general motivation is for the assumption that the semantic process must have this structure. Is it then an empirical question (analogous to a question about the structure of universal grammar)? If so, then the evidence seems to suggest that the ban on monsters is empirically incorrect. But I have just argued that in the CI framework, with its abstract and unconstrained concept of an index, the imposition of this structure (the ban on monsters) puts no substantive constraint on the semantics. If the evidence shows that some parameter shifts, compositionally, then one can just put it (or a copy of it) into the index. This seems right, and unproblematic, for isolated parameters of a kind that are determined by context such as the agent parameter that is shifted in propositional attitude ascriptions in languages such as Amharic. But what if it is the whole "context" that is shifted? Can we preserve the form of the CI framework by putting a "context" coordinate into the index, and if we can, is there any point in doing so? Let's look at an example of a putative monster and see how the CI framework accommodates it. The example comes from a defense of monsters by Paolo Santorio.

The protagonists in Santorio's story are familiar from the literature on indexical belief, with ancestry that goes back to Frege, but this time they are involved in a new and desperate situation. Rudolf Lingens and Gustav Lauben are two amnesiacs who each know that they are one of the two, but do not know which. They have been kidnapped and will be subjected to the following experiment:

> First, they will be anesthetized. Then a coin will be tossed. If the outcome is tails, Lingens will be released in Main Library, Stanford, and Lauben will be killed. If the outcome is heads, Lauben will be released in Widener Library, Harvard, and Lingens will be killed. Lingens and Lauben are informed of the plan and the experiment is executed. Later, one of them wakes up in a library.[3]

The statements Santorio considers in this context are two indicative conditionals, and two corresponding epistemic possibility statements made by the person who wakes up.

(1) If the coin landed tails, I am in Main Library, Stanford.
(2) If the coin landed heads, I am in Widener Library, Harvard.
(3) I might be in Main Library, Stanford.
(4) I might be in Widener Library, Harvard.

The datum is that all of these statements are felicitous. If we take them to be statements that say something true or false, relative to a context, it seems clear that they are true in the scenario described, and known to be true by the speaker since he knows that the scenario is as described. The problem is that if we give them a compositional semantics in the CI style, we do not get the result that both conditionals, and both "might" statements are true unless we allow for a compositional "shift" in the context. If we do allow such a shift, we get the results we want easily and naturally, at least in this case. Intuitively, even in the world in which the coin landed heads, where the speaker is Lauben, his statement, "I might be in Main Library, Stanford" is true, since he does not know that he is not Lingens in the world where the coin landed tails. (More to the point,

[3] Santorio 2012, 363.

it is an open possibility in the context that he is Lingens, and is in such a world.) If the possible worlds that are in the domain of the "might" are the *context* worlds, with the contextual parameters fixed as they are in that context world, then both statements come out true. That is, suppose the rule for the epistemic "might" were something like this:

$$[\Diamond \phi]\langle c,i\rangle = 1 \text{ iff } [\phi]\langle c^*,i^*\rangle = 1$$
for some c^* and i^* such that $w_{c^*} \in g(c)$, and $w_{c^*} = w^*$

where $g(c)$ is the context set of the conversation taking place in K-context c. (We need to shift both the context and the world of the index in order to get the right result: that statement (2) is true when it is made by Lingens in the world where the coin landed tails, and where he is in fact in Main Library, Stanford.)

This rule gets the right result, but it turns the "might" into a monster. Could we avoid monstrosity and preserve the purity of the CI semantics by putting a copy of the "context" into the index? Yes we can, but the required change will be more radical than it is in the case of the first-person pronoun in a language that works the way we are told that Amharic works. We will need to modify other rules so that values of indexicals and modifiers such as "now" and "actually" are defined in terms of the "context" coordinate of the index rather than the K-context itself. Is there any point in doing this, rather than simply removing the structural restriction that rules out compositional context shifts? From a technical point of view, it may make no difference exactly how one formulates the rule, but copying a context into the index and preserving the ban on Lewisian monsters has this conceptual point: the notion of a K-context is playing two different roles: (1) it models the *context of utterance*: the concrete situation in which the utterance being interpreted takes place. Contexts, in this sense, determine a body of information (the common ground). But (2) the elements of the common ground (in the given context of utterance) are themselves K-contexts, or something that, given an utterance, determines a unique K-context. A K-context, in its first role, cannot shift, compositionally, but there is no reason why K-contexts, qua abstract objects that are members of a set used to characterize an information state, cannot be subject to compositional shifts.

I have acquiesced in using the word "context" to refer to centered possible worlds since the usage is so firmly entrenched, but in fact I think this is extremely misleading terminology. K-contexts deserve the title, and can play their role in explaining how content is sensitive to context, only because they determine the common ground (since it is a fact about the world in which a speech act takes place that certain information is common ground among the relevant people at the relevant time). That is, a K-context contains or determines the contextual information to which context-sensitive expressions are sensitive, since it is a representation of a whole world, plus a center that determines the conversation in which certain information is common ground. But calling this abstract object (a centered possible world) a "context" tends to blur the line between the distinctive information that is contextual information and other facts that may play a role in the compositional semantics. And it obscures the fact that centered possible worlds, in the general case, are not suitable to be contexts, since they need not be centered on an utterance, or on a conversation. If we were to stay with the intuitive idea motivating Kaplan's character/content semantics, we would take character to be a function from the CG-context (rather than the K-context) to content. Where a CI semantics appeals to a feature of "context" that is not available in the common ground (such as the world of the context, or in cases where the identity of the speaker or addressee is in question, or "at issue", the agent or addressee of the context), then we should say that what the context itself—the common ground—determines is not the specific feature (a world, or an agent), but instead a function whose argument is an element of the CG-context (a sequence-centered world), and whose value is the feature in question (a world, an agent, or an addressee). This is what happens, for example, with the first-person singular pronoun when one applies a CI semantics in the context of our sequence-centered worlds model of common ground. What context (CG-context) provides are the I-concepts, which are functions from elements of the common ground to agents. But if the semantic value (determined by context) of an indexical pronoun is a nonrigid individual concept, then we seem to have some deviation from the direct reference picture, and violations of the Kaplanian dogma that indexicals are always rigid designators. This deviation is what Santorio's examples, which are robust and, I think, decisive, show.

The ban on monsters and the doctrine that indexicals such as "I" and "that" are always rigid designators are tied together as a package in Kaplan's theory, but they can be pulled apart. If our semantic theory says that what context determines, for the interpretation of the pronoun "I" is a possibly nonrigid individual concept (a function from possible worlds to individuals), then we have rejected the doctrine about indexicals, but we have not thereby lifted the ban on monsters—semantic rules that shift the context—even in the Kaplan framework. Santorio's examples are compatible with a compositional semantics for epistemic "might" in which context determines the content of the prejacent, and then the semantics for the "might" determines that this proposition is true in one of the contextually determined possible worlds. No context shifting need be involved.

3 Assertoric content

Lewis's semantics deliver a truth-value for the utterance of a sentence as a function of the context of utterance: it is the value of the function that is the meaning of the sentence for the argument pair whose terms are the context of utterance and the index of that context. Lewis noted (somewhat dismissively) that, if you like, you can extract a proposition (a function from possible worlds to truth-values) from the semantics in either of the following two ways. First, for a given K-context, initialize all the coordinates of the index except the world coordinate, and abstract on the world coordinate. That gives you a function from K-contexts to propositions, and he labels the value of this function "the *horizontal* proposition". A second way to extract a proposition from the semantic value of a sentence, which he calls "the *diagonal* proposition", is a little more complicated. Here is what he says: "Let c^w be that context, if there is one, that is located in world w and indistinguishable from c; then for all the speaker knows, he might inhabit w, and c^w might be the context of his utterance. (I ignore the case of two indistinguishable contexts in the same world.)" He then defines the diagonal proposition for a sentence φ as the function that takes a world w to the truth-value of φ, relative to the context/index pair $\langle c^w, i_c w \rangle$, where $i_c w$ is the index of the context c^w. Now as I have noted, propositions do not play any role either in the compositional semantics, or in his pragmatic story about conventions of truth and trust, but if we want to identify a proposition that is the *assertoric content* of an utterance, which of these should it be? Lewis's diagonal proposition comes closest to what we want for the following reason: the role of assertoric content, according to the general pragmatic theory that I am promoting, is to determine which are the possibilities that are to be eliminated from the context set when an assertion with that content is accepted. As Michael Dummett wrote, in introducing the distinction between assertoric content and ingredient sense, "to grasp the content of an assertion, one needs to know only what possibilities it rules out."[4] In cases where the diagonal and horizontal propositions defined by Lewis differ (for possible worlds in the relevant context set), it is intuitively clear that the point of the assertion is to rule out those possible worlds in which the diagonal proposition is false. (I will give an example to illustrate this below.) Furthermore, this is not just a fact about usage that might have been different. As I have emphasized throughout the discussion of the role of context in determining content, the contextual features on which what is said depends must, in any appropriate speech act, be presumed to be available to the addressee. A K-context, centered on a speaker in a conversation, contains all of the information that is available, and that might be relevant, but it also determines information that is not available. To put the point in a slightly different way, a CG-context in which an utterance event is presupposed to be taking place is compatible with many K-contexts, and the information that distinguishes between the different K-contexts compatible with common ground is not presumed to be available. So we need a notion of assertoric content that meets the condition that the content of a speech act, relative to one K-context, is the same as the content relative to a different K-context that determines the same CG-context. The horizontal proposition, as defined by Lewis, does not, in general, meet this condition, but a version of the notion of a diagonal proposition does.

The definition of the diagonal proposition that I will give is slightly different from Lewis's, relying on the notion of common ground, rather than a notion of indistinguishability, but the idea is essentially the same. Before stating the definition, I need to make some remarks about the relation between three things: (1) the uncentered possible worlds that *propositions* distinguish between, (2) the multiply-centered worlds (call them "s-worlds") that are the elements of the common ground, and (3) the singly-centered worlds that are K-contexts.

---

[4] Dummett 1991, 47.

According to the account developed and defended in Chapter 5, the elements of the common ground are possible worlds centered on a time and a sequence of individual agents—one individual agent for each of the participants in the conversation. It is an assumption of that account, which I defended in Chapter 5, that each uncentered world occurs only once in a common-ground set of s-worlds, and so there will be a one-one correspondence between the elements of the common ground and the context set, C—the set of uncentered possible worlds that are compatible with the common ground. When an utterance event occurs, it takes place in each of the elements of the CG-context, and this determines a set of *singly-centered* worlds (K-contexts), centered on the speaker. So where C is the context set (the uncentered worlds compatible with the context) and ϕ is the sentence uttered, it will be true that for each $w \in C$ there will be a unique K-context, c_w, which is the world w centered on the time of utterance, and the speaker. The *diagonal proposition* for the utterance of ϕ (defined relative to C) will be the proposition that takes w to $[\phi]\langle c_w, i_c w\rangle$. That is, the diagonal proposition is the one that is true at w if and only if ϕ is true, relative to the K-context determined by w. This specifies only a *partial* proposition—a function from possible worlds to truth-values that is defined only for the context set. We will consider below the ways in which the proposition can be extended.

Here is a simple example to illustrate the contrast between the horizontal and diagonal propositions, and to show that what is asserted is the diagonal. Clara, on a game show, can choose to have the contents of one of two boxes, A or B. One contains a million dollars ($M), while the other contains only a thousand dollars ($T), but she has no idea which box is the one with the big prize. She chooses box A, but before she opens the box, the game show host observes to the audience, "Clara could have gotten more money than she actually got." It seems clear that this statement tells the audience that box A (the one Clara chose) is the one containing only $T. Now let us apply the CI semantics to the host's observation, which we will formalize this way: S is the sentence "Clara got more money than she actually got," so the sentence used to make the statement is formalized ☐S. (I use a solid diamond for the kind of causal modality that is expressed by the "could".) Since it is known that Clara chose box A, there are two relevant possible worlds compatible with the prior context—the CG-context as it was before the host made his statement. Call them α and β. In world α there is $M in box A, and $T in box B, while in world β there is $T in box A and $M in box B. In both α and β, Clara chose box A. (It is common ground, in the prior context, that box A was chosen.) Since the sentence we are interpreting involves a (nonepistemic) modal "could", we will need to consider two other possible worlds that are outside of the context set: worlds γ and δ are like α and β, respectively, in the amount of money in the boxes, but they are both worlds in which Clara selected the other box, B. Since Clara could have made either choice, but had no control over the amount of money in the boxes, α and γ will be possible with respect to each other, as will β and δ, but neither α nor γ will be possible with respect to β or δ. Let us assume that the world of the *context* (the K-context) is world β. So sentence S will be true (in that context) in index world *x* if and only if Clara gets more money, in world *x*, than she got in the context world, β. So S will be true (in the β context) in worlds α and δ, and false in β and γ. Since α is possible relative to itself, and δ is possible relative to β, ♦S will be true, relative to both α and β. So the horizontal proposition expressed (in context world β) does not distinguish α from β; if this proposition were the assertoric content of what the host said, he would not have told the audience anything about where the money is. But if we evaluate the sentence relative to context world α, the result will be that it is false in both possible worlds. Since the sentence is false in world α, in context α, and true in world β, in context β, the diagonal proposition will be the one that excludes possible world α, and so it is intuitively clear that it is the diagonal that is the assertoric content of the host's statement.

"It would be a convenience, nothing more," Lewis wrote, "if we could take the propositional content of a sentence in context as its semantic value. But we cannot. The propositional contents do not obey the compositional principle, therefore they are not semantic values."[5] The point (to use Dummett's terminology) is that we need to distinguish ingredient sense (the semantic value required for compositional purposes) from assertoric content (what a sentence is used to say). The main consideration Lewis appeals to in arguing for the need for this distinction is that to get the compositional semantics right, the index must contain coordinates other than a possible world, since the language contains operators that "shift" other features of the situation. One might think

---

[5] Lewis 1980, 39.

that if we could somehow get rid of these other operators, and so get rid of the need for other coordinates of the index, we could preserve the simpler and more convenient semantics, where the semantic values (in context) of sentential clauses that are parts of more complex sentences were all the same as the assertoric contents that the corresponding sentences would have on their own. As noted in Chapter 1, Jeffrey King argued that we can and should eliminate temporal and locative sentential operators by using a semantics with variables in the logical forms of sentences that range over times and places, with tense and temporal and locative modifiers analyzed as object-language quantification over domains of times and places.[6] He argues that we have independent motivation for adopting this kind of semantics, and that if we did so, we could avoid the distinction between assertoric content and ingredient sense. I am skeptical about the independent motivation, but I think that is a question best left to the syntacticians. (Despite its name, "logical form" is a syntactic notion.) I am also unclear how it would help to reduce all temporal and locative modification to explicit quantification over times and places, since in Lewis's CI framework, quantifiers are themselves treated as index-shifting operators. (The CI semantics for quantification has a certain elegance, since it treats deictic pronouns and bound pronouns in a uniform way. Unbound, a pronoun's reference is fixed by the initial index—the index of the context. But when it is bound, the index value is shifted by the quantifier rule, and so depends on a domain supplied by the context, rather than specific values for the variables.) So even if we eliminate time and location coordinates, we will need, in the index, values for the variables that range over times and places—values that are shifted by quantifiers. But my main point is that even in a CI semantics where the only coordinate of the index is a possible world, we still will need a distinction between assertoric content and ingredient sense. The point is made by the game show example, which does not involve temporal or locative modification, or quantifiers. It is essential to get the compositional semantics right that the argument of the causal "could" be the "horizontal" proposition (or the function from index to truth-value, determined as a function of the context). But as the example made clear, the assertoric content of the whole sentence must be the diagonal proposition.

[6] King 2003.

The distinction between assertoric content and ingredient sense is obviously related to the issue about monsters, but the distinction does not by itself introduce monsters into the compositional process, or require that a "context" coordinate be included in the index, since one can think of the extraction of assertoric content as a post-semantic operation. It is when assertoric contents appear in the scope of an operator, as seems to happen with epistemic modals and propositional attitudes that we get (in the CI framework) the problem about monsters.

I noted that the definition I have given for the diagonal proposition (the assertoric content) determines only a partial proposition: as specified so far, the function from possible worlds to truth-values is defined only relative to the domain of possible worlds in the context set. If we stop there, we have a semantic/pragmatic account that is essentially like the dynamic semantics that takes semantic values to be context-change potentials—functions taking prior contexts into posterior contexts. I have resisted the move to dynamic semantics, favoring instead a dynamic pragmatic story, and part of my reason for the resistance, as I have said, is that I think we need a notion of propositional content that is defined for possible worlds beyond those compatible with the current local context. We want to be able to detach information we have been told from the immediate context in which we were told it, and we want at least in some cases to be able to assess statement (as true or false) in a retrospective context that is different from the one in which the statement was made. So it is important for my general view that the assertoric content expressed in a speech act be defined, at least in some cases, for a wider range of possibilities. In many cases, the extension of the domain of the function that is the proposition will be unproblematic, since with many expressions the semantic value may not depend on context, or may depend only on features that are shared by a wide range of possible contexts. But the extension of the assertoric content of even paradigm indexical sentences will often be unproblematic. For example, the context (the common ground) may provide a natural extension of the relevant I-concept to possible worlds outside the context set. In contexts where the identity of the speaker is not "at issue", (which is the normal case) the relevant I-concept will be the ordinary rigid concept, picking out the actual speaker in all possible worlds. Even when the identity of the speaker *is* at issue, the relevant I-concept clearly picks out the actual speaker in the actual world (or in any possible world compatible with a retrospective context in which the proposition is assessed), even if the worlds in the retrospective context are not compatible with the context in which the statement was made. In the derived contexts relevant to the interpretation of subjunctive conditionals, the extension of the relevant I-concept is clear, since the derived context is defied by an imaging function (a mapping of worlds to worlds), and the referent of "I" in the image world will be the referent in the base world. To interpret propositional attitude ascriptions (such as, for example, "Ralph believes that I am a spy," said by Ortcutt), a proposition will be determined in the relevant derived context only if the basic context—the common ground—determines a uniquely most salient way that the subject identifies the speaker. A salient I-concept *may* be undetermined for some possible worlds (outside of the basic context set), and so the assertoric content of utterances of sentences with this pronoun in the scope of a attitude verb may remain partial, but appropriate speech will require that the I-concept be defined, not only for all the possible situations compatible with the basic context, but also for possible situations compatible with any of the subordinate contexts that are relevant to the interpretation of what is said.[7]

4 Two-dimensional "semantics"

In distinguishing the two ways of determining a proposition, and in using the "horizontal/diagonal" terminology for this distinction, Lewis was, as he said, "borrowing and modifying" some apparatus that I used in my "Assertion" paper. But I put this apparatus to use, in that paper and others, in a somewhat different way. I thought of the two-dimensional structures (what I called "propositional concepts'"—functions from possible worlds to propositions, which were themselves functions from possible worlds to truth-values) as a descriptive apparatus for representing the different ways in which what is said is a function of the facts. That a particular utterance expresses a proposition is a matter of fact, which means that the truth-value of an utterance will depend on the facts in two different ways: the

---

[7] The extension of the domain of possible worlds over which a proposition is defined beyond those in the context set (to possible worlds incompatible with what is being presupposed) is related to the notion Stephen Yablo develops of "noncatastrophic presupposition failure" (see Yablo 2006).

facts determine what is said, and the facts also determine whether what is said is true or false. (The directional terminology derives from the matrices used to represent the two dimensions: vertical for the dimension that represents the role of facts in determining what is said, and horizontal to represent the role of the facts in determining whether what is said is true or false.) This application of the apparatus is not a part of the semantics for any language in which propositions are expressed—it abstracts away from that, representing the facts on which the determination of propositional content depends simply by a function from possible worlds to propositions. So at this level of abstraction, the representation is neutral on the question, what sort of fact is it that determines content, and it says or assumes nothing about the compositional semantics that determines what propositions are expressed. The facts that determine content will presumably include facts about the semantics of the language in which the content is expressed, as well as facts about the context, however that notion is understood, in cases where the expressions of the language are context-sensitive.

The word "semantics" is in quotation marks in the title to this section in order to highlight a way that this label for the two-dimensional apparatus, in the use to which I put it, may be misleading. The two-dimensional apparatus was taken from a formal semantics, or model theory, for a two-dimensional modal logic. This semantics gives compositional rules for the interpretation of sentences of an artificial language with two-dimensional modal operators, but in the use to which I put them, the structures defined in that model theory were not used to give a two-dimensional semantics for any natural language. Whether natural languages are appropriately given any kind of two-dimensional semantics is a separate and independent question. In both Kaplan's semantics in *Demonstratives* and Lewis's CI theory a two-dimensional framework *is* used for a different and complementary purpose: for giving a compositional semantics for a language. The two ways of using two-dimensional structures interact and may overlap, but it is important not to conflate them.[8]

In the abstract two-dimensional model theory that I used in "Assertion",[9] the two parameters (the two dimensions relative to which truth-

---

[8] See Stalnaker 2004 for discussion of contrasting uses of the two-dimensional framework.
[9] I was drawing on Segerberg 1973.

values are defined) were the same: truth was defined relative to an ordered pair of possible worlds. A two-dimensional concept associated with a particular utterance token can be defined for any set of possible worlds in which that utterance event occurs, including worlds that are not compatible with the common ground, or with what a speaker is presupposing. The set of worlds relative to which a propositional concept is defined will include all the worlds compatible with the common ground, since it is assumed that it is common ground that the utterance event took place. But one can use a propositional concept to represent ignorance and error about what is said, either the ignorance or error of a participant in a conversation, or of an outside observer. The example used in Chapter 1 (and in my original "Pragmatics" paper) to illustrate the contrast between the two roles that factual information plays in determining the truth-value of an utterance was this kind of case: Daniels thinks I said something false when I said "You are a fool" to O'Leary, because he mistakenly thought that I was talking to him. In this example, the speaker was *presupposing* that O'Leary was the addressee, so the worlds that are compatible with what Daniels believed were outside of the context set. Perhaps O'Leary misunderstood as well, in which case I might correct him this way: "Hey! O'Leary! I'm talking to *you.*" The assertoric content of this correction statement is that O'Leary is the addressee. Since I recognized that O'Leary had misunderstood me, I am no longer presupposing, in making this statement, that O'Leary is the addressee. This assertion was intended to exclude possible situations in which the "you" refers to Daniels, which means that the "you" refers to Daniels relative to the possible situations that are excluded. Of course there are no limits to what O'Leary can misunderstand, so he might miss the point, even of my correction, and remain ignorant of the assertoric content of what I said. One might use a two-dimensional matrix to represent O'Leary's further misunderstanding, in which case the "horizontal" propositions in this representation will be the alternative assertoric contents that for all O'Leary knows, are the contents of what I said. These same propositions—the "horizontals" of one representation—might be determined as diagonal propositions of the kind defined for a two-dimensional, CI semantics.

In calling some semantic theory (either for a formal language, or for a natural language "two-dimensional" I mean only that it defines truth as a function of two parameters. In Segerberg's abstract two-dimensional modal semantics, and in my original application of it, the two parameters were drawn from the same domain—a set of possible worlds—so truth is defined relative to an ordered pair of things of the same kind. In this case, the concept of a diagonal is straightforward: if f is a propositional concept (a binary function taking an ordered pair of possible worlds to a truth-value), then the corresponding diagonal proposition is the singular function $\lambda x f(x,x)$. If "†" is the diagonalization operator (in a formal language such as the one defined by Segerberg), then the rule for this operator will be this: $[†φ]\langle x,y \rangle = [φ]\langle y,y \rangle$. But in the more general case, the two dimensions (the two arguments of the binary function) may be drawn from distinct domains, as is the case with a CI semantics, where the dimensions are K-contexts (centered possible worlds) and indices (sequences of coordinates of a kind that context determines). In these cases, there is no straightforward notion of a diagonal, and whether a notion of a diagonal can be defined at all depends on the relationship between the two different domains of the binary function. The definition of a diagonal proposition defined in section 3 above depended on the fact that one component both of a K-context and of an index is a possible world, and on the constraint that within the set of possible worlds compatible with the common ground, there is a function from index worlds (of the index of the context) to context worlds. In David Chalmers's two-dimensional framework[10] one parameter is a centered world, and the other is an uncentered world. The diagonal is not a proposition, but a centered-worlds proposition—a function from K-contexts to truth-values. If f is a two-dimensional function taking a centered world c and an uncentered world w to a truth-value, and if w_c is the world of c, without its center, then the diagonal (centered-world) proposition is defined as follows: $\lambda c f(c, w_c)$.

In Seth Yalcin's semantics for epistemic modals, which I will discuss just below, he defines both a diagonal and a horizontal, but in this case, neither is a proposition. The diagonal is, as in Chalmers's two-dimensional semantics, a centered-worlds proposition, or a function from centered worlds, or K-contexts, to truth-values. Yalcin's horizontals are functions from indices to truth-values; the semantics determines a horizontal for an utterance as a function of its K-context.

[10] Chalmers 2006.

5 Yalcin's semantics for epistemic modals

Seth Yalcin (in Yalcin 2007) proposed a semantics for epistemic modals in Lewis's CI framework. The main innovation was to include as one coordinate of the index an information state parameter, represented by a set of possible worlds and a probability function on it. Assuming for simplicity that the only elements of the index are a possible world and an information state, the rule for the epistemic "might" is this:

$$[\Diamond \phi]\langle c,w,s \rangle = 1 \text{ iff } [\phi]\langle c,w',s \rangle = 1 \text{ for some } w' \in s.$$

The information state coordinate may shift when the "$\Diamond$" occurs within the scope of a supposition or propositional attitude operator. Specifically, a supposition will shift the information state to the set of possible worlds compatible with what is being supposed.

The abstract semantics leaves open the specific question, (a)—what determines the value of the information parameter, in application?—as well as a more general question about the role of an epistemic modal claim in communication. Yalcin puts the general question this way: "What informational content do utterances of epistemic modal sentences communicate?" (p.1006), and he contrasts two ways of answering it, which he calls "the diagonal view" and "the informational view".

The diagonal view follows the general pattern of Lewis's story about the role of assertive utterances in discourse: the context of utterance c provides an "initial" index, i_c, the index *of* the context. An utterance of a sentence in a context c will be true just in case it is true relative to the context-index pair, $\langle c, i_c \rangle$. To complete the story, we need to specify the initial information state coordinate—the information state of the index of the context. (This is question (a).) Yalcin leaves this open, in his characterization of the diagonal view, but a natural proposal that he considers is that it should be the context set—the possibilities compatible with the common ground of the K-context.[11] To get the informational content of the epistemic modal statement, we follow the general account of assertoric content. Yalcin takes this to be a centered-worlds proposition: a function from K-contexts to truth values, defined as follows for

---

[11] There is a problem for this suggestion, noted by Yalcin, when the world of the context is not itself compatible with the common ground (that is, when something false is being presupposed). We can set this problem aside by restricting the proposal to the case where the K-context is compatible with the common ground.

arbitrary sentence φ: $\lambda c[\phi]\langle c, w_c, s_c \rangle$. So the diagonal view treats utterances of epistemic "might" sentences exactly as it treats ordinary assertions.

The contrasting informational view rejects the assumption that epistemic modal sentences have propositional content, and are used to say what the world is like. The relevant abstract object, in application, is not a function from centered worlds to truth-values, but a function (defined relative to a given context c) from *information states* to truth-values, defined (again, for arbitrary sentence φ) as follows: $\lambda s[\phi]\langle c, w_c, s \rangle$. On the informational view, the role of the utterance is to put a constraint on the context set: it must be an information state s that this function takes to the value 1 (true). On the informational view, there is no need to specify an initial value for the information state of the index of the context.

Yalcin remarks that if we add to the neutral diagonal view (which leaves it unspecified what the initial information state is), the proposal to identify the information state of the context as the context set of that context, then we "effectively collapse it into the informational view.... The two pragmatic views technically come to the same thing." (p. 1012) Let me spell out the sense in which this is true:

For any K-context α and any sentence φ, ◊φ will be true in K-context α (according to the diagonal view) if and only if the context set of α meets the constraint, in context α, imposed on the informational view. Formally,

$$\lambda s[\Diamond \phi]\langle \alpha, w_\alpha, s \rangle(s_\alpha) = \lambda c[\Diamond \phi]\langle c, w_c, s_c \rangle(\alpha)$$

Yalcin expresses a preference for the informational view, but given this equivalence, why do we have to choose between the two views?

There remains a difference between the *neutral* diagonal view (that leaves open the question, what is the information state coordinate of the index of the K-context) and the informational view (that makes no use of an initialized information state), but the difference is that the diagonal view retains a flexibility that is not available to the informational view. That is, the informational view is equivalent to a special case of the diagonal view. If the special case is the only one with any application, then we can ignore the general case, and treat the two views as two ways of representing the same thing. But if there are cases where an epistemic "might" should be interpreted relative to an information state that is different from the context set, then there is an advantage to the formulation that allows the additional flexibility. The account of epistemic modals sketched in Chapters 6 and 7 suggest that in cases of disagreement, we need to allow for this divergence.

Let me elaborate on this last point. The equivalence of the special case of the diagonal view and informational view might be put this way: a modal sentence is *acceptable*, relative to a given K-context α if and only if it is true in that K-context (on the diagonal view) and if and only if the context set of α conforms to the constraint on information states (on the informational view). These two characterizations of acceptability are equivalent. But what happens if an epistemic modal claim is made in a (prior) context in which it is unacceptable? On either way of viewing the situation, there are two options: (1) the context will adjust so as to make the statement acceptable; or (2) the statement will be rejected. Case (2) has two subcases: (2a) the statement is then retracted; or (2b) the speaker sticks to her claim, while the interlocutor sticks to his rejection. (2b)—the disagreement case—is the case where (I argued in Chapter 7) the information state relevant to the interpretation of the epistemic modal comes apart from the common ground—the kind of case for which we need the flexibility of the diagonal view.

I suspect that one reason for Yalcin's resistance to the diagonal view is that by treating epistemic modal sentences exactly like ordinary assertions, it fails to explain the expressive character of epistemic modals. I agree that one needs to clarify the sense in which epistemic modal sentences are (often at least) used not to make claims about what the world is like, but to guide the direction of the discourse, and to express epistemic priorities. The account I sketched tries to explain the expressive character of epistemic modals and indicative conditionals in terms of the prospective character of the speech acts. But the application of this explanation of speech act force to cases of disagreement led us to make distinctions between the possibilities that may go beyond what there is a fact of the matter about. In a case where Alice accepts that it might be that ϕ, while Bert rejects this possibility, we need a possibility in which she is right and he is wrong. I described this refinement of the points of evaluation relative to which the contents of speech acts are defined as a kind of projection of epistemic priorities onto a world. Sometimes this kind of projection is a way of getting richer resources for describing the facts, but sometimes the projection is temporary, and disappears in a retrospective context. That is, sometimes when we ask later about such a disagreement, "Who turned out to be right?" the question has no answer. Yalcin's semantics for epistemic modals provides a way to model the more fine-grained possibilities as possible-world/information-state pairs. I will say a little more about this below in the section on expressivist semantics.

A second reason, I think, for Yalcin's preference for the informational view is that he is concerned with questions about logical structure and semantic consequence, and the informational view goes naturally with a conception of informational consequence that is useful for explaining some of the subtleties and puzzles about reasoning with epistemic modals, and other constructions that involve the kind of index shifting that epistemic modals illustrate. But just as the equivalence between the two views (in the special case of the diagonal view) means that we don't have to choose between them (at least in contexts that don't involve disagreement), it also means that we don't have to choose between a more classical notion of consequence and the notion of informational consequence that Yalcin defines. We can use both of them, and explore in rigorous detail the relations between them.

6 Expressivist semantics

The semantics for Lewis's language game of command and permission involves a normative component—a function whose value is a "sphere of permissibility" determining what the slave is obliged and permitted to do. As Lewis defines the game, the normative component is wholly determined by (and so supervenient on) the nonnormative facts about a possible world. Specifically, what is required and permitted at a given time in a given world is wholly determined by what utterances the master has produced at or before that time in that world. But one might have a more flexible semantics. After all, in these enlightened times, we might question whether the slave is really obliged to do what the master commands. (Imagine the subversive kibitzer saying to the slave, "You know, you don't really have to do what the master tells you to do." Even the conservative, who thinks the kibitzer's subversive claim is false could allow that it is not a contradiction.) We might keep the game the same (with it being a rule of the game that the slave must do what the master commands), but generalize the semantics so that this rule is not a *semantic* rule, but a substantive normative claim (!the slave does whatever the master commands). This more flexible semantics would be essentially the same as the semantics that Allan Gibbard proposed in his original presentation of a semantics for normative discourse.[12] A system of norms, in Gibbard's sense, can be defined as a function taking a world-time pair to a sphere of permissibility. The points of evaluation for the interpretation of the sentences of the mixed factual/normative language will be pairs consisting of a possible world and a system of norms. The "propositions" expressed by the sentences of this language will be functions from points of evaluation of this kind to truth-values.

It is a substantive meta-normative question what it means for an agent to *accept* a set of norms, just as it is a substantive question in the philosophy of mind what it is to *believe* a proposition. But both factual propositions and systems of norms are abstract objects definable independently of any propositional attitudes, or any substantive account of what it is to have a cognitive, conative, or evaluative attitude.[13]

Yalcin describes his account of epistemic modals as "expressivist", and it is natural to see his semantics for epistemic modals as a variation on the kind of semantics that Gibbard proposed for normative discourse. As with Gibbard's semantics, in Yalcin's the points of evaluation will be pairs of a possible world and a nonfactual component, but in this case the nonfactual component is an information state. Just as Gibbard's general meta-normative theory needs an account of what it is to accept a system of norms, so Yalcin's needs an account of what it is to accept a "proposition" defined in terms of this kind of point of evaluation. But the compositional semantics does not depend on the way this substantive question is answered.

---

[12] Gibbard 1990, Ch. 5.

[13] Mark Schroeder (in Schroeder 2008) takes it to be a commitment of an expressivist theory that the semantics must be done by associating sentences with attitudes, and then giving compositional rules for those attitude states. The problems for expressivism that he develops in the book all derive from this commitment. But I think this is not a commitment that an expressivist need or should accept. If one does the compositional semantics for abstract objects that are definable independently of any attitudes, and separates the semantics from substantive meta-normative and meta-semantic questions about what it is to accept or to communicate a proposition, in the extended sense of proposition defined in the semantics, then one avoids all of the problems that he explores in the book, problems that he argues cannot be given a satisfactory solution. I take the main lesson of Schroeder's book to be that one should not do expressivist semantics in this way.

As should be clear, I am sympathetic with both kinds of expressivist semantic frameworks, though I would emphasize, in both cases, that the sharp separation of the factual and normative components of a point of evaluation is a severe idealization. One benefit of doing semantics in terms of points of evaluation that mix factual and normative elements is that one can explain how discourse and inquiry can proceed without answering in advance questions about what there is a fact of the matter about.

7 Common ground contexts, basic and derived

I have made a number of distinctions between different kinds of common-ground contexts, basic and derived. This section aims just to summarize in one place these distinctions, and some of the formal properties of the different kinds of context sets.

In the formal representation of common ground developed in Chapters 2, 4 and 5, the elements are possible worlds centered on a sequence of individuals—the participants in the communicative situation. The worlds are those compatible with the shared information of the participants—with their presumed common knowledge, including common knowledge of who and where they are. The centering represents the presumed shared ways that they all locate themselves and each other in the relevant possible worlds.

So the elements of a common-ground context are multiply-centered worlds (which I labeled s-worlds), but any given (uncentered) possible world occurs only once in such a set. So there is a one-one correspondence between the s-worlds that define a CG-context and a corresponding set of uncentered worlds. "The context set" sometimes refers to this corresponding set of uncentered worlds.

The common ground is a state defined in terms of a propositional attitude (acceptance for the purposes of the conversation) of the parties, but it is not itself any one person's propositional attitude. What a party to a conversation *presupposes* is defined as what that party accepts to be common ground: in a conversation involving just Alice and Bert, Alice *presupposes* that ϕ if and only if Alice accepts that Alice and Bert commonly accept that ϕ. The iterative structure implies that if what Alice and Bert presuppose is the same, then the set of possibilities compatible with what each presupposes will be the same as the set that is compatible with what the other presupposes. Their presuppositions diverge if and only if at least one is mistaken about what is common ground. Since successful communication depends on agreement about shared information, we say that a context is *defective* if the presuppositions diverge.

Presupposition and common ground are not factive notions: even in nondefective contexts, what is presupposed may be factually false, which means that a (centered) possible world in which certain things are common ground may not itself be a possible world that is compatible with the common ground. Where pretense is involved, it may be known, even common knowledge, that some presuppositions are false. Even in nondefective contexts without any pretense or error where all parties know and accept that the common ground is what it in fact is, it may not be *common ground* that the common ground is what it in fact is.

In the idealized model, we assume that the basic attitude in terms of which common ground and speaker presupposition are defined (acceptance for the purposes of the conversation) is a *transparent* attitude, conforming to the principles of positive and negative introspection. (If Alice accepts that ϕ, she accepts that she accepts it, and if she does not accept it, she accepts that she does not accept it.)[14] Positive introspection carries over to the iterated attitudes: If it is common ground that ϕ, then it is common ground that it is common ground that ϕ. Negative introspection does not, however, carry over: ϕ might fail to be common ground, even though one of the parties mistakenly thinks that it is. In this case, it will not be common ground that it is not common ground that ϕ. The negative introspection principle for common ground may fail even in some nondefective contexts,[15] although it is true that if an agent *presupposes* that the context is nondefective, then the negative introspection principle will hold for that agent's presuppositions. (And if it is

---

[14] This is of course an idealization, but even in the idealization, it does not imply that she can reflect on or articulate that she does or does not accept what she accepts. Higher order attitudes can be tacit and inarticulate, just as easily as ground level attitudes can be.

[15] This last remark conflicts with a claim made in Stalnaker 2002: "If a speaker believes the context is nondefective, then that speaker's presuppositions will satisfy both negative and positive introspection. In terms of the possible worlds model, this is equivalent to the assumption that if world y is compatible with what the agent is presupposing in world x, then what the agent is presupposing in world y is the same as what she is presupposing in world x." Thanks to Harvey Lederman, who constructed some models that are counterexamples to this claim. But I believe the weaker claim is sufficient for the points made in that paper.

common ground that the context is nondefective, then the negative introspection principle will hold for the common ground.)

I defined various kinds of subordinate or derived contexts. While these are relevant to the interpretation of complex expressions of a language, and may be appealed to (as the basic context is) in the compositional rules of a language, the subordinate contexts are information states that are definable wholly in terms of features of the basic context—of what is taken to be common ground. That is why they are appropriately called "derived contexts". First, there are derived contexts used in the interpretation of propositional attitude ascriptions. In a context in which what Charlie believes is at issue, it will be true in each of the possible worlds compatible with the basic context that Charlie is in a particular belief state, represented by a set of possible worlds, those compatible with what Charlie believes in that world. The derived context will be the union of all of those sets. That is, if the basic context set is C and R is the accessibility relation for Charlie's belief states in a simple Hintikka-style "semantics"[16] for belief, then the derived context is defined as follows: $\{y: xRy \text{ for some } x \in C\}$.[17] In doing the compositional semantics for an attitude ascription, one must determine a value (a proposition) denoted by the clause that is the object of belief. If context-sensitive expressions occur in the clause, one may appeal to information in either the basic context or the derived context to fix the content or reference of those expressions. Although this kind of derived context is an information state determined by the basic context that is available for the interpretation of clauses embedded in propositional attitude ascriptions, it is only part of the information about what is presupposed about the attitude state of the subject of the ascription. It might, for example, be presupposed that Ralph believes that a particular person is a spy without it being presupposed of any particular person that Ralph believes that he or she is a spy. That kind of information will not be reflected in a set of

---

[16] "Semantics" is in scare quotes for the same reason as it was put in scare quotes in the heading of section 4 of this appendix: the Hintikka-style semantics is a semantics for a formal language used to represent relationships between propositional attitude states. It may also play a role in the compositional semantics for belief ascriptions in a natural language, but we are not appealing to semantics, in that sense, here.

[17] In using the classic Hintikka-style framework, I am oversimplifying, since to account for attributions of self-locating belief, we need the kind of modified centered-worlds account discussed in Chapter 5.

worlds that is the union of those that might, for all that is presupposed, be compatible with Ralph's beliefs.

One special case of a propositional attitude context that got some attention, both in Chapter 4 and in Chapter 7, was a case where the attitude was *acceptance* (the same kind acceptance whose iterated extension is used to define the common ground) and the subject of the attitude was one of the parties to the conversation. In this case, the derived context, defined as above, will be a simple one, which is to say it will be a subset of the basic context set.

We also considered derived contexts determined by a supposition (either counterfactual or epistemic). In the general case, this kind of derived context is defined by an imaging function that takes a possible world from the basic context set to a possible world in which the content of the supposition clause is true. An imaging function of this kind must be determined by the basic context; that is, in order for suppositions to be interpretable, it must be presupposed in the basic context that a certain imaging function is uniquely salient, though it may be a "blurred" imaging function (to use terminology David Lewis introduced), which means that it may be only partially defined. In the case of indicative suppositions, it is a constraint that from any base world within the basic context set, the image must also be from that set. The upshot is that the derived context set determined by an indicative supposition will be simple in the sense defined.

So there are two kinds of derived contexts whose context sets are subsets of the basic context set. I labeled these "*simple* derived contexts". Simple derived contexts contrast with others (labeled "*parallel* derived contexts") in that the full iterative structure, and the centering, is preserved. In the possible worlds in counterfactual context sets, and in the context sets relevant to propositional attitude ascriptions for agents that are not parties to the conversation, the utterance event whose content the semantics is aiming to determine is not necessarily taking place, and so these possible worlds are not components of a "context of utterance". This means that the contextual features determined by a K-context (for example a speaker and time of utterance) are not determined. But in determining the proposition expressed in a subordinate clause, one may appeal to the information in either the basic context or the derived context. Suppose, for example, the consequent clause of a counterfactual contained the pronoun "I". There may be no speaker in the possible worlds in the parallel derived context, but we can and will take the indexical "I" to refer to the speaker in the base world. That is, if world y is the image of world x (from the basic context), then the "I" will denote, in y, the speaker in world x.

In Chapter 7, I introduced one further distinction between different basic common-ground contexts. Even a *nondefective* context may fail to be an *equilibrium* context. A context is in equilibrium when the parties agree, not only about what they accept in common, but also agree about what they *ought* to accept in common—what they are in a position to accept. A context is in equilibrium when what is manifestly accepted by the different parties is the same. That is, a context is in equilibrium when a proposition is common ground if and only if it is common ground that each party accepts that proposition. This is the same as to say that the simple derived contexts, what it is common ground that X accepts for each X that is a party to the conversation will all be the same, and will coincide with the common ground.

References

Abbott, B. 2008. "Presuppositions and common ground," *Linguistics and Philosophy* **31**: 523–38.

Abbott, B. 2010. "Conditionals in English and first order predicate logic," in D. Shu and K. Turner (eds.) *Contrasting Meaning in Languages of the East and West*. Oxford: Peter Lang, pp. 579–606.

Anderson, A. 1951. "A note on subjunctive and counterfactual conditionals," *Analysis* **12**: 35–8.

Austin, J. 1962. *How to Do Things with Words*. Cambridge, MA: Harvard University Press.

Bennett, J. 2003. *A Philosophical Guide to Conditionals*. Oxford: Clarendon Press.

Chalmers, D. 2006. "The foundations of two-dimensional semantics," in D. Carpentiero and J. Macia (eds.) *Two-dimensional Semantics*. Oxford: Oxford University Press, pp. 55–141.

Chemla, E. and P. Schlenker. 2009. "Incremental vs. symmetric accounts of presupposition projection: An experimental approach." Institut Jean-Nicod, LSCP & NYU (unpublished manuscript).

Clark, E. and H. Clark. 1979. "When nouns surface as verbs," *Language* **55**: 767–811.

Donnellan, K. 1966. "Reference and definite descriptions," *Philosophical Review* **75**: 281–304.

Dummett, M. 1959. "Truth," *Proceedings of the Aristotelian Society* **54**: 141–62.

Dummett, M. 1991. *The Logical Basis of Metaphysics*. Cambridge, MA: Harvard University Press. (Reference to assertoric content/ingredient sense distinction: pp. 47–50.)

Edgington, D. 1986. "Do conditionals have truth-conditions?" *Critica* **18**: 3–30.

Edgington, D. 1995. "On conditionals," *Mind* **104**: 235–329.

Edgington, D. 2004. "Counterfactuals and the benefit of hindsight," in P. Dowe and P. Noordhof, eds., *Cause and Chance: Causation in an indeterministic world*. London and New York: Routledge, pp. 12–27.

Egan, A. 2007. "Epistemic modals, relativism and assertion," *Philosophical Studies* **133**: 1–22.

Egan, A. 2000. "Self-locating belief and the Sleeping Beauty problem," *Analysis* **60**: 143–7.

Fagin, R. et al. 1995. *Reasoning about Knowledge*. Cambridge, MA: MIT Press.

Field, H. 2009. "Epistemology without metaphysics," *Philosophical Studies* **143**: 249–90.
von Fintel, K. 2001. "Counterfactuals in a dynamic context," in M. Kenstowicz (ed.) *Current Studies in Linguistics 36: Ken Hale: A Life in Language*. Cambridge, MA: MIT Press, pp. 123–52.
von Fintel, K. 2004. "Would you believe it? The king of France is back! Presuppositions and truth-value intuitions," in M. Reimer and A. Bezuidenhout (eds.) *Descriptions and Beyond*. Oxford: Oxford University Press, pp. 315–41.
von Fintel, K. and A. Gillies. 2011. "'Might' made right," in A. Egan and B. Weatherson (eds.) *Epistemic Modality*. Oxford: Oxford University Press, pp. 108–30.
Fogelin, R. 1967. "Inferential Constructions," *American Philosophical Quarterly* **4**: 15–27.
van Fraassen, B. 1966. "Singular terms, truth value gaps, and free logic," *Journal of Philosophy* **63**: 481–95.
Geach, P. 1967. "Intentional identity," *Journal of Philosophy* **64**: 253–5.
Geurts, B. 1996. "Local satisfaction guaranteed: A presupposition theory and its problems," *Linguistics and Philosophy* **19**: 259–94.
Gibbard, A. 1980. "Two recent theories of conditionals," in W. Harper, R. Stalnaker, and G. Pearce (eds.) *Ifs*. Dordrecht: Reidel, pp. 211–47.
Gibbard, A. 1990. *Wise Choices, Apt Feelings*. Cambridge, MA: Harvard University Press.
Grice, P. 1989. *Studies in the Way of Words*. Cambridge, MA: Harvard University Press.
Heim, I. 1983. "On the Projection Problem for Presuppositions," in M. Barlow, D. Flickinger and N. Wiegand (eds.), *Proceedings of WCCFL 2*, Stanford University, pp. 114–25. (Reprinted in S. Davis (ed.) *Pragmatics*, Oxford: Oxford University Press, 1990; pp. 397–405. Page references are to the reprinted version.)
Heim, I. 1992. "Presupposition and the semantics of attitude verbs," *Journal of Semantics* **9**: 183–221.
Higginbotham, J. 2003. "Conditionals and compositionality," in J. Hawthorne and D. Zimmerman (eds.) *Philosophical Perspectives, 17, Language and Philosophical Linguistics*. Oxford: Blackwell, pp. 181–94.
Hintikka, K., 1962. *Knowledge and Belief*. Ithaca, NY: Cornell University Press.
Howell, J. (forthcoming). "On Modal Interpretations of the French Conditionnel," in *Proceedings of the 39th Annual North East Linguistics Conference*.
Iatridou, S. 2000. "The grammatical ingredients of counterfactuality," *Linguistic Inquiry* **31**: 231–70.
Kamp, H. 1971. "Formal properties of 'now'," *Theoria* **37**: 227–73.

Kaplan, D. 1989. "Demonstratives," in J. Almog, J. Perry, and H. Wettstein (eds.) *Themes from Kaplan*. New York and Oxford: Oxford University Press, pp. 481–563.

Karttunen, L. 1973. "Presuppositions of compound sentences," *Linguistics Inquiry* 4: 169–93.

Karttunen, L. 1974. "Presupposition and linguistic context," *Theoretical Linguistics* 1: 181–94.

King, J. 2003. "Tense, modality and semantic value," in J. Hawthorne and D. Zimmerman (eds.) *Philosophical Perspectives, 17, Language and Philosophical Linguistics*. Oxford: Blackwell, pp. 195–245.

Kölbel, M. 2002. *Truth Without Objectivity*. London and New York: Routledge.

Kölbel, M. 2011. "Conversational score, assertion, and testimony," in J. Brown and H. Cappelen (eds.) *Assertion: New Philosophical Essays*. Oxford: Oxford University Press, pp. 49–77.

Kratzer, A. 1986. "Conditionals," *Chicago Linguistics Society* 22(2): 1–15.

Kratzer, A. 2012. *Modals and Conditionals*. Oxford: Oxford University Press.

Kripke, S. 1979. "Speaker reference and semantic reference," in P. French et al. (eds.) *Contemporary Perspectives in the Philosophy of Language*. Minneapolis: University of Minnesota Press, pp. 6–27.

Kripke, S. 2009. "Presupposition and anaphora: Remarks on the formulation of the projection problem," *Linguistic Inquiry* 40: 367–86.

Landman, F. 2000. *Events and Plurality: The Jerusalem Lectures*. Studies in linguistics and philosophy, 76. Dordrecht: Kluwer.

Lasersohn, P. 2005. "Context dependence, disagreement, and predicates of personal taste," *Linguistics and Philosophy* 28: 643–86.

Lewis, D. 1969. *Convention*. Cambridge, MA: Harvard University Press.

Lewis, D. 1973. *Counterfactuals*. Cambridge, MA: Harvard University Press.

Lewis, D. 1974. "Semantic analysis for dyadic deontic logic," in S. Stenlund (ed.) *Logical Theory and Semantic Analysis Essays Dedicated to Stig Kanger on his Fiftieth Birthday*. Dordrecht: Reidel. (Reprinted in Lewis 2000, 5–19.)

Lewis, D. 1975a. "Languages and language," in K. Gunderson (ed.) *Minnesota Studies in the Philosophy of Science, VII*. Minneapolis: University of Minnesota Press, pp. 3–35. (Reprinted in Lewis 1983, 163–88.)

Lewis, D. 1975b. "A problem about permission," in E. Saarinen et al. (eds.) *Essays in Honour of Jaakko Hintikka*. Dordrecht: Reidel, pp. 163–75. (Reprinted in Lewis 2000, 20–33. Page references to the reprinted version.)

Lewis, D. 1976. "Probabilities of conditionals and conditional probabilities," *Philosophical Review* 85: 297–315.

Lewis, D. 1979a. "Attitudes *de dicto* and *de se*," *Philosophical Review* 88: 513–43. (Reprinted in Lewis 1983, 133–59.)

Lewis, D. 1979b. "Scorekeeping in a language game," *Journal of Philosophical Logic* 8: 339–59. (Reprinted in Lewis, 1983, 233–49. Page references to the reprinted version.)

Lewis, D. 1980. "Index, context, and content," in S. Kanger and S. Öhman (eds.) *Philosophy and Grammar*. Dordrecht: Reidel. (Reprinted in Lewis, 1998, 21–44. Page references to the reprinted version.)

Lewis, D. 1983. *Philosophical Papers* 1. New York and Oxford: Oxford University Press.

Lewis, D. 1986. *On the Plurality of Worlds*. Oxford: Blackwell.

Lewis, D. 1998. *Papers in Philosophical Logic*. Cambridge: Cambridge University Press.

Lewis, D. 2000. *Papers in Ethics and Social Philosophy*. Cambridge: Cambridge University Press.

MacFarlane, J. 2003. "Future contingents and relative truth," *Philosophical Quarterly* 53: 321–36.

MacFarlane, J. 2011. "Epistemic modals are assessment sensitive," in A. Egan and B. Weatherson (eds.) *Epistemic Modality*. Oxford: Oxford University Press, pp. 144–78.

Montague, R. 1968. "Pragmatics," in R. Kiblansky (ed.) *Contemporary Philosophy: A Survey*. Florence: La Nuova Italia Editrice, pp. 102–22. (Reprinted in Montague 1974, 95–118.)

Montague, R. 1970. "Pragmatics and intensional logic," *Synthese* 22: 68–94. (Reprinted in Montague 1974, 119–47.)

Montague, R. 1973. "The proper treatment of quantification in ordinary English," in J. Hintikka, J. Moravcsik and P. Suppes (eds.) *Approaches to Natural Language: Proceedings of the 1970 Stanford Workshop on Grammar and Semantics*. Dordrecht: Reidel, pp. 221–42.

Montague, R. 1974. *Formal Philosophy: Selected Papers of Richard Montague*, ed. R. Thomason. New Haven: Yale University Press.

Moss, S. 2012. "The pragmatics of counterfactuals," *Noûs* 40: 561–86.

Neale, S. 2005. "Pragmatism and binding," in Z. Szabo (ed.) *Semantics versus Pragmatics*. Oxford: Clarendon Press, pp. 165–285.

Ninan, D. 2005. "Two puzzles about deontic necessity," in J. Gajewski, V. Hacquard, B. Nickel and S. Yalcin (eds.) *New Work on Modality, MIT Working Papers in Linguistics* 52. Cambridge, MA: MIT Press, pp. 149–78.

Ninan, D. 2010. "Semantics and the objects of assertion," *Linguistics and Philosophy* 10: 355–80.

Ninan, D. 2012. "Counterfactual attitudes and multi-centered worlds," *Semantics and Pragmatics* 5: 1–57.

Perry, J. 1977. "Frege on demonstratives," *Philosophical Review* 86: 474–97.

Perry, J. 1979. "The problem of the essential indexical," *Noûs* 13: 3–21.

Plato, 1990. *Theaetetus*, transl. M. J. Levett, revised by Myles Burnyeat. Indianapolis: Hackett.

Railton, P. 2003. "Practical competence and fluid agency," in D. Sobel and S. Wall (eds.) *Reasons for Actions*. Cambridge: Cambridge University Press.

Recanati, F. 2003. "Embedded implicatures," in J. Hawthorne and D. Zimmerman (eds.) *Philosophical Perspectives, 17, Language and Philosophical Linguistics*. Oxford: Blackwell, pp. 299–332.

Richard, M. 1983. "Direct reference and ascriptions of belief," *Journal of Philosophical Logic* 12: 425–52.

Richard, M. 2004. "Contextualism and relativism," *Philosophical Studies* 119: 215–42.

Richard, M. 2008. *When Truth Gives Out*. Oxford and New York: Oxford University Press.

Richard, M. 1989. "Modal subordination and pronominal anaphora in discourse," *Linguistics and Philosophy* 12: 683–721.

Roberts, C., M. Simons, D. Beaver, and J. Tonhauser. 2009. "Presupposition, conventional implicature, and beyond: a unified account of projection," in N. Klinedist and D. Rothschild (eds.) *Proceedings of Workshop on New Directions in the Theory of Presupposition*, ESSLI.

Rothschild, D. 2008. "Presupposition projection and logical equivalence," *Philosophical Perspectives* 22: 473–97.

Russell, B. 1905. "On denoting," *Mind* 14: 479–93.

van der Sandt, R. 1992. "Presupposition projection as anaphora resolution," *Journal of Semantics* 9: 333–77.

Santorio, P. 2012. "Reference and monstrosity," *Philosophical Review* 121: 359–406.

Schaffer, J. 2007. "Knowing the answer," *Philosophy and Phenomenological Research* 75: 383–403.

Schiffer, S. 1972. *Meaning*. Oxford: Oxford University Press.

Schlenker, P. 2003. "A plea for monsters," *Linguistics and Philosophy* 26: 29–120.

Schlenker, P. 2010. "Local contexts and local meanings," *Philosophical Studies* 151: 115–42.

Schroeder, M. 2008. *Being For*. Oxford: The Clarendon Press.

Searle, J. 1965. "What is a speech act?" in M. Black (ed.) *Philosophy in America*. Ithaca, NY: Cornell University Press, pp. 221–39.

Segerberg, K. 1973. "Two-dimensional modal logic," *Journal of Philosophical Logic* 2: 77–96.

Simons, M. 2001a. "Disjunction and alternativeness," *Linguistics and Philosophy* 24: 597–619.

Simons, M. 2001b. "On the conversational basis of some presuppositions," *Semantics and Linguistic Theory* (SALT) 11.

Simons, M. 2005a. "Dividing things up: the semantics of *or* and the modal/*or* interaction," *Natural Language Semantics* 13: 271–316.

Simons, M. 2005b. "Semantics and pragmatics in the interpretation of *or*," *Semantics and Linguistic Theory* (SALT) 15.

Simons, M. 2005c. "Presupposition and relevance," in Z. Szabo (ed.) *Semantics versus Pragmatics*. Oxford: Clarendon Press, pp. 329–55.

Simons, M. 2013. "On the non-independence of triggering and projection." Unpublished manuscript.

Stalnaker, R. 1968. "A theory of conditionals," in N. Rescher (ed.) *Studies in Logical Theory*. Oxford: Blackwell, pp. 98–112.

Stalnaker, R. 1970. "Pragmatics," *Synthese* 2: 272–89. (Reprinted in Stalnaker 1999, 31–46.)

Stalnaker, R. 1974. "Pragmatic presupposition," in M. Munitz and P. Unger (eds.) *Semantics and Philosophy*. New York: New York University Press. (Reprinted in Stalnaker 1999, 47–62.)

Stalnaker, R. 1975. "Indicative conditionals," *Philosophia* 5: 269–86. (Reprinted in Stalnaker 1999, 63–77.)

Stalnaker, R. 1978. "Assertion," *Syntax and Semantics* 9: 315–32. New York: Academic Press. (Reprinted in Stalnaker 1999, 78–95.)

Stalnaker, R. 1984. *Inquiry*. Cambridge, MA: MIT Press.

Stalnaker, R. 1998. "On the representation of context," *Journal of Logic, Language and Information* 7: 3–19. (Reprinted in Stalnaker 1999, 96–113)

Stalnaker, R. 1999. *Context and Content*. Oxford: Oxford University Press.

Stalnaker, R. 2002. "Common Ground," *Linguistics and Philosophy* 25: 701–21.

Stalnaker, R. 2004. "Assertion revisited: on the interpretation of two-dimensional modal semantics," *Philosophical Studies* 118: 299–322.

Stalnaker, R. 2005. "Saying and meaning, cheap talk and credibility," in A. Benz, G. Jager, and R. van Rooij (eds.) *Game Theory and Pragmatics*. New York: Palgrave MacMillan, pp. 83–100.

Stalnaker, R. 2006. "On logics of knowledge and belief," *Philosophical Studies* 120: 169–99.

Stalnaker, R. 2008a. *Our Knowledge of the Internal World*. Oxford: Oxford University Press.

Stalnaker, R. 2008b. "A response to Abbott on presupposition and common ground," *Linguistics and Philosophy* 31: 539–44.

Stalnaker, R. 2011a. "The essential contextual," in J. Brown and H. Cappelen (eds.) *Assertion: New Philosophical Essays*. Oxford: Oxford University Press, pp. 137–50.

Stalnaker, R. 2011b. "Conditional propositions and conditional assertions," in A. Egan and B. Weatherson (eds.) *Epistemic Modality*. Oxford: Oxford University Press, pp. 227–48.

Stalnaker, R. and R. Thomason. 1973. "A semantic theory of adverbs," *Linguistic Inquiry* **4**, 195-220.

Stanley, J. 1997. "Rigidity and content," in R. Heck (ed.) *Language, Thought, and Logic: Essays in Honour of Michael Dummett.* Oxford: Oxford University Press: pp. 131-56.

Stephenson, T. 2008. "Judge dependence, epistemic modals, and predicates of personal taste," *Linguistics and Philosophy* **30**: 487-525.

Strawson, P. 1964. "Intention and convention in speech acts," *Philosophical Review* **73**: 439-60.

Thomason, R. 1970. "Indeterminist time and truth-value gaps," *Theoria* **36**, 264-84.

Vlach, F. 1973. *"Now" and "Then": A Formal Study in the Logic of Tense Anaphora.* Unpublished Dissertation, University of California, Los Angeles.

Williamson, T. 2009. "Conditionals and actuality," *Erkenntnis* **70**: 135-50.

Wittgenstein, L. 1953. *Philosophical Investigations.* New York: MacMillan.

Yablo, S. 2006. "Non-catastrophic presupposition failure," in J. Thomson and A. Byrne (eds.) *Content and Modality: Themes from the Philosophy of Robert Stalnaker.* Oxford: Oxford University Press, pp. 164-90.

Yablo, S. 2011. "A problem about permission and possibility," in A. Egan and B. Weatherson (eds.) *Epistemic Modality.* Oxford: Oxford University Press, pp. 270-94.

Yalcin, S. 2007. "Epistemic modals," *Mind* **116**: 983-1026.

Yalcin, S. 2011. "Nonfactualism about epistemic modality," in A. Egan and B. Weatherson (eds.) *Epistemic Modality.* Oxford: Oxford University Press, pp. 295-332.

Yalcin, S. and J. Knobe. 2010. "Fat Tony might be dead. An experimental note on epistemic modals." Unpublished manuscript.

Index

Abbott, Barbara 141, 159
acceptance 4, 38–9, 45, 49
acceptance (system of norms) 201
accessibility 45
accommodation 6, 47–50, 69, 157
actualism 194
actuality-operator 29–33, 209
adding possibilities 127
adverbs 16
Alice, Bert, and Charlie 92–3
Amharic 211
"and" 95
Anderson, Alan 184–5
anticipatory presupposition 50, 57
appropriateness 52
assertion 50–3, 89
assertion (Bayesian account) 164
assertoric content 23, 216–22
asterisks 63
aunt's cousin 72
Austin, J. L. 37, 50
autonomy of pragmatics (thesis) 1, 35
available information 24

bathroom 99
Bennett, Jonathan 185–6
Blakemore, Diane 76
boring books 156–7
boy in the purple t-shirt 50
branching time structure 195–6

Camp, Elisabeth 46, 112–14
cancer test 171
Casteñeda, Hector-Neri 111
centered worlds 9, 24, 195, 218
CG-context 4, 10, 26, 215, 217, 231–2
Chalmers, David 225
change of state verbs 74
character 5, 18, 34, 211–12
Chomsky, Noam 61
CI framework 19–23, 88, 208–10
Clara, game show 218–19
Clark, Eve and Clark, Herbert 85
clefts 72

cloud of contexts 166
cognitive competence 82
cognitive significance 34
command 129–30
common ground 2, 3, 25, 121–2, 218
    disagreement 165–6
common interest 41
common knowledge 3, 25, 44
compositional vs. pragmatic
    considerations 17, 22
conditional assertion 148, 150–1, 164, 170
conditional supposition 28
conditionals 11
constitutive rules 36–7, 51–2
context change potential 64
context of assessment 194, 196
contextualism 192, 203
convention 37, 40
conventional acceptance 38
conventional implicature 84
conventions of truth and trust 21
conversational implicature 8, 41, 61–2,
    82–3
conversational tone 89
cooperative activity 7
cooperative principle 41–3, 52, 82
counterfactual 130–1, 184

dedicated presupposition triggers 75–7
defective contexts 47
definite description 55, 71, 145
deontic logic 131
deontic modal operators 11, 129–36
deontic must 133, 147–8
derived context 97
diagonal proposition 216–18, 225
Dick Cheney's dream world 193
dictiveness condition 87
Didi, Mary and Naomi 202–5
direct argument 158, 164
disagreement 90, 138, 165–6, 195,
    203–4, 228
    faultless 205–7
    practical 200

disjunction 98–101, 132
disobedient slave 147–8
Donnellan, Keith 49
doxastic accessibility 43, 114, 118
doxastic alternatives 93
Dummett, Michael 23, 67, 218
dynamic semantics 64–5, 96, 145–6

Edgington, Dorothy 148, 158, 172
Egan, Andy 195
Elga, Adam 117
English 27
epistemic accessibility 43, 121
epistemic modals 11, 137–49
   contextualism 168
   disagreement 165–6
   embedded 142–3
   semantics 144–5, 226–9
epistemic priorities 170–1, 205–7, 228
essential indexical 34, 110–11
expressivism 11, 139, 161, 201–2, 229–31
extensional semantics 15–16

factives 73
felicity 52
fiat/taif 129
flight 007 172
Florence quits job 29, 33
flouting maxims 83
force 51, 128–9, 136–7
formal languages 180–4
formality condition 87
fragile truth conditions 163
Frege, Gottlob 7
future contingents 195–8

Geach, P. T. 94
generative grammar 60–1
Geurts, Bart 67–70, 95
Gibbard, Allan 162, 201–2, 230
gradable adjectives 202–5
grammatical notions 91–3
grammaticality 61
Grice, P. 1, 2, 37
   on conversational implicature 8, 61–2
   on pragmatic presupposition 56
Gricean program 39–42
Gricean reasoning 8, 80

Heim, Irene 64–5, 71, 95
hey wait a minute 73, 106

Higginbotham, James 153–6
Hintikka, Jaakko 43–4
Hintikka models 10, 114
Howell, Jonathan 175

I-concept 120–1, 124, 215, 221–2
Iatridou, Sabine 185
illocutionary act 50
implicature 82
index 17, 208–9
indicative conditional 12, 30–3, 148–60
   embedded 152–3
   quantified 153–60
   restrictor analysis 154–5
Individual concept 119–20
Infinite Jest 157
informal context 14
information 36, 65
   objective 112
   self locating 112–14
informational content 16
intensional generalization 15–16
intentionality 39
inter-personal attitudes 114–15
iterated attitudes 26, 113–14, 119–20, 232
iterative structure 25, 38, 44, 178

Jim two meters tall 30
John Perry/Fred Dretske 119
Justice Stewart 59, 66

K-context 4, 10, 24, 26, 123, 208–9, 217
Kamp, Hans 18
Kant 42
Kaplan, David 4, 5, 27–9
   index 17–18
   monster 27
   semantics 63–4, 123, 211–12
Karttunen, Lauri 55–7
king of France 55, 66, 71
King, Jeffrey 22, 220
knowledge attributions 73
Kolbel, Max 38, 205
Kratzer, Angelika 180, 183
Kripke, Saul 58, 59, 65, 70

language game 36
Lewis, David 4, 5
   accommodation 6, 57
   actuality operator 32
   centered worlds 9, 111–14, 195

CI framework 19–23, 27, 216
common knowledge 3n
convention 41
conventions of truth and trust 21
conversational score 38
counterfactuals 131
  deontic modals 11
  modal realism 194
  permission 128–31
Lingens the amnesiac 112, 114, 118, 179
  kidnapped 213–16
linguistic presupposition 53
local context 8, 9
logic of belief 43
logic of common knowledge 45
logic of knowledge 43

MacFarlane, John 12, 193, 194
man drinking martini 49, 145
manifest event 47, 52
master, slave, kibitzer 129–31
material conditional 32, 149, 151, 158, 229–31
meaning$_{NN}$ 39–40
metaphor 86–7
"might" statements 186
minimal difference 131, 150
modal horizon 169
modal operator 128
modus tollens 185
monsters 27, 210–16
Montague, Richard 4, 15
  framework 4, 5
  grammar 15
  index 17
Moore's paradox 138–9
"most" 104
Mr. D'Arcy 186
multiple centers 26, 122–3, 231
"must" statements 187
mutual belief 3

natural gestures 41
Neale, Stephen 81
Ninan, Dilip 23, 122
nondefective context 4
norm of agreement 46
nouns used as verbs 85–6

O'Leary the fool 18, 24, 224
Once-operator 27, 208

"or else" 100–1
Ortcutt 120–1
Oswald 174

parking garage 115–17
Partee, Barbara 99
partial functions 64
performance/competence 61
permission 128–36
Perry, John 111
phone booth 123–5
Plato 190
possible world semantics 15–16
possible worlds 36, 43, 110, 196–7
posterior/prior context 136–7, 140
pragmatic
  presupposition 7, 95
  processes 78–79
  sentence presupposition 56, 59, 63
predicates of taste 198–202
pregnancy 204–5
presupposition 7
  cancellation 101
  projection 94–107
  rejection 48
  suspension 184–8
  triggers 8, 94
pretense 46
professors retiring early 155–6
projection 168, 170, 228
projection problem 8, 55, 94–107
pronoun 17
proposition 5, 21, 193–5
propositional attitudes 2, 110–11
propositional concept 222–3
prospective assertion 136–7, 140, 152
Protagoras 190–1
proviso problem 67–70

quantifiers 28, 103–7, 143–4, 154–5, 181
questions at issue 141–2
Quine, W. V. 120, 181, 203

R-propositions/O-propositions 194
Railton, Peter 81
Recanati, Francois 83, 84
Red Sox/Yankees 146–7
regimentation 181–2
rejection 51, 140–1
relational claims 191–2

relative truth 192–5
reminders 141
"rich" 202–5
Richard, Mark 123–5, 191, 202–5
rigidifying operator 31–3
Roberts, Cragie 89
Rothschild, Daniel 102
Russell, Bertrand 29
  theory of descriptions 67

S5 logic 140
Santorio, Paolo 213
Sarkozy, Nicolas 55, 103
satisfaction theory 67–70, 95
Schiffer, Stephen 3
Schlenker, Philippe 95, 97, 100, 211
Schroeder, Mark 230
score 6
Scrooge and Cratchit 132–3
Searle, John 37
Segerberg, Krister 224–5
selection function 150, 176–7
self-locating information 9, 10, 34, 113–14
semantic presupposition 7, 63–4
semantic processes 78–9
semantic relativism 12
semantics/pragmatics distinction 13, 79, 183
shiftable features 19, 27, 88, 210–11
Simons, Mandy 74–7, 100
Sleeping Beauty 117, 179
Sly Pete 162–3, 206
Snodgrass 159–60
speaker meaning 2, 39, 87
speaker presupposition 3, 6, 25
speech act 15
sphere of permissibility 129
standard of taste 198–9
Stanley, Jason 23
stopping smoking 74, 101, 104–5
Strawson, P. F. 37, 67

subjunctive conditional 12, 32, 173–80
  future 185–6
subjunctive tense 184
subordinate context 8, 9, 28, 90–4, 97, 107, 134–6, 150–1, 167, 233–5
  simple/parallel 92, 177–9, 234–5
subtraction 130–1
supposition 90–2, 150–1
  indicative/subjunctive 92
surface phenomena 60–2, 65
system of norms 230

tacit reasoning 81, 83–4
temporal operators 19
temporalist metaphysics 195
tense 17, 174–5, 182, 186
Theo, who hates sonnets 68–9
theoretical concepts 60–2
theory of communication 23
Thomason, Richmond 16, 58
Tebow, Tim 86
timing 49–50
"too" 70–1
transitive closure 44
truth-value gaps 55, 64, 95
two-dimensional semantics 222–6

van der Sandt, Rob A. 79
Vlach, Frank 18
von Fintel, Kai 67, 73, 75, 106, 184
von Fintel, Kai and Gillies, Thony 138, 166

what is said 5, 20
whodunit case 163–71, 206–7
Willamson, Timothy 30–1
Wittgenstein, Ludwig 36, 138

Yablo, Stephen 127, 222
yacht 29
Yalcin, Seth 89, 138–9, 141–3, 225, 226–9